Mindpieces
A Collection of Short Works

Marianne Tong

authorHOUSE®

AuthorHouse™
1663 Liberty Drive
Bloomington, IN 47403
www.authorhouse.com
Phone: 1-800-839-8640

First published by AuthorHouse   01/25/2012

ISBN: 978-1-4567-2485-6 (sc)
ISBN: 978-1-4567-2487-0 (hc)
ISBN: 978-1-4567-2486-3 (e)

Library of Congress Control Number: 2011901869

Printed in the United States of America

To Leighton, my husband, lover and soul-mate, who has remained level-headed throughout
my agonies and ecstasies.

Not only are these short works Pieces of my Mind, but writing them gave me Peace of Mind.

Please refer to the Author's Notes for certain numbered titles.

Contents

America, It's all Your Fault

During the years when I was writing lots of letters to various editors, I found an article in a Success Unlimited magazine that I questioned in a short letter. One of the editors corresponded with me and eventually invited me, an immigrant, to write about my life. I was taken aback and wrote the following letter that was published in the October 1978 edition:

To the Editor:

You asked why don't I try writing an article for your magazine? Because I don't know how I could possibly express my thoughts about success in this country in one short article.

How can I consider myself a success when I owe all that I am to millions of people? If I am anything, I am the result of the efforts of the farmers who produce my food, of the drivers who carefully avoid hitting me as I share the highways with them, of the teachers who take the time to answer my questions, of the pilots, drivers and mechanics who transport me safely from place to place and of the military people who allow me to get an untroubled night's sleep as well as of the enemies who failed to harm me permanently during World War II.

I am also the result of the efforts of those who have cared enough to cheer me when I was sad, to cure me when I was ill, to correct me when I was wrong and to let me be a whole person.

So, you see, America, if I am a success, it's all your fault!

Once is Enough[1]

1979

Just for a moment let's
Transcend all space and time,
Enjoy each other's company
And not disclaim, "But, I'm..."
Let's clear away those hazy mists
And realize, "The Universe exists!"

The Chinese Merchant's Wife

Chapter 1 In the Village

"You are my wife, and you **will** go with me!" declared Wong Hoo Chun to the eighteen-year-old trembling in front of him. There were no tears.

Ng Shee's beautiful face revealed none of the terror in her heart. She had been brought in a Sedan chair from Nai Yau, her family's village. As the only daughter of a village elder, she had bound feet because she was not expected to work hard. Servants and concubines would be doing the cooking and other housework. Her only duty would be to please her husband, a man thirty years older than the young bride.

"Yes, husband," she whispered dutifully as she wondered where they would be going. She had been told that she would be living in Hoo Chun's house in the Yew Tin village. Where were the servants? A young girl peeked shyly through the kitchen door.

"This is my daughter, Kum Hing," declared Hoo Chun matter-of-factly. "She will be going with us."

"Where are we going, father?" at nine years old, Kum Hing was quiet but unafraid to speak up. She had inherited much of her father's spirit in facing the unknown. Kum Hing had grown up with the teasing and rough-housing of her two older brothers, Mo Yin and Yoke Choy. Their mother, Ng Hai, had died just four months earlier. While the boys secretly expressed their resentment of the young bride in angry whispers, Kum Hing accepted Ng Shee as a new-found friend.

"It is not your business to know such things!" Hoo Chun dismissed the young girl sternly. "You will tend to your clothing, and prepare to take a long journey!" he added with a wave of his hand.

Kum Hing disappeared back into the kitchen. An elderly woman was nervously stirring the juk (rice soup). "Por-por, is the soup almost done?" Kum Hing was always full of questions. "Do you know what father is talking about? Is he leaving again? Will he come back?"

Yow Ping just shook her head, "Child, ever since your mother died I've been helping here in this house, but he tells me nothing. You must do as your father says. First go feed the chickens, and then come in to eat. Later we will take care of your clothing."

In the tiny parlor, Hoo Chun had lowered his voice in an attempt to calm Ng Shee. "I will explain my situation to you, but do not ask any questions. My business is not to be interfered in. do you understand?"

Ng Shee nodded. She was well aware of her position as the third wife even though the others were no longer living. "I am prepared to do what my husband expects of me," she replied.

Hoo Chun smiled. He had chosen well. Perhaps this woman would be the companion he had needed in the faraway land on the other side of the vast ocean. He called into the kitchen, "Yow Ping, bring my wife a cup of tea. We have some important matters to discuss."

Settling down at the tiny table, Ng Shee could feel the tension leave her. Perhaps this man would protect her after all. What mystery was about to be revealed?

Hoo Chun cleared his throat. It was not in his nature to discuss events with a woman, but it had to be done. "You know that I have been away for a long time. I have been in America. In 1880 I left this village of Yew Tin and sailed on a ship across the ocean. In San Francisco, I worked in a medicine shop called Fook Wah Tong as a bookkeeper. Soon I became manager and was called a merchant. A Chinese merchant is an important person in America. Laborers are not important. Laborers are not allowed to bring their families to America; however, merchants are allowed."

Ng Shee's heart was beating a bit faster. Was he talking about her sailing to America? What would she do there? Would she have someone to help deliver her babies? Would she understand the language? She tightened both her hands around the tea cup to hold it steady.

Not seeming to notice his wife's anxiety, Hoo Chun went on, "Next month we will take the train to Hong Kong, and then we will sail on a beautiful ship to America. Perhaps the winter weather will make great waves in the ocean, but the tickets are not so expensive in January. My daughter Kum Hing will come with us, but my sons are not welcome. Their place is in the home village. They must make their own fortune!"

Relief mixed with the terror in Ng Shee's heart. Kum Hing had been friendly ever since her wedding, but the boys still smirked at her whenever they thought their father was not watching. Ng Shee's mind reeled with the information she had just received. Thinking wildly, "One month! Sailing on the ocean in the winter! I must have warm clothes!" She looked shyly at the imposing man who now sat silently across from her.

"Very well, husband. Will there be time to go to my village and take leave of my family before we travel?" She spoke so softly that he barely heard her.

"I will go with you to Nai You on the second day of next week. On the way back we will stop in the Sun Tong market district to make some necessary purchases," he had assumed his authority again. Ng Shee could tell that the discussion was over. She silently sipped her tea and waited patiently for dinner.

Chapter 2 Why Can't We Land?

Kum Hing bounded into the cabin. "You must come! I can see a city in the distance!" Despite the biting cold, she was excited and eager to show her discovery.

Hoo Chun grumbled, "Yes, yes, I've seen it before. It's San Francisco, but we won't be allowed to land for several days."

Throwing a warm shawl around her shoulders, Ng Shee caught some of Kum Hing's excitement although she was walking slowly because of her feet. "Are we close? Can you see your father's store?"

Kum Hing laughed, "There are many buildings and many boats, but I can't tell what I'm looking at."

Most of the other passengers were crowding onto the deck. After a long cold voyage from Hong Kong, they were as eager as children to get a glimpse of land. Luckily the fog had already lifted on that February morning as they sailed into the Bay.

"Why aren't we going to the city?" Kum Hing was confused. "I thought we were going to San Francisco," she complained.

"Don't you remember what your father told you?" Ng Shee reminded her. "The ship will stop over there first. Then we must answer questions before we can go to San Francisco."

"But why?" Always inquisitive, Kum Hing asked for an explanation.

They had reached the railing where they could get a good look at the island on one side and the city on the other. "Your father told me that this country has a law. Not all Chinese are allowed to land here. I really don't understand everything he told me, but it has something to do with Exclusion." Ng Shee was trying her best to explain.

Kum Hing had already lost interest. "You are speaking words I don't understand," she said as she started to move away. "Besides, the people are making too much noise. I just want to watch the ship sail into the harbor."

Ng Shee was trying hard to remember what Hoo Chun had told her about Exclusion. About sixty years earlier there had been a discovery of gold in California. Many people came to mine the gold. Even more people came to California to grow food, to start businesses and to build cities. Then other people wanted a railroad across the whole country so they could travel back and forth. There were not enough people to build the railroad, so they asked people in China to come work on the tunnels, bridges and tracks. Many Chinese came to do the hard work. These were the laborers who were not allowed to bring their wives, and they were not allowed to marry American girls. They were expected to go back to China after the work was done. The immigration laws of the time allowed people from other countries to come to America with their families, but the Chinese laborers were excluded. Certain Chinese, however, were allowed to stay in America and even bring their families from China. For instance, a merchant who did no other work on a railroad or in the fields was allowed to stay. That is why her husband Hoo Chun, who was a merchant, was allowed to bring his wife and daughter. He had explained everything to her. He told her to be very careful when the inspectors asked questions. He said the Exclusion Law was very strict, and they might have to stay on the ship and be sent back to China! Ng Shee shuddered. She wanted to be back in her village, but the thought of another three weeks on the ship back to China did not appeal to her. Besides, she would shame her family if she returned.

"Look, look! There is a mountain right in front of us!" Kum Hing was tugging at her sleeve to bring Ng Shee out of her reverie.

"It looks very nice, but we won't be allowed to get off the ship today. First we must answer lots of questions," Ng Shee explained. Kum Hing was already skipping away.

Just then Hoo Chun walked up behind Ng Shee. "It will be good to tend to my business again," he casually commented. Ng Shee noticed that his face had a completely changed expression. There was an excitement that had nothing to do with him looking at his young and beautiful wife. He was already preoccupied with managing Fook Wah Tong & Co. He had left a good man in charge, but the business required his own steady hand. Surely, his customers would appreciate dealing with him personally again. Also, his members were waiting for their dividends.

The ship had stopped and was being tied up at the dock. "Who are those men coming up the ladder?" asked Ng Shee with nervous anticipation.

"Those are the inspectors I told you about," Hoo Chun answered. "They will call each and every one of us to a room. It will take a long time, maybe several days before it's our turn."

Two days later, Hoo Chun was called to testify. An interpreter posed short questions, and Hoo Chun gave concise answers. It was clear that the inspectors were familiar with his case. He had already made one trip in 1895 back to China, returning in 1897. One of the inspectors was studying his file. The photographs matched, and the answers matched. Hoo Chun was cleared for landing.

"Tomorrow they will call you," he told Ng Shee. "Just tell them the truth. If you don't know an answer, say so."

Immigration Inspector Gassaway noticed her nervous shaking as she walked into the interrogation room. He pointed to a chair, so she quietly took her seat and waited.

"What is your name?" he asked in a kindly voice. The interpreter translated.

"Ng Seung Yee," responded Ng Shee. Her given name had been replaced by the general term for a married woman, Ng Shee.

"How old are you?"

"Nineteen today," her birthday was of no significance. Her husband had not even acknowledged it.

A hint of a smile passed between the Inspector and the Stenographer. On the previous day they had questioned her husband Hoo Chun who admitted to being forty-seven. After a few more questions, she was dismissed.

Inspector Gassaway's handwritten letter to the Inspector in Charge of the United States Immigration Service, Chinese Bureau stated,

"I have taken the testimony of the Applicant, the husband and the daughter by the first wife, they all state the applicant and Wong Ho, were married in 3rd month of last year. –there are no material discrepancies in said testimonies.- this woman has bound feet, and seems to be a very respectable person. The testimony of husband and daughter will be found in cases E.S. 3425 and 3427 of this same steamer."

On the next day, permission to be landed in the exciting city of San Francisco was granted to Ng Shee.

Chapter 3 Dupont Street

Baby Ging Ching had been cranky most of the night. She was a little over one year old and usually slept through the night. What could be wrong? As Ng Shee comforted the child in her arms, she felt the new life stirring within her. She didn't mind living in the cramped room behind the Fook Wo Tong store, but it was difficult to keep the little girl quiet. She stared out of the window into the dimness of the pre-dawn, gently rocking the baby in her arms. Another movement rocked her whole body. Then a chunk of the plaster ceiling fell just behind her.

The loud sound woke Hoo Chun, "Can't you keep that baby under control?" he yelled from his makeshift bed.

Ng Shee was confused, "It wasn't the baby!" she said just as the building began to tremble even harder.

In one jump Hoo Chun reached the window, "It's an earthquake. We must leave." Grabbing the bag with important papers, he started for the door in his night clothes. "Come, wife! Bring the child."

Ng Shee stood rooted to the floor. Even though she was swaying with the movement, she held the baby even tighter. Her eyes were mesmerized by the red glow starting in front of the window. Finally she forced her legs to move toward the door. The shaking had stopped, but things were still falling all around her. At the door, Hoo Chun yelled, "Kum Hing, wake up, we must leave! The building is burning!" Wrapped in a blanket, Kum Hing, grabbed Ng Shee's hand to lead her out.

People were gathering in the street. Hoo Chun was already shouting orders. "The fire is blocking our escape to the north! Go south toward the ferries!" Suddenly he remembered his wife and daughters. He saw them coming through the store, "Stay close to me. There are too many fires. Many people will crowd into the streets. We shall go to the waterfront."

Scores of people, some still in their night clothes, flooded into the street. Dupont Street had been their home, and now it was on fire. Shouts and screams streamed like a wave toward the waterfront. In the general hubbub, all their possessions had to be abandoned.

"Husband, what shall we do?" The truth began to sink in. Kum Hing was still hanging on to Ng Shee's hand as they arrived on the dock.

"We shall wait here until we can board a ferry. I know a merchant in Alameda. We shall go there." Hoo Chun was determined not to show his fear.

Ng Shee nodded, and then she looked around. Hundreds of people had gathered at the wharf. Behind them a deep red glow mixed with the rising sunlight. Shivering in her flimsy night dress, she realized the horror that had just happened and the horrors that were to follow. Their store and home were going up in smoke. How could she care for the child in her arms and the child in her body?

Now the jostling of the crowd began to push them closer to the water. Hoo Chun stayed close to his wife and daughters. "Follow me!" he whispered. Hoo Chun had taken something from the bag. He approached a ferryman with an envelope of money. "Take this!" The ferryman quickly allowed the little family to board the ferry.

Within the hour, they were on the way to Alameda. Ng Shee handed the child to Kum Hing, "My body continues to feel the quaking," she explained. "Please take care of Ging Ching if anything happens to me." Soon she was hanging over the railing retching uncontrollably.

Hoo Chun looked away. "Am I to lose another wife?"

Chapter 4 Johnson Alley

Quan Fat Yin's grocery store on Johnson Alley in Alameda had become a refugee center. A near-by vacant lot was dotted with make-shift shelters. Although Alameda had sustained heavy damage in the earthquake that devastated San Francisco, people were willing to share what they had left. Quan Fat Yin was one of Wong Hoo Chun's customers when Fook Wo Tong and Co. was a thriving herbal shop on Dupont Street. Now he shared what little he had.

"Will your wife help Ng Shee when she is ready to give birth?" Hoo Chun resented that he had been humbled into a position of asking for help.

"We have a small room in the back of the store where Ng Shee can sleep. When will the baby be born?" Fat Yin was concerned about the coming cold weather.

"It will be November before Ng Shee needs to lie down," Hoo Chun played down the urgency.

In the tent Kum Hing was preparing a pot of juk (rice soup) for the ailing Ng Shee and the little girl who was almost two years old. A biting October storm had passed through, and coughing could be heard throughout the camp. Now the rain had stopped and the sun was spreading some welcome warmth over the misery.

Throughout the summer, Hoo Chun had been gone most of the time. He spent hours and hours each day walking the streets of Alameda and Oakland trying to find a job and a suitable place for his family to live. He noted with satisfaction that a vigorous reconstruction was taking place, but he was not allowed to take on a laborer's job. He had to be a merchant in order to stay in the United States. The ferry service between Oakland and San Francisco had become quite efficient. Hoo Chun had returned to Dupont Street several times, but it would be a long time before he could reopen his store.

Now he faced the imminent birth of another baby!

"Husband, it's my time," Ng Shee calmly explained. Hoo Chun walked with her to Fat Yin's store. Quan Shee, his wife, received Ng Shee with a sympathetic face. She had given birth to six children herself and was not easily flustered.

"I've prepared a bed for you in here," Quan Shee pointed to a tiny closet behind the store.

Ng Shee briefly stopped to let a contraction pass over her.

"I think the baby will come soon. I have felt the pains since last night. Now I feel a pain every few minutes," Ng Shee was very pale, but her voice was strong. She lay down, and only a few moments later another pain passed over her. Quan Shee was washing her hands at a bucket.

"We shall have a strong child!" she commented. "November 14 is an auspicious date," she assured the groaning mother. "Did your first child come easily?"

"Ging Ching was born in my husband's room behind his store. It was warm, and the baby came quickly. I am comfortable here, and the baby has been strong within me." Ng Shee and Quan Shee chatted about giving birth while getting some clean towels ready.

Before dark, a tiny voice announced its arrival on Johnson Alley.

Chapter 5 Oakland

Hoo Chun was slurping his hot soup when he suddenly made a casual announcement. "Fook Wo Tong & company is in business again." Ng Shee smiled quietly, but she was hesitant to respond.

Kum Hing, in her usual inquisitive style beset her father, "Are we moving? Will we have a real house? Will there be room for our two babies? Will I be able to go to school?"

"We must not promise ourselves too much," Hoo Chun responded. "There is a large park at Harrison Street, and special shelters have been built there for Chinese people who are engaged in legitimate employment. There is room for me to set up a small shop," he explained. "We shall all sleep there when I have worked in the herbal shop for one month." Then he went back to slurping his soup, and the conversation was over.

Ng Shee was breast-feeding her little daughter, Yoke King. Ging Ching was playing with a rag doll at her feet. "Husband, we shall be grateful to have some shelter against the terrible spring rain storms." She was not one to complain about the miserable conditions she and hundreds of others had been enduring on the land near Quan Fat Yin's store.

At the Harrison Street refugee camp, a small Chinese school had been established for children ten years old and over. Kum Hing begged her father to let her go to school, "Please father, I shall help Ng Shee with the babies as soon as I come back."

Ng Shee agreed, "I am strong enough now to care for the two babies. Let Kum Hing learn to read and write. She will be able to walk there and come back only three hours later."

Hoo Chun became thoughtful, "Why must a girl read and write?"

Neither Ng Shee nor Kum Hing had an answer for that question. In the home villages in China boys were expected to learn reading and writing while girls had to limit their skills to gardening, handicrafts and cooking.

"Very well, we are in a new world! I will arrange for you to attend, but you must work hard to be a good student!" Hoo Chun conceded.

"Oh, Father! I promise, and I will help with the babies, too!" Kum Hing quickly left the rickety little hut to share her good news with a friend.

By midsummer, Ng Shee had made a cozy home for her family at 666 Harrison Street. Even though it was only a temporary building, of the type constructed throughout many refugee camps in the Bay Area, it was more comfortable than the room behind the Dupont Street store. There was even a small cook stove that didn't smoke up the air in the kitchen, and the babies had a soft place to sleep.

The year went by quickly. Kum Hing was doing well in school and also had time to practice the sewing skills she had learned in her home village in China. Whenever Hoo Chun had some time, he ferried over to San Francisco to get new supplies and check on the rebuilding progress.

"Dupont Street is no more!" he declared one day.

"I don't understand," replied Ng Shee.

"You know that Dupont Street was not a good place for a family. Too many businesses dealt in opium. Also there were places where females sold their services. Dupont Street was a place where sailors and other men stopped for a short time only to leave again. Our store was one of very few on that street that had a good reputation," he explained.

Ng Shee remembered that she had been afraid to go outside on Dupont Street. "What do you mean when you say that Dupont Street is no more?" she asked.

"New buildings, and the street has been repaired, but it is now called Grant Avenue in honor of President Grant. Firms with a bad reputation will not be allowed to do business there. The Fook Wo Tong & Co. will have to prove that it is a reputable firm before we are allowed to move back." Hoo Chun took a sip of his tea. He was confident that he would be able to reestablish Fook Wo Tong & Co. to its former place in the business world of San Francisco. He was prepared to bide his time. It would happen!

The following winter brought several severe storms, but their little house remained strong against the rains and winds. Though the earthquake remained in people's hearts and minds, the earth began to feel solid under their feet again. With new flowers and green leaves on the trees all around them, Ng Shee and her family thrived.

"Perhaps this next child will be a son," Ng Shee commented casually just as Hoo Chun was about to take a sip of tea.

Some of the tea spilled on the Chinese newspaper he was reading. "When?" was all he could utter.

"The child will arrive in the first month of next year," she responded. Knowing how difficult it was for him to provide for his family of five, she feared bringing another child into the world, especially another girl.

Hoo Chun quickly regained his composure. "You know that it will be a long time before we can return to San Francisco. We shall have to be satisfied here."

"Yes, husband." The conversation ended.

On January 19, 1909 a robust little girl made her appearance. She was named Choy Ping, in the hope that "choy" (prosperity) would not be too far away.

Chapter 6, Finally, a Son!

Hoo Chun's home was anything but quiet. With three little girls and an inquisitive teenager in the tiny house, life was hectic. Some of the people in the temporary community at Harrison Street had already moved away. Others had formed friendships in the hustle and bustle of everyday life. It was a dynamic time, especially when the summer sun afforded the warmth to remain outside for long pleasant evening conversations.

As the fall approached, Ng Shee felt new life stirring inside her. "Not again!" she thought to herself, but to her husband she showed a brave face. "We shall have that son next year!" she announced one day.

Hoo Chun remained calm. "How can you be certain?"

You named our third daughter Choy, so we will have "choy," she declared steadfastly. He smiled.

"We shall see," he stated matter-of-factly. He had already chosen an American name for a boy, Harry. Now all he had to do was wait a few months to see whether he would have a son or another daughter.

A mild winter that year was a blessing because Ng Shee's pregnancy was not easy. She spent much of her time on the bed, directing Kum Hing to care for the children and do some cooking. Hoo Chun was working long hours, and when he had some time, he went to San Francisco to see about reestablishing the Fook Wo Tong & Co. there.

Despite her difficult labor, Ng Shee delivered a healthy boy on May 8. He was named Wong Sum Foo, and he was also given the name of Harry. Now Hoo Chun was more determined than ever to get back to San Francisco as soon as possible.

Chapter 7, Fook Wo Tong

"Pack up, wife, we are moving back to San Francisco. My store is ready. " Hoo Chun announced unexpectedly at dinner. His tone of voice revealed that he had regained his confidence.

Ng Shee was surprised. She had become accustomed to the cramped quarters and made several friends in the camp. She had almost forgotten that she was living in temporary housing.

She wanted to know more, but she knew how annoyed he could become about too many questions. Kum Hing could not contain her curiosity, "Where shall we live, Father?"

"I have arranged for an apartment on Stockton Street. I shall be able to walk from there to my store," he could barely avoid shouting. "My store!" He had gone at every opportunity to see that Fook Wo Tong & Co. moved to a suitable location on what was becoming known as Grant Avenue. "Our store will be at 940 Grant Avenue. I have already written to our suppliers in Hong Kong that they can begin shipping the larger stock of herbs and medicine."

Kum Hing and Ng Shee had stopped eating. "When?" they both asked in unison.

"Full of questions, are you?" Hoo Chun was in such a good mood, he joined them in the fun. "When I said 'pack up' I meant right now!" he joked.

As Ng Shee, holding Choy Ping on her lap made a move away from the table, he said, "Wife, finish your dinner first," with a twinkle in his eye. Even Ging Ching and Yoke King noticed their father's happiness and competed for his attention. He patted them on the head. Then he reached into the crib for his son. Raising him up and holding him high over his head, he exclaimed, "Harry, my son, you will learn the herb business!" Quickly, he dismissed thoughts about the two sons he had left in China. He did not want to admit that he missed them; furthermore, he did not want be reminded that they could not immigrate under the strict laws of the United States.

Chapter 7 New Life in San Francisco

"Look, this stove has places to cook two things at once," Kum Hing was astounded. "You put coal in this firebox. When it burns, these round things on top get very, very hot. Then you can put a pot of soup on one of the round things, and something else on the other round thing. It's like magic!" She had never seen such a modern cook stove in the refugee camps. Their food had to be cooked over an open fire near Quan Fat Yin's store. At Harrison Street, the stove was a tiny cylindrical contraption with one burner. This apartment in the Stockton Street building seemed very luxurious to her childlike innocence. Even though the building was old, it had survived the earthquake. "I will make a wonderful dinner for tonight! Father will be proud!" Kum Hing exclaimed.

Wong Hoo Chun was proud, indeed. He had succeeded in renting a store with a basement at 940 Grant Avenue. The Quong Lun Company had already owned the building long before California enacted the Alien Land Law of 1913 that prohibited Chinese ownership of land or property. After the earthquake, the Quong Lun Company completely rebuilt the heavily damaged building. Several apartments and offices occupied the upper floors while the street level store was just what Hoo Chun had been searching for. He hired an artistic friend to paint a sign that declared "Fook Wo Tong & Co." As manager, Hoo Chun proudly submitted a list of the active and silent partners to the City of San Francisco. Each partner owned a $1000 interest in the firm. He was determined to manage a legitimate business.

The shop dealt in herbs, such as bok kay, chai foo, fong dong, wai sun, fook shun, and ling gee. One of the active partners acted as bookkeeper and another as salesman. One partner was particularly talented in concocting Chinese medicines from the herbs right in front of a customer. Fook Wo Tong & Co. was officially in business again!

Ng Shee heard the footsteps of her husband coming up the rickety stairs. She was pleased that his success put him in a good mood at dinner time, but those stairs severely restricted her own movement. Her bound feet kept her a virtual prisoner in the apartment full of children. Seven-year-old Ging Ching was a quiet girl, but five-year-old Yoke King was rambunctious. The crying and squabbling of three-year-old Choy Ping and one-year-old Harry occasionally caused a neighbor to bang on the walls. Keeping the noise down in the Stockton Street apartment building was difficult. There was another issue she would have to discuss with Hoo Chun: her pregnancy.

"What? Another child?" Hoo Chun kept his voice under control. He had mixed emotions about all these children. A man of his well-respected stature in the community rises in the eyes of his peers with the birth of each living child, but how was he to support his ever-growing family? "You know that Kum Hing will leave us soon. She will be married next year. I have been negotiating with the Lee family. You shall have to take care of the children yourself."

Ng Shee was well aware that her new life in San Francisco was becoming more difficult with each child, the cramped quarters and her cramping feet. The glittering promise of her first view of San Francisco from the ship at Angel Island had faded into a depressing obscurity. Her tear-filled eyes longed to see Nai You, her home village, again. Even her husband's village of Yew Tin in the Sun Tong Market near Canton City would be a welcome sight.

Quietly, she averted her eyes as she served Hoo Chun the dinner that Kum Hing had prepared. She had learned that letting him see her feelings would bring her nothing. He lived in a different world. After the meal, he left to spend the evening with several of his partners as usual at the Fook Wo Tong & Co. store.

15

Chapter 8 A Big Move

When his daughter Suey Ping was born in May 1912, Hoo Chun realized that the tiny flat on Stockton Street was no longer acceptable for the family of a man of his standing. Some new apartment buildings had been erected just around the corner on Washington Street, so he decided to move his family.

"Wife, you won't have to climb too many stairs, and there is another Chinese family living on the same floor," Hoo Chun explained.

Ng Shee was still weak from giving birth to her fifth child, a healthy little girl. "Husband, I will gather up our things and prepare for the move." She had packed up and moved so many times in the past few years that she hadn't accumulated very much. Some clothes and bedding was all they needed. Then there were a few cooking utensils, some rice bowls and chopsticks. "Will the new place have a good cook stove like this one?" she asked.

"The new apartment has a kitchen with a good stove and, most important, a sink with running water!" Hoo Chun proudly proclaimed.

"Running water? Does it flow all the time? Is there a way to stop it?" Now Ng Shee's curiosity had been aroused. She had heard of running water and remembered how it worked on the ship, but she had never seen a sink and a faucet in an apartment before.

"You will see how convenient the new apartment is. We will have two bedrooms, one for the children and one for us," he added, already thinking that perhaps more sons would be born there. "Did you know that Washington Street is named for President George Washington? He was the first president of the United States." Hoo Chun seemed unusually talkative.

Ng Shee just shook her head. She had never heard of George Washington. In fact, she had very little time to think about the United States government, presidents or any other topic except her children. Now and then images of China flickered through her mind, but she was too busy with her children to dwell on them. Was there no old woman in this city to teach her the Chinese traditions and remind her of home? Ng Shee longed to talk with someone about her youth in China that now seemed so far away.

Their household was soon bundled up and moved to 901 Washington Street. A friendly Chinese woman with three children peeked out of one of the two apartments on the first floor above a jade jewelry store that occupied the ground level. Ng Shee gratefully smiled back.

"This is my wife, Ng Shee," Hoo Chun introduced her to the woman.

A man also appeared in the doorway. "This is my wife." he smiled. "She, too, is called Ng Shee." Traditionally, a married woman from some of the villages in the Canton province gave up their maiden names and became Ng Shee at the wedding. The two women immediately knew that they would be able to speak Cantonese and understand each other.

Feeling much stronger, Ng Shee set to work in her new home. Even Ging Ching, who was now eight years old, was helping. She carefully tended to three-month old Suey Ping. Yoke King at six and Choy Ping at four were trying to stack some clothing onto a shelf while two-year-old Harry teased them by pulling on their braids.

Hoo Chun attempted to calm the three young ones, "I shall apply my paddle to your behind if you cannot stop teasing your sisters!" Harry scurried away. He had not yet found a corner of his own in this unfamiliar room. "Harry, this will be your special place," Hoo Chun pointed to a nook near a window. "Your sisters will not be allowed on this side of the room," he looked sternly at the two crestfallen girls. "Do you understand?"

"Yes, Father," replied Yoke King and Choy Ping in unison. "Isn't Kum Hing helping us anymore?" they wanted to know.

"Kum Hing is at school. She will not be living with us anymore. She has moved to a Chinese family in Berkeley.

Ng Shee looked up from her work at the shiny enameled kitchen stove, "When will the wedding take place?"

"Next year on her eighteenth birthday," he replied.

Now Ging Ching and Ng Shee were totally alert. "Has the marriage been arranged?" Ging Ching asked.

"Kum Hing has not yet seen the young man, but I am told that he comes from a good family named Lee," Hoo Chun's tone clearly indicated that the discussion had come to an end.

Harry had fallen asleep in his special corner, and the girls quietly tended to their work. Ng Shee served Hoo Chun a cup of tea and then went back to her food preparation. She would miss Kum Hing, but she would be able to spend many tea times with her new friend across the hall.

Perhaps 901 Washington Street would be an open door to a life in this country, after all!

Chapter 9 George Washington Wong

"Alright! We're lucky to have such a nice summer day on laundry day!" Ng Shee was looking out of the window and speaking to no one in particular. The girls anticipated the excitement of the weekly trips to the laundry room in the basement of the building.

"Yoke King and I will carry the basket of diapers," volunteered Choy Ping. Ging Ching was in charge of taking baby Suey and Harry downstairs. Just outside the laundry room door the small enclosed lawn was a safe place for the little ones to get some fresh air. She would have to watch the babies play on the lawn while the other two girls were allowed to help with the sorting and folding.

"Be careful going down the stairs, and don't forget to stop at the toilet first, so you won't have to tramp up and down too many times. The toilets were located a half flight of stairs lower than the apartments. Each family had its own locked stall. Choy Ping, at age four was still afraid of the strange-looking water tank far up on the toilet wall. She refused to flush by pulling on the chain. "It might fall on me," she yammered. Yoke King, being almost six and brave, always had to accompany her and pull the chain for her.

Several baskets of clothes and all the children made the trip to the laundry room into quite an adventure.

"I'll have a nice cup of tea waiting for you when you are finished," smiled Shao Ying, Ng Shee's neighbor. They had become good friends over the year and decided to call each other by their given names rather than the formal Ng Shee.

Seung Yee answered, "Wonderful! I have some news to talk about, but first I must get these clothes washed and hung up to dry."

The laundry room had recently been modernized. Two deep sinks for washing and rinsing with running water were attached one side of the wall. A hose could be used to put water into a large tub on a low coal-fired stove in the middle of the room. This tub was used for items that needed to be boiled, such as diapers. Just below that tub at the side of the stove was a drain pipe, so that the tub could be easily emptied. On the other side of the room was a long table top for ironing and folding. The flatirons could be heated on the low stove when the boiling tub was no longer in use.

Ng Shee reminded the children, "You can all go play on the lawn outside. The weather is nice and warm today. I'll call you when I need some help."

The children enjoyed the time outside even though the yard was quite small. Two tall T-poles held the clothes lines. Six lines were strung between the poles, but as long as there were no clothes hanging on them, they were high enough, so the children could play on the lawn without noticing them.

A couple of hours and lots of work later, Ng Shee and her children made their way back up the stairs.

"Seung Yee, don't forget to come over for tea," Shao Ying, peeking out of her door, reminded her.

I'll be over as soon as I put Suey Ping and Harry down for their naps."

With her children taken care of and the laundry hung up to dry, Ng Shee was happy to have a half hour to herself before she had to think about dinner. She had been tiring easily for the past few weeks.

"Shao Ying, I believe I'm pregnant again," Ng Shee was nearly in tears.

"This will be your sixth child!" her neighbor exclaimed.

"My husband will be quite upset," Ng Shee feared.

"Perhaps it will be a boy; then he won't have any reason to get angry," Shao Ying offered.

"He gets so impatient with the girls. Do you think that's why he spends so much time at the store Shao Ying?" Ng Shee, close to tears, already knew the answer to her own question.

"It is better not to talk about these things too much. What choice do we have? Our husbands have come to this country for their own reasons. They have brought us to this country, and now we are here! Having babies, babies and more babies." Just then one of Shao Ying's sons ran into the room with a bloody nose.

"Brother Chuk Mun and I were wrestling! I bumped my nose on the floor," he wailed.

Ng Shee excused herself, "I'll let you take care of Yin Kwong. I need to start dinner now."

Hoo Chun came home to eat. When he was ready to leave again, Ng Shee stopped him, "Husband…"

He looked at her, "Didn't you have laundry day today? Won't you have to go get the clothes off the lines and fold them?" He was clearly not in the mood for a conversation.

"The clothes can wait. I have an important matter to tell you."

Hoo Chun could tell by the look on her face what was coming. "Will it be a boy this time?" was all he asked.

"I can't tell. The child is strong within me. It will be born in February."

Hoo Chun smiled unexpectedly, "If it is a boy, we will call him George Washington!" he announced. Then he left for the evening in his store.

Chapter 10 The Last Straw

1916 started like any other ordinary year. The cold air of San Francisco kept the children indoors. Despite her bound feet, Ng Shee had to carry the washed laundry painfully up to the attic where it was hung up to dry. Cooking smells permeated the apartment building, and the place fairly buzzed with shrill voices. It was difficult to find a moment of peace in the hubbub of everyday life at 901 Washington Street. Ging Ching and Yoke King attended the Oriental School in the adjacent building for four hours a day. Shao Ying's two older sons and one daughter also attended the same school, but there were plenty of younger children to make noise.

The two Ng Shee's kept their regular tea times in the afternoon, but the strain of keeping twelve children from bothering their busy fathers after work was beginning to line their faces.

"I can't believe that I've missed my period again!" Seung Yee commented into her tea cup.

"Have you tried taking wild yam tea?" Shao Ying asked. "Surely, your husband can recommend something from his herbal shop to prevent another pregnancy."

"I've tried some herbs, but I must be so fertile that all he has to do is hang his underwear on the bed post for me to have another baby," joked Seung Yee.

"Funny! But are you sure another child is on the way?"

"Yes, but I haven't told my husband yet. When George was born he was happy to have another son, but he barely looks at any of the children now. Sometimes I get the idea that he wishes they were all grown up already and out of the house," Seung Yee seldom offered this much information.

"Men don't realize that it takes years and years of child care before a baby becomes a woman or a man," Shao Ying's wisdom was apparent. "They make a baby, and then they go to work in fields, in stores or wherever, leaving the women to raise the children. It's the way of the world." She added for emphasis.

Seung Yee nodded, "Yes, I've understood that for a long time, but that doesn't help me now."

Shao Ying smiled and poured another cup of tea. "Here, let's have an almond cookie and enjoy a few moments of quiet time. Soon we will have to cook dinner."

"Look, Mother! I can write my name now," Ging Ching proudly dipped her calligraphy pen into the ink and demonstrated what she had learned.

"Here, let me try it," Yoke King, though two years younger always tried to keep up with her sister.

"You are both doing a fine job," Ng Shee conceded although Yoke King had dripped some ink on the table.

She was proud of her healthy family. The child within her frequently announced his presence with strong kicks against her tight belly, and Hoo Chun had not been nearly as upset as she feared.

With a thoughtful expression, he said, "I shall find a way to take care of my family."

His composure puzzled Ng Shee. What could he be thinking? Find a way? Their routine life was already established. At this point another child was simply another child. There was not much difference between six children or seven children.

On a warm August day their third son, Tsun Choy, was born. He was also given the name Alfred at his red egg and ginger party. Shao Ying had told her about this tradition after the birth of George. One month after the birth of a son, the family celebrates with red eggs to denote fertility and ginger to denote good health. Seung Yee had not known of this tradition, and it would have been difficult in the refugee camps.

"Husband, you have been very quiet and secretive in the past few weeks. Is there something I should know?" Ng Shee felt an uneasy strain in their marriage.

"You will be taking the children back to China!" He stated without a flicker of emotion on his face.

Ng Shee dropped the rice bowl with a loud clatter.

"Can't you be more careful, woman?" Hoo Chun shouted. The room became completely silent. All the children looked up in surprise. They had not seen their father so agitated before.

"Mother, what's wrong?" Choy Ping put her arms around Ng Shee.

"Father says that we'll be going to China, and it just surprised me, that's all," Outwardly calm, Ng Shee had all she could do to keep from screaming.

"Yay! China!" Harry was jumping up and down and infected the toddler George with his joy. Neither of the boys knew what China was, but it sounded exciting to go there.

Ging Ching looked puzzled. "Why does father want us to go to China?" Shaking her head, Ng Shee had no answer. An uncomfortable silence among the girls stopped Harry and George's jumping.

Hoo Chun surveyed his family. They were all looking expectantly back at him. He felt the need to explain his decision.

"Back in the village I own a house. You will live there and go to school. When you are old enough, you will be able to return to the United States because you were born here. I will obtain all the necessary documents, so that you can always prove that you are U.S. citizens."

All the children, except baby Alfred, understood the gravity in their father's voice and listened quietly while he explained. Ng Shee held Alfred in her arms, but she trembled inside. "Will you go with us?" Ng Shee wondered.

"I cannot leave the store at this time." He dismissed the idea of the whole family traveling together.

"Will I have time to prepare for such a journey?" Ng Shee was hesitant to ask, but she needed to know what to do.

Hoo Chun realized that he needed to explain a bit more, "I have investigated the matter. A ship is leaving for China in December. I will have time to write to the village elders and let them know that you are coming. I will also have time to prepare the documents. You will have time to prepare the clothing and other things to take with you."

"So December! That gives me two months to think about going back to China. I wonder what Shao Ying will have to say about these news," Ng Shee's mind was reeling. She could barely wait until the next day's tea time with Shao Ying.

The two months went by quickly. Passport pictures had to be taken, and trunks packed. Ng Shee was ready to take her seven children on the long journey across the Pacific Ocean. She had told them that they might not feel well on the ship, comparing the ocean voyage to the ferry boat they had on occasion taken from San Francisco to Oakland and back. "There will be a lot of movement, and you may not feel like eating," she prepared them. "But you will like living in the village!"

As the family gathered on the dock, ready to board the SS China, Ng Shee looked around for her son Harry.

"Husband, I thought you were bringing Harry with you. You took him with you to the store this morning to say Good-bye to your partners," Ng Shee said.

"He will not be leaving with you," Hoo Chun declared. He seemed not to notice the tears gathering his wife's eyes.

"Will he stay with you in the store?" Ng Shee barely whispered the question.

"He has already left on a train to Georgia. Ng Yow Gum is traveling with him. Harry will be living with my brother Kam Chen in Augusta, Georgia. He will go to school there."

Ng Shee was momentarily stunned. Suddenly she aired all her pent-up emotions.

"You have not said one word about Harry staying in Georgia. He is not yet seven years old! How can you be so cruel? Your brother is living with a woman who is not Chinese! Is this an example you want your son to follow? You bring me to a land where the very earth rebelled against us. You drag our family through refugee camps. You give me seven children in twelve years, and now you tear our family apart. You…"

A shrill whistle interrupted her rampage and announced the embarkation of the passengers. Yoke King is holding little Suey Ping's hand. Ging Ching and Choy Ping are guiding little George up the gangplank. Ng Shee carries baby Alfred as she reluctantly climbs the steps to board the ship.

With a satisfied expression Hoo Chun waves to his family at the railing as the ship pulls away from the dock. Then he heads back to Fook Wo Tong and Co.

Wong Hoo Chun[2]

Living in the Yew Tin village in the Sun Tong market of the Canton Province, the Wong clan produces one young man on August 8 in 1858 who could not be fettered by the local walls. Hoo Chun is only eighteen years old when he takes his first wife, Ng Hai, who gives birth to two sons. While he was still married to Ng Hai, he takes a concubine, Jang Shee. This young woman dies soon after she gives birth to a daughter. The little girl is not given a name because she dies before she is one month old. Shortly after that, Hoo Chun, leaving a surprised wife and two little boys, sails to America! In 1880, he has no trouble being admitted as a merchant. There is no restriction on immigration of merchants yet. Only two years later the U.S. Congress passes The Chinese Exclusion Law that complicates immigration, especially for laborers, for years to come.

Knowing that he might want to return to the U.S., Hoo Chun secures a Re-entry permit in 1895 before he sails back to China on the Steamer "Coptic." As a bookkeeper for the Fook Wah Company on Dupont Street in San Francisco he has saved up enough money for a trip back home. Not long after he arrives, his wife becomes pregnant and gives birth to a little girl. Hoo Chun divides his time between the ancestral village of Yew Tin, Canton City and Hong Kong. After only two years of moving around within China, he yearns for another adventure. He returns to America on the SS "Gaelic" in January 1897 without his wife and three children. In San Francisco he works on establishing his own business. By the time he applies for permission to make another trip to China in 1901, he has already been the respected manager of Fook Wo Tong & Co. on 711 Jackson Street in San Francisco for more than a year. The company formerly owned by Lou Chong and six other members of the Lou clan has been bought out by ten new stockholders, including Wong Hoo Chun. All the new members are Wong's from the Yew Tin village, some still living in China and some in America. Hoo Chun has become a businessman! He has four white witnesses vouch for him at the immigration hearing.

While Hoo Chun is in China, his wife, Ng Hai, dies. A man with a nine-year old daughter must have wife, so he marries Ng Seung Yee, age 21, from a neighboring village, Nai You. Even though her name changes from Ng Seung Yee to Ng Shee in subsequent documents, she is the same person. In early 1904, Hoo Chun sails back to America with his young wife, Ng Shee and his daughter, Kum Hing, on the Steamer "SS China." His sons, Mo Yin and Yuk Choy are left in China. They may have been too old to immigrate as his children. Perhaps Hoo Chun miscalculates how long ago he was in China, but he claims their ages to be 20 and 18, respectively; perhaps, he had other motives. In any case, Hoo Chun and his pregnant new wife, Ng Shee, are admitted by the immigration authorities. An inspector who investigates Ng Shee at Angel Island describes her as a young woman with bound feet who "seems to be a very respectable person." Ng Shee even signs her own name, demonstrating that she has been educated in her village. She testifies that the nine-year-old girl is Kum Hing, the daughter of Wong Hoo Chun by his first wife who is now dead. The family is approved for landing, and their life in San Francisco begins.

In December of the same year, Ng Shee gives birth to her first child, Ging Ching, a daughter with the American name Rosie. Their small home is in the back of the store on Dupont Street which burns down in the April 1906 San Francisco earthquake. Fortunately, Hoo Chun is an efficient bookkeeper and manager. He has cautiously kept all his documents, including Ging Ching's birth certificate, in his possession. He carries them with him when the small family flees to the other side of the San Francisco Bay.

A temporary refugee camp for the surviving Chinese community has been set up in Alameda, so Hoo Chung takes his pregnant wife and his two daughters there. In November Ng Shee gives birth to another girl, Yoke King, at the store of Quan Fat Yin, 26, Johnson Alley in Alameda. One can only imagine Hoo Chun's face when he finds himself surrounded by three daughters and no sons. According to his testimony in 1922, his two sons in China have died from a sickness around the time of the great San Francisco earthquake. Despite his current predicament, Wong Hoo Chun keeps his composure. He and Ng Shee have two more children before moving back to San Francisco. On January 19, 1909, Wong Choy Ping, American name Mae, is born at 666 Harrison Street in Oakland. On May 8, 1910, Wong Sum Foo, American name Harry, is born at 666 Harrison Street in Oakland. A son! At last!

In May 1912, another daughter, Suey Ping, is born at 1047 Stockton St. in San Francisco. In July of the same year, Hoo Chun submits a document of the Fook Wo Tong & Co., at 940 Grant Avenue, listing him as the manager. It appears that he and his family has recovered from the blow dealt by the earthquake. Celebrating their good fortune, Hoo Chun and Ng Shee have two more sons. George Washington Sum Quong Wong is born on February 22, 1914 and Alfred Tsun Choy Wong is born on August 11, 1916 while they are living at 901 Washington Street in San Francisco. Naming his son George Washington, born on the first U.S. President's birthday, Hoo Chun displays a sense of humor that soon leaves him. With seven children plus a seventeen-year-old daughter, his life becomes too hectic. He makes the decision to send his wife and children back to China!

Testimony is taken at Angel Island to obtain Re-entry permits for his wife and children in case of their return to the United States. No mention is made of the fate of Kum Hing, his seventeen-year-old daughter. In later testimony, he states that she is married and has lost track of her. In his testimony he gives the following reason for sending his family to China, "Because there is nobody now looking after my home back there, and I sent my wife back there to look after it." He is referring to his home in the ancestral village of Yew Tin. On December 21, 1916, Ng Shee sets sail on the SS China with six of her seven children. Harry, age 6, remains behind, but he is sent with Ng Jow Gum (perhaps a friend) the very next day to Georgia to be raised by his uncle Kam Chen and go to school there.

Kam Chen (also known as Wong Gum Chuen) lives in Augusta, Georgia and runs two businesses, a grocery store called Wong Gum and a laundry called Gum Sing. Hoo Chun testifies that Kam Chen has a son in China who has never been to the United States. That boy's mother is dead. Answering the inspector's questions, Hoo Chun admits that his brother married a white woman in Georgia and has a boy, age 21, and a girl with her. The inspector is surprised, "And you sent your son down to Augusta to live with a brother who married a white woman?" Hoo simply answers, "Yes." The inspector presses a little further, "How many brothers have you?" Hoo Chun then names two more brothers who have remained in China. His married brother, Wong Yee Hung, is about 40 years old and has a son and two or three daughters. His other brother, Wong Chit Yee, and his wife are dead, but they have a daughter about fifteen or sixteen who is still living.

Clearly, Hoo Chun has become a dispassionate witness. He answers questions in a stunningly robotic way. When asked about the two sons he left in China, he coldly answers, "The boys are dead." He endures the further questioning about their names and ages. The inspector suddenly asks him, "Why do you try to tell us now that you had no children born in China, except that girl that you landed in 1904?" Hoo Chun answers, "Since they were dead I didn't want to mention them." The inspector finds this difficult to believe, so he presses further, "If your wife should come here from China on her return and say that you have two sons in China, what would you say?" Hoo Chun's shocking answer is, "If that is the case, deport her."

For the next few years, life at the Fook Wo Tong & Co. goes on. The 940 Grant Avenue address has become a well-known stopover for immigrating Chinese, especially those from the Canton area. With no children to get in his way, Hoo Chun throws himself into developing his business in the rented building. In 1919, Hoo Chun submits another document listing the members who have invested money in the business. He is still the manager who rules with an iron fist, distributes dividends and keeps meticulous records.

Suddenly, a family member arrives from China as servant of a Chinese Government Diplomat. This family member is Wong Yat Chew (later identified as Wong Yoke Choy), the son of one of Hoo Chun's cousins in the Yew Tin village. Later, both Yat Chew and Harry Wong (Hoo Chun's son) testify that their grandfathers were brothers from the Yew Tin village. Unfortunately, the Diplomat dies in 1922, and Yat Chew seeks refuge at the Fook Wo Tong store. Shortly before that, Hoo Chun and his son Harry had planned a trip back to China, so they sailed on the SS Nanking in April. Yat Chew finds that the people left in charge at the store during Hoo Chun's absence don't have enough work for him, so he becomes a street vendor with a vegetable cart. This does not suit a young man of dignity, so he sets out for Augusta, Georgia where he expects to make his fortune in a grocery store under the guidance of his other uncle, Wong Kam Chen.

In Yew Tin village, Hoo Chun and Harry are welcomed back into the family. He moves his family to Canton City. In May 1923, Ng Shee gives birth to her eighth child, Wong Gum Quen (Howard) in Canton City. Three of the sisters, Ging Ching, Yoke King and Choy Ping, move back to the Yew Tin village. Suey Ping, being the youngest of the girls, plus George and Alfred remain in Canton City to go to school.

In November 1923, Hoo Chun and Harry return to America on the SS President Cleveland, bringing nine-year-old George with them. While Hoo Chun hurries off to tend to his business, Harry offers to stay on Angel Island with his younger brother until he is released for landing. Soon after their arrival at 940 Grant Avenue in San Francisco, the two brothers, Harry and George are sent to Augusta, Georgia. They will continue their education and help out in the Chinese grocery stores there. In China Ng Shee moves back to the village with Alfred, leaving the baby Howard and young Suey Ping in Canton City.

In 1924, Hoo Chun learns that his wife, Ng Shee has died in January, leaving the four daughters, ages 20, 18, 16 and 12 to care for the two little boys, Alfred and Howard. Suey Ping, 12, and Howard, 8 months old, are still in Canton City while the older three girls, Ging Ching, Yoke King, Choy Ping with Alfred are living in the family-owned house in Yew Tin village. There is no record of the family or boarding house with whom Suey Ping and Howard are living in Canton City. Choy Ping returns to Canton City to go to school there for two years. Suey Ping attends school in Canton City as well.

Two years later Hoo Chun decides that it's time for his son Alfred, age 9, to return to the U.S. to get an American education. He makes the arrangements for Choy Ping to accompany the child. On December 2, 1926, Choy Ping and Alfred arrive via the SS President Cleveland in America. During her interrogation at Angel Island, Choy Ping testifies that her sister Suey Ping and her little brother Howard are living in Canton City, while her two older sisters are living in Yew Tin village. Hoo Chun is aware that he has another son, Howard, in China who should also be brought to America; however, that son was not born in the U.S. Would there be problems with his immigration? Hoo Chun decides to depend on his excellent reputation as a domiciled merchant.

After filing appropriate documents, including an application for a visa in October 1927, Hoo Chun sails back to China on the steamer Taiyu

Maru on November 22, 1927. On October 16, 1928, Hoo Chun obtains an extension of his visa from the U.S. Consulate in Hong Kong. It can be assumed that he is determined to follow all the immigration rules in order to bring Howard to America. Such an endeavor takes time. The extension of his Re-entry permit allows Hoo Chun to remain in China until October 19, 1929. Meanwhile in San Francisco Harry and Choy Ping make plans to travel to China. Alfred is sent to Augusta, Georgia to live with Yat Chew, the distant cousin who showed up in 1919. Alfred is expected to go to school as well as help in the grocery store, Wong Choy. On December 21, 1928, Harry and Choy Ping set sail on the SS President Jefferson.

On August 19, 1929, Howard (Gum Quen or Yue Quan) Wong arrives with his father Hoo Chun at Angel Island on the SS President Madison. On September 18, Howard is released from Angel Island. In China, Harry marries Ng Hoy Chee. Plans are made for Harry to accompany the family of Yat Chew (wife So Shee, son Kam Ling and son Kwock Ling) back to the U.S. Harry's sister, Suey Ping, is to travel with them, but Harry's wife, Ng Hoy Chee is to remain in Yew Tin Village with Ging Ching, Yoke King and Choy Ping. No reason is given for this turn of events.

In Hong Kong So Shee Wong, the wife of Yat Chew (aka Yoke Choy) and her son Kam Ling, are diagnosed with hookworm, so Harry takes them to a doctor every other day for about two weeks. Finally they board the SS China, arriving at Angel Island on March 6, 1930. So Shee and Kam Ling are held and treated for hookworm for about a month while the younger brother Kwock Ling, Harry Wong and Suey Ping are released to Hoo Chun's store on 940 Grant Avenue. Fook Wo Tong & Co. has become a safe haven for immigrating Chinese from the Canton area.

As soon as everyone is healthy, Harry takes Yat Chew's family to Augusta, Georgia. Hoo Chun arranges a marriage for Suey Ping. A widower named Jack Hoo Tong who is a merchant in Los Angeles apparently meets his approval. The wedding takes place on November 29, 1930. Jack Tong is very secretive about his arrival in the United States because he immigrated with purchased papers a few years before. His family name is Ho (or Hall) and his given name is Chuck Mun, (also pronounced Guen Suet) according to the registry in his home village of Ying Nam. Jack Tong is his assumed name which serves him for the remainder of his life. Suey and Jack soon make their way to Los Angeles, where their first son, Allen Hall Luen Tong is born in 1932. In Augusta, Georgia, So Shee, also gives birth to a son, Larry. For the next few years both Suey Ping and her traveling companion So Shee have babies at least every other year.

In Los Angeles, Jack establishes a butcher shop-grocery store. His wife, Suey presents him with three more sons and a daughter, Leighton Hall Lai Tong, born in 1933, Eugene Hall Jeun Tong, born in 1935, Jerome Hall Chew Tong, born in 1937 and Emily Neyrong Tong, born in 1938.

In Augusta, So Shee gives birth to three more children, Rachel (1932), Edward (1934) and Ginger (1935) Wong.

In China, Yoke King gets married in the Dai Dung village to Lo Mun Sang (also known as Chi Isaing Lo) in 1932. Their son, Clifford Lo Gam Chew is born in 1933 and their son, Calvin Lo Chor Chew is born in 1935. Sadly, the oldest of the Wong sisters, Ging Ching, has died. Family lore has it that her husband killed her.

In San Francisco, Hoo Chun's business is growing. A new list of members of the Fook Wo Tong & Co. is submitted on September 10, 1932. It includes Wong Sum Foo (Harry) as an active member. It also lists Wong Yock Chou (Yat Chew or Yoke Choy) as a silent member living in Georgia. Yat Chew's two sons, Wong Kwock Ling (Ted) and Wong Kang Ling (Robert) are also listed as silent members residing in Georgia. Surprisingly, Hoo Chun's two sons George and Alfred are not listed while his young son, Wong Kum Quan (Howard), is listed as a silent member residing in San Francisco.

Harry is eager to get back to his wife in China. In March 1934, he applies for permission to travel to Hong Kong through Seattle, Washington on the Steamer "Empress of Japan" and to return via the San Francisco port. Harry departs on March 9. By the time he leaves China, he is the father of two children, a daughter, Wong Ngon Hoy (or Gum Yong or Joyce) and one son, You Jeung (or Yue Chong). Harry does not know that his wife, again left in Hong Kong, is pregnant. On May 6, 1936, Harry arrives in San Francisco via the SS President Hoover. Gum Foo (Jeff) their third child, is born in December 1936.

While Harry is in China, Hoo Chun plans to take his two sons, George and Alfred to China. Both boys are of marrying age, and Hoo Chun wants to make sure that they marry girls from the Sun Market area in the Canton Province. All three, Wong Ho Chuen, alleged Merchant; Wong Jong Choy (Alfred Wong) and Wong G. Washington (Wong Sum Quong) alleged natives are listed as applicants for a Re-entry permit, and a hearing is scheduled for May 21, 1936. The three are to proceed to the Angel Island Station via the SS "Angel Island," leaving at 8:45 A.M. on the date mentioned. An intensive interrogation of Hoo Chun and one of his business partners follows.

Wong Lai Shue, the bookkeeper at Fook Wo Tong & Co., testifies at the immigration hearing that there are sleeping quarters at the store. According to this witness, Hoo Chun, his sons, and the witness, Lai Shue, all sleep at the store. Later that afternoon, Hoo Chun also testifies that Alfred is the hired cook for the firm. He earns $35 a month!

A new list of members of the Fook Wo Tong & Co. is submitted by Wong Lai Shue, listing Wong Hoo Chun as Manager on his way to China on the SS President Coolidge. He lists himself as Acting Manager and Harry as an active member. When questioned about the finances of Fook Wo Tong & Co. he testifies that the business has an account at the Bank of America, and that Hoo Chun is the one who pays the bills by check. Lai Shue says that either he or Harry will be authorized to pay the bills in Hoo Chun's absence.

At a later testimony Hoo Chun also testifies that he is the only one who is authorized to draw on the two company accounts, at the Bank of America and at American Trust, both in Chinatown. When the inspector asks who will write the checks while Hoo Chun is in China, he says, "No one." The inspector asks, "How will bills and salaries be paid then?" Hoo Chun answers, "They will be paid in cash." George's and Alfred's names are still noticeably missing from the members list. Harry is an active member. Hoo Chun has called Wong Yat Chew from Augusta, Georgia to San Francisco to become an active member and manage the firm, and perhaps to keep an eye on the acting manager who is not a very close relative of Hoo Chun.

Because of the conflicting testimonies of Lai Shue and Hoo Chun regarding the firm, the Immigrant Inspector, E.I. Sims reacts unfavorably. In his May 23 report Sims notes the discrepancies and adds this comment to the report, "From the foregoing I do not believe that WONG HO CHUEN has established his mercantile status within the meaning of Section 2 of the Act of November 3, 1892 and I am therefore unable to recommend favorable action in this case."

The immigration authorities request additional documentation on a June 12, 1936 Memorandum; however, another inspector adds a June 17, 1936 Memorandum to the page:

Herewith a new partnership list of FOOK WO TONG & COMPANY, 940 Grant Avenue, also another photo of Wong Ho Chuen. It is not signed by the applicant. Wong Ho Chuen departed for China on the S.S. "President Coolidge on June 12, 1936 without waiting for return permit."

Harry, believing that his father may want to return to the U.S. one day, hires a lawyer, Walter F. Lynch, to obtain the very important document: A Re-entry permit. Hoo Chun, being Chinese, is not a Citizen. The laws of the time did not permit immigrants from China to become citizens, while their children born in the U.S. have the constitutional right to U.S. Citizenship. Hoo Chun's official status is "domiciled merchant," and as such, he must obtain a dated and limited Re-entry permit each and every time he travels abroad.

The July 7, 1936 letter from Attorney Lynch to the District Director of the Immigration & Naturalization Service, Angel Island Station, California, clearly explains why Ho Chun did not wait for the paperwork.

Dear Sir:

In re: WONG HO CHUEN, applicant for Form 631, #12017/58631.

The above named Wong Ho Chen departed from this port for China on June 12, 1936, S.S. "President Coolidge". He filed a verified affidavit with the Immigration Officials at the pier at the time of his embarkation. The affidavit stated, among other things, that the applicant's mercantile status had been preinvestigated and that he was about to depart for China and his intention to return to the United Sates.

Your letter of June 11th, 1936, addressed to applicant has been referred to me. I have been informed that one of the applicant's sons complied with the request contained in said letter some time ago and, therefore, I presume that the case has been completed by this time and forwarded to Washington. I have been asked to communicate with you for the purpose of requesting that the applicant's return permit, if and when issued, be mailed to the applicant's foreign address, in care of the American Consulate at Canton, China, with instructions that they, in turn notify the applicant of the arrival of the return permit and to call for it in person. The applicant's foreign address is the following: Wong Hoo (Ho) Chuen, c/o Quon Hing Co., Sun Tong Market, Kwong Kow Railway's Post Office at Sung Tong Station, Canton China.

I have been informed that the applicant had to depart when he did because of necessity, and without waiting to receive his return permit, for the reason that he had made arrangements to sail on the S. S. "President Coolidge" on June 12th, 1936, and his return permit (Form 631) was delayed because of the fact that one of his sons, who had filled out the typewritten application for Form 631 had failed to include the matters referred to in your letter of the 11th, ultimo, and the omissions deferred the closing up of the case until the matters omitted had been supplied. Inasmuch as the applicant had made, so I am informed, his application more than 30 days prior to June 12, 1936, he supposed that the return permit would be delivered before the date of his departure on June 12th, ultimo, and had purchased a ticket, along with his son, who was to and did accompany him on the voyage. The applicant, according to my information, had also written to his family and relatives in China advising them that he was departing on the 12th day of June, 1936, and would see them on or about a given time. He also had his trunks and baggage conveyed to the pier in contemplation of his embarkation on that date. So, there would seem to be some real necessity or emergency for his departing without awaiting the arrival of his return permit.

I am herewith enclosing, in duplicate, a memorandum giving the foreign address of the applicant in Chinese as well as in English so that the delivery of the return permit at his foreign address may be facilitated, if and when it is issued, and if the present request is granted. Please find herein enclosed an additional unmounted photograph similar to the one originally submitted of the applicant.

Kindly inform the undersigned when the applicant may be expected to receive his return permit, if it is issued, and if the present request is granted.

Very truly yours, Walter F. Lynch

The July 15, 1936 response from the District Director to Attorney Lynch is as follows: "You are advised that return permit No. 1106191 has been issued to Wong Hoo Chun (Chuen) and is today being forwarded to him in care of the Quon Hing Company, Sun Tong Market, Jung Shing District, China." Short and sweet!

Wong Hoo Chun, now seventy-nine years old, and his son George arrive in China. Alfred is not with them even though he was supposedly one of the departing applicants. For some reason he has changed his mind and remains in San Francisco. He never sees his father again. Hoo Chun does not return to the United States.

George Washington Sum Quong Wong leaves China on the SS "President Taft" and arrives on Angel Island on March 1, 1938 a changed man. He testifies that he married Ng Shee (actually Ng Wan Gow or Yow) on August 25, 1936. He has one son, Wong Ting (Tang) Chor, born on July 15, 1937, and his wife is three months pregnant. They are living in the Yew Tin village where their second son is born on September 1938.

Both Harry and George have left their wives and babies in the village. Hoo Chun remains in China, but he decides to move the two young women with their babies to Hong Kong. Ng Wan Yow, George's wife, testifies several years later that,

"Before my husband's father died he, my two sons, Ng Shee, the wife of my husband's brother, Wong Sum Foo, and her daughter, Wong Ngon Hoy and her two sons, Wong You Jeung and Wong Gum Foo all lived in the same house together. After my husband's father died, Ng Shee and her three children returned to the You Ting village to live. My two sons and I remained in Hong Kong until the end of CR-30 (1941) when we returned to the You Ting Village."

(editor's note: apparently, the name Ng Shee is the name for a married woman. So far several women have been called Ng Shee: two of Wong Hoo Chun's wives, Ng Hai and Ng Seung Yee, are both called Ng Shee in several documents. Harry calls his wife Ng Shee although her name is Ng Hoy Chee, and George calls his wife Ng Shee even though her name is Ng Wan Yow.)

On July 7, 1940, Alfred Wong and Rosie Choy are married in San Francisco. They plan to make their home in Hawaii, and Alfred departs San Francisco via the SS "President Coolidge" on December 4, 1940. Rosie joins him, but they return to the U.S. in April, 1941 on the SS "Matsonia." Their daughter, Rebecca, is born in San Francisco in 1941, assuring her American citizenship.

Storm clouds are gathering in China, with the invasion by Japanese armies in 1937, and winds of war are blowing in Poland and spreading across all of Europe, with the invasion by German armies in 1939. While life in the United States remains relatively peaceful, the U.S. government enacts draft registration in preparation for difficulties to come. In July, 1941 Washington declares a total economic embargo against Japan and freezes its assets in the United States. U. S. policies trigger Japan's December 7th attack on Pearl Harbor, and Washington declares its entry into World War II. The Flying Tigers, a volunteer troop of American aviators led by American General Clare Chennault, is formed in China to combat Japanese aggression. The Chinese civilian community is not immune to the violence. Several members of the Wong family are directly affected:

In March 1939, Choy Ping writes to the American Consul General in Hong Kong that her Form 430 (an important Identity document with an attached photo) was "stolen from her by Japanese soldiers when the village in which she was living in South China was captured." She values her American Citizenship and wants to assure her future return.

During World War II Alfred Tsun Choy Wong enlists in the U.S. Merchant Marines in 1942. He serves as an Oiler on Liberty ships that participate in Pacific Ocean actions. Around the same time Edward Vann Wong (a nephew of Hoo Chun) joins the Flying Tigers, an American Volunteer Group of Aviators, serving in China against the Japanese. He and Colonel Ma, a Chinese pilot, befriend each other, but Colonel Ma is killed in action and leaves a widow and two daughters. In 1943 Harry and George are drafted into the U.S. Army. Their families have to remain in China. While Harry is going through training near Chicago, Illinois, he meets Harriet Moy. He has never felt romantic love before. When he gets a short vacation, he takes Harriet to Augusta, Georgia to introduce her to his village cousins there. While they know that he has a wife in China, they are very supportive of Harry and Harriet. He takes her back to Chicago and serves out his military service. He cannot forget his love, so after the war Harry and Harriet get married on September 1946 in Chicago. At the first opportunity Harry goes to Hong Kong, where he and Ng Hoy Chee sign divorce papers.

In Los Angeles, Jack Tong, a family man raising four sons without their mother, is exempt from military service. He has an opportunity to buy a Japanese-owned grocery store at a low price. Hoo Chun's son Howard, in San Francisco is also exempt from military service for health reason.

Somehow, family life at home goes on despite the hardships and disruptions. In the Dai Dung village in China, Yoke King has two more children, a son, Lo Jun Chew (later named Herbert), is born in 1938 and a daughter, Lo Kwun Jun, is born in 1939.

In 1940 Wong Hoo Chun dies of old age in Hong Kong, and Wong

Yat Chew carries on the managerial duties at the Fook Wo Tong & Co. in San Francisco until he also dies in 1941 of unknown causes. Wong Yat Chew's wife, So Shee and her adult sons, exempt from military service because of family responsibilities, run the store in Augusta, Georgia and never see their father again.

Jack Tong has committed his wife, Suey Ping Tong, to a State Hospital for unknown reasons. Mrs. Quan, number eleven sister of his first wife, takes three-year-old Emily to China in May 1941, and Jack depends on neighborhood women to help raise his young sons. The boys are somehow managing to develop into mature young men without their mother. In Germany one little girl is running from one bomb shelter to another with her mother, surviving the horrors of war without her father, to become the wife of one of Jack Tong's sons.

After World War II, all the scattered pieces of the Wong Hoo Chun family overcome a variety of difficult circumstances in order to restore the American Dream of the man who sailed into the unknown on that unnamed steamer from China so long ago.

Throughout the 1940's and 1950's four pieces of the family are still living in now-Communist China. Ng Hoy Chee, Choy Ping, Yoke King and Emily Tong are raising their families in separate villages. Occasionally, they visited each other. Were they aware of their connection to America?

Choy Ping gets married to Meichi Ou. Her first-born daughter, Jianxiong is born the following year. At age thirteen, Jianxiong falls out of a tree and dies two years later. In 1948, Choy Ping's second daughter, Jianxi is born on September 14, and her son, Zuo Xian is born in 1951.

Yoke King loses her daughter, Kwun Jun, in 1945. A year later, her son Guey Chew (later named Herman) is born in the Dai Dung village in 1946. Her second son, Calvin, wants to move to America, but immigration restrictions on the children of American mothers, prevent him from fulfilling that dream. Using the birth certificate of Harry's deceased son, Yue Chong, Calvin arrives on December 29, 1950 in the United States on a PanAm plane. Clifford, Yoke King's oldest son arrives only two years later under his own name. The matter of whether the U.S. Citizen parent is male or female has been changed.

On September 24, 1947 Harry's 11-year-old daughter, Joyce Nam Hoy Wong, arrives at Angel Island (perhaps accompanied by her aunt, Ng Wan Yow), but his wife remains in China. Yue Chong, one of Harry's sons, has died in infancy. Harry's son Jeff Gum Foo Wong arrives on February 25, 1951 on the "SS President Wilson."

On October 8, 1947, George's wife, Ng Wan Yow is admitted into the United States, but she has to leave her two sons in China with her mother, Lau Shee. In 1948, she gives birth to another son, Kenneth. Their son William Wong is born in 1950 and their daughter Sharon is born in 1953 while they are still living in San Francisco.

In another village, Emily Neyrong Tong loses her stepmother, Mrs. Quan, in 1948. Mr. Quan remarries, and Emily remains with them until 1952 when she is sent to a boarding school in Hainan, China. Emily marries Zhou Mian Liang on July 17, 1960.

Meanwhile, the other pieces of the family are living and thriving in California and Hawaii. The family of Yat Chew has moved to Oakland. Edward Vann Wong, the son of Wong Kam Chen, has returned from his service in China with a wife, Jessie Ma, and two stepdaughters, Vera and Winnie. They make their home in Oakland. With the help and influence of Edward Vann, Suey Ping is released from the Norwalk State Hospital in 1954 into the care of her husband Jack. Her grown sons, Allen and Leighton have joined the military service. Eugene and Jerome, graduating from high school in 1953 and 1955, respectively, are almost ready to move on with their lives. Suey and her husband Jack own a big house, so they invite George and his family to move in with them in Los Angeles after their unsuccessful attempt to bring their son Tang Chor to America. All the blood tests are taken and the paperwork is completed, but something prevents Tang Chor's departure. George eventually opens his own liquor - grocery store and buys a home of his own in Los Angeles, but he never mentions his two sons born in China again.

After being honorably discharged from the Merchant Marines on January 14, 1946, Alfred invests in some acreage in Waianae, Hawaii. He builds a home for his family and starts a chicken farm to supply Hickam Air Force Base and Pearl Harbor with poultry products.

Harry and Harriet settle down in Oakland, where Barbara is born in 1948 and Dennis is born 1951. Harry remains with the U.S. Civil Service working as an instrumentation specialist.

In 1954, Allen Tong, Suey and Jack's oldest son, marries a white woman, Rose Zduniak! Even though miscegenation laws have been struck down as unconstitutional, Allen remains estranged from the family for several years. When their second son, Leighton, approaches Jack about a German girl he met while stationed at Kindley Air Force Base in Bermuda, Jack comments, "There's a nice Chinese girl living on our street!" Leighton doesn't take the bait. He and Marianne are married on November 17, 1956.

The Civil Rights Era has finally removed the last barrier to full Citizenship rights, and all those "nice Chinese girls" (and boys!) have become Americans.

Over the years all of Wong Hoo Chun's children (except Ging Ching who died young) have returned to the United States.

"Oh, Brave New World, that has such people in it!" Shakespeare's, The Tempest, Act 5, Scene 1.

Parallel Lives [3]

On September 22, 1888 a baby girl came into the world. Her parents were a sturdy German couple who owned a small restaurant and some acreage in the Hunsrück Mountains. They were just getting by in a village of seventy or eighty families. With their seven children they lived a peaceful life among the cows and chickens, moving through the seasons with faith in God. In time the little girl grew to be a healthy young woman.

Only seven months after the birth of this little girl, on April 21, and about 400 miles to the south, a little boy was born to another German couple. With no other children they had the resources to provide him with books and an education as he grew into a healthy young man.

The two never met, yet both have influenced my life in immeasurable ways.

Does anyone know whether the sun had stopped shining? How did the storm clouds gain enough strength to crowd the human spirit? Not only these two children but millions of others were being born into a world which was just becoming industrialized. Babies had to compete with machines for the attention of their parents, and the machines were winning.

By 1914, the spiral had gone out of control. Bombs were flying against bombs, flame throwers were throwing flames against each other, and poison gases suffused everything. The world didn't know whether it was made out of gaseous, liquid or solid elements, but there was no doubt that its plasma had become toxic.

The young woman, who had become a maid to a city family, kept her illegitimate child a secret from her married lover. She eventually married a widowed railroad engineer and bore three more children.

The young man failed to qualify for the professional art schools he hoped to enter and eventually became a member of a large group of malcontents.

The young woman's background of hard work and strong family ties, no doubt, helped her endure the hardships of giving birth and nurturing children in the midst of chaos. In the meanwhile, the young man served as a volunteer in an infantry regiment, operating mostly as a headquarters runner. He endured a leg wound and a gassing in the hostilities.

After relative peace was restored, the young woman raised a family which remains strong to this day. The young man was awarded high honors for bravery in action and found a new purpose (horrifying, to be sure) which his hitherto unsuccessful youth had failed to yield.

Maria, my indomitable grandmother, lives in me but occasionally seems to succumb to Adolf, her spectral contemporary, who has not yet relinquished his evil influence on my life.

The struggle between them continues to fuel my rage.

Forty Steps to the Balcony [4]

1997
1997 'Twas the day after Christmas and time to look back
The 1996 Santa had emptied his sack
For forty years as the family grew
Now the challenge was to find something new.

Suddenly a wondrous thought occurred
It was something from friend Della I'd heard
They had gone to Disneyland for Christmas before
And now the Tong's weren't too poor anymore!

1957 Baby Vivienne's first holiday in Bermuda was sparse
All we had was one present and a couple of paper stars.
1958 With two tiny babies the following Florida year
In a trailer we managed to keep the Christmas cheer.

1959 Little by little our finances improved
So the holidays became a time to be loved.
Despite lots of toys to occupy little hands,
Kathy enjoyed banging Mom's new pots and pans.

1960 The following Christmas went by in a blur
Because Marianne's third pregnancy preoccupied her.
But once Lisa was born the real fun began
A family of five requires a plan.

1961 We felt the girls were old enough now
So shiny red bikes brought a big Christmas "Wow!"
The park was a safe place to pedal their bikes
While Lisa had time to spend riding her trike.

1962 It's hard to remember what happened in sixty-two, you see
We had spent several months in Illinois and D.C.
California-bound and our eyes full of hope
We no longer had any reason to mope.

1963 For two or three years there was more than enough
Because grandparents could now be part of our love
Besides goodies and toys and holiday fun
1964 Our family was also blessed with a son.

1965 But shortly after Christmas a change in our life
Took us to Denver then Maine in sixty-five.
Marianne missed her Mom on Christmas Day,
So she forgot she had hidden John's trike away.

Since children view Christmas through rose-colored lenses
No one noticed that Mom had lost her senses.
We all enjoyed Maine and our beautiful home
While the war in Viet Nam was worrying some.

1966 In November Lee took Marianne's breath away,
"How would you like to spend Christmas in Californi-ay?"
She knew what that meant: a year without Lee!
With tears she accepted "what will be, will be."

1967 A bittersweet Christmas with a picture as proof
That the sleigh occasionally descends from the roof.
The holidays were stressful that year
Oma and Opa tried to dispel the fear.

Who knew whether Lee would return safe and sound?
The stress took its toll: lumps formed, blue and round.
They say, "Every cloud has a silver lining."

Eventually, Marianne found plenty of reasons to stop whining.

1968 Lee returned to take care of his brood,
And Marianne returned to her happier mood.
In Indiana life was good, and Christmas was better.
The children were healthy and perfect the weather.

When word of another move came in sixty-nine,
"Christmas in Germany" sounded just fine.
For nineteen years Marianne had not seen her father
There had previously been too many hard feelings to bother.

1969 With the Christmas spirit and maturity a good combination
Marianne attempted a friendly brief communication.
That Christmas brought us a priceless gift:
Marianne and her father finally healed the rift.
1970 Just before Christmas the following year
Emergency surgery filled our hearts with fear.
Marianne had been stopped by gall bladder trouble,
So her recuperation caused the joy to double.

1971 One of next year's gifts for the family
Was a trip to the Alps where we could ski.
1972 When we directed the Teen Club in Trier
We played Santa and Elves on the "Hill" that year.

1973 One precious memento of the Christmas loot
Is a picture of Großvater in a Santa suit.
After four years in Germany we had to move out
Orders for North Carolina caused us to pout.

1974 Our names had been placed on the "Naughty" list
So on Christmas we all felt that we had been missed.
Our hearts yearned for Fairfield, so the time had come
To get out of the Air Force and move closer to home.

1975 Once again the holidays became a happier time
With relatives to visit and choirs to chime.
The Junior Music Makers went caroling

And we went to hear <u>The Nutcracker</u> sing.

1976 How could anything ever be better made?
Our daughters would march in the Rose Parade!
1977 We thought we had reached the top of the hill
Nothing could ever top that thrill.

1978 For the holidays during the next few years
There were lots of parties and no time for tears
One memorable moment was caught for us
In an Elks Christmas picture with Leilani and Gus.

1979 We had two grandchildren the following year
Little Teddy had brought us more reasons to cheer.
He would carry our love to Germany
While the rest of us treasured our Family.

1980 Each Christmas brought happiness to all of us
1981 With Oma and Opa to make a fuss.
1982 They traveled each year to celebrate
1983 Starting out early so they wouldn't be late

1984 We missed Kathy and Teddy and also big Ted
Even though it helped to have Kaala and Les instead.
Then one day we heard the exciting news.
They were coming home with Janine to chase away the blues.

Elks parties, family parties and good Christmas health
Made our life very happy and increased our wealth.
When Ted had to go to Turkey one year
Kathy, Teddy and Janine would join us here.

1985 Just as we were together on Christmas Eve,
A shock came by phone, I didn't want to believe.
Großvater had died after an accident
My heart wasn't broken, but it was seriously bent

It is said that "Time marches on," so when things occur
One looks at one's blessings up front and quite near.

Our children stood by me and grandkids gave hugs,
So I got over the pain and the heartstring-tugs.

1986 The holidays in nineteen eighty-six were fun again,
Our new little grandson Keoki made up for the pain.
Besides, Ted had returned no worse for the wear,
And John and Katie were a newly-wed pair.

1987 After Oma's death in eighty-seven,
It was hard to pretend we were living in heaven.
Yet Christmas was good and we caroled alright.
With Opa included, we sang, "O Holy Night!"

1988 In eighty-eight Christmas was also fun
The family had grown by another one.
With Kimo and Keoki, the two little boys,
We had to make sure there were plenty of toys.

1989 A year later a great time was had,
With Vivienne's music, our hearts sang out glad.
So many good things to look forward to,
We almost didn't know what else to do.

1990 A motorized Jeep for the kids hit the spot
They could hardly wait till the weather got hot.
The Christmas party with Na Huapala was great,
And a new baby was coming for John and Kate!

1991 Little Eric fitted right in with the rest
Our living room felt like a small cozy nest.
That year we also got new dishes for dinners
Our wonderful family made us feel like real winners.

Since we all liked computers, there was only one thing to do.
We needed to find a way to come through.
Santa would bring each family one!
One request to the boss, and the purchase was done!

1992 Just when one thinks that everything's fine,

45

Life somehow manages to draw the line.
With the holidays coming, my face began to sag,
Though my heart filled with joy, I looked like an old bag.

1993 After I healed and stopped working so hard
It was time to start thinking about Christmas cards.
This time we could include the good news
That we have a new girl named Kelli Rose.

1994 Each Christmas since then has been filled with love
1995 We sing carols and give presents like angels above.
1996 We appreciate our family for coming together
And return back home through all kinds of weather.

1997 So this year we're having a wonderful time
A new granddaughter Leah has made life sublime
On Christmas Eve with Bob and Viv.
They certainly have a nice place to live.

We went! It was Disneyland for three wonderful days
I don't want the good times to disappear in a haze.
This one not-so-secret wish for a long time I've had:
To watch the Fantasmics from the balcony, real bad!

Thank God! From a couple from poverty town!
It's a lesson: Don't let anything get you down.
From Christmas to Christmas is just one short step,
All you need to do, is approach it with pep!

A Bear Named Bowling Shoes

"No, don't buy 'em," said Dave.

Annie, his wife, was disappointed, but said, "Okay." Secretly she thought, "He'll probably get 'em for me for Christmas." She was willing to wait, so she asked the saleslady in the Bowling Lanes Pro shop to hold those beautiful bowling shoes for her for a couple of weeks.

Those gorgeous bowling shoes with the metallic green leather with stitching around the soles and suede trim on the sides made Annie's eyes shine. Not only were they good-looking, but they fit Annie's difficult feet just right. The soft buttery insides and a padded top edge would surely improve her bowling. They were the Cadillac of bowling shoes with interchangeable soles and heels to make sliding on different lane surfaces more efficient. Annie thought, "I'll be able to bowl like crazy with those shoes."

As they were driving home, Annie asked, "Why didn't you think I should buy those shoes?"

Dave answered, "I don't like to get gouged. Besides, those shoes were way too expensive for the average once a week bowler. Only professional bowlers would consider paying that much for shoes, and you're not a professional." Annie was mad but didn't say anything.

She thought, "Christmas is coming. Maybe Dave was only teasing me and plans to get those beautiful shoes for my Christmas present." She let the idea of the bowling shoes go.

With the whole family around her on Christmas Eve Annie opened a huge box on Christmas Eve. Surprise, surprise! It was a soft, cuddly Teddy bear! She looked at Dave with disappointment and said, "I love it, but I thought for sure it would be something else."

He wondered, and asked in all honesty "Why, what did you think it would be?"

Annie said, "You know what I wanted."

"No, I don't."

She realized he was serious but reminded him. "Remember in the pro shop when I tried on those beautiful bowling shoes? I thought you'd get me those for Christmas."

He said, "If you wanted those bowling shoes, you should have bought 'em. I was just making a comment."

"Oh never mind. I have this lovely bear. I'll just name him Bowling Shoes. Come here, Bowling Shoes. You're a sweet, wonderful bear. You get to sit on my bed every day."

Every night, Annie says, "Hi, Bowling Shoes. How the heck was your day?" as she moves the bear from the bed to his special place next to her beautiful metallic green bowling shoes.

I Dreamed a Boy [5]

> Take the fruit of my womb, Lord.
> Let the milk of my breasts spill as bloody guts
> Onto the precious Earth in your infernal wars with Man.
> My tears will not be wetter than the others'.

Awestruck, I witnessed his birth, and twenty-one years later I helplessly watched him die.

Now and then, a vision comes into focus and thrills us with its significant three-dimensional reality. Such a vision was the birth of my first grandson. I was in the delivery room to support my daughter with little thought of anything else. Twenty-one years earlier when I first saw my baby girl, I had thought about the lives that would one day spring forth from her body. Now my body reacted viscerally as I watched our family tree grow a new branch. My mind reeled with memories and thoughts while I watched this part of me take a breath and become a soul unto itself.

My daughter and her husband Ted named this man-child Theodore Leighton after his two grandfathers. Immediately, "Teddy" became one of our household words. Reluctantly, I went back to my daily routine at UC Berkeley. I wanted to stay and play grandma, but I had committed to my studies, so I left. By phone my husband told me that Kathy would be able to come home soon, but that Teddy had to remain in the hospital because of jaundice. Kathy would go back to breast-feed Teddy every three hours.

I headed back home for the weekend. There I witnessed a miracle. Great pools of glistening tears gathered in Kathy's eyes when she talked about her little boy in the hospital. Those were the same eyes which had remained dry whenever she said good-bye to any number of friends and relatives as we moved away during our military years. Those were the same eyes which had looked upon the world with child-like wonder. Those were the eyes that had seemed so self-centered during her teen years. Now the tears in those beautiful eyes magnified the lovely soul which had just given birth to a son.

For twenty-one years my husband Lee and I enjoyed Teddy's appearances in our lives. When his daddy, big Ted, was transferred to Germany, the Air Force allowed him to take along his family. We tearfully said good-bye to Kathy and little Teddy who was only an infant. We missed those cute years when he learned to walk and talk, but we were grateful for the pictures. I was comforted by the thought that our loss was my father's gain. Ted was stationed at Hahn Air Base which was located less than an hour's drive away from Trier where my father lived. He kept me informed of Teddy's progress and enjoyed the visits with this little family and especially his precocious great-grandson.

In February 1983 it was time to leave Germany. Grossvater (as Kathy called my father) was sad to see the young family leave. Big Ted's tour of duty at Hahn Air Base was finished. Teddy's precious little sister Janine had been born five months earlier, and now we would finally get to experience this sweet addition to the family.

At the airport Auntie Lisa got a big kick out of Teddy. Teddy was bouncing around just like all three-year-olds ought while his baby sister was getting all the attention from the rest of us. We were all so very happy to have Kathy and her family back. Teddy and I bonded right away. The first night at home, everyone except Teddy was exhausted. He was wide awake, so I stayed up to keep him company. We were watching a movie on TV. When a fire was shown on the screen, Teddy yelled, "Gramma, fire!"

"It's in the movie, Teddy. Just blow it out," I assured him.

He puckered his cute little lips and blew and blew till the fire went out.

Teddy and his cousin Leilani, who was eleven months older and lived next door, thoroughly enjoyed each others' company. They played for hours in the same cul-de-sac where their mothers, Lisa and Kathy used to play with their friends.

For a whole month, we renewed family ties and even had a big baptismal party. Leilani and Kaala, our daughter Lisa's children, and Teddy and

Janine were baptized in one ceremony at Holy Spirit Church. Afterward we had a great big family party. Far too soon we had to say good-bye again. Ted was stationed at Plattsburg AFB in upstate New York. Now that they were on the same continent and not on the other side of the Atlantic Ocean, we planned a visit. We traveled across the United States and parts of Canada in our brand-new Buick Regal in the summer of 1984. On the way we talked about getting four-year old Teddy a small bicycle. In my mind's eye I could see him tooling down the street. I quickly suppressed fears of an accident with thoughts of the security of base housing. He was living in a fairly safe place, but I wished he were living with us.

About a year later I got my wish. "Mom, Ted is being transferred to Turkey, and we can't go with him. Can we come and spend the year with you?" Kathy's voice on the phone raised my hopes.

"Oh, I'm sorry that Ted has to leave, but I'm glad that you've decided to come live with us," I told her.

We had lots of fun during the year Kathy, Teddy and Janine were living with us. We repainted the small bicycle for the younger children and Teddy rode my larger one. We enjoyed small adventures, such as tracking Humphrey, the humpback whale, who had lost his way into the Sacramento River. Among other activities, we visited Lawrence Hall of Science with Auntie Vivienne, took a trip to Disneyland and started a whole new tradition: Gramma's Summer School.

When big Ted returned from Turkey, he was stationed at Travis Air Force Base, only ten miles away. I was very happy to have them live so close because it meant that I could continue to with our Gramma's Summer School. Eventually Ted and Kathy bought a house in Dixon, about a half hour's drive away, where both Teddy and Janine graduated from high school.

For more than ten years I continued "Gramma's Summer School" teaching them to play the piano, speak, sing, read and write German as well as bowling, banking, swimming, and lots of other things. At the end of each summer vacation, we staged a piano recital and poetry readings at our Annual September Party. Proudly, I watched as Teddy and his cousins developed into accomplished teenagers. Teddy excelled at several school sports as well as league bowling. He played the tenor sax and piano. He loved reading classic literature and became a computer whiz. His high school GPA (Grade Point Average) reached 4.21 because he attended several Honors classes.

Just before Christmas 1996 in his senior year at high school, Teddy lost his hearing. We were puzzled. Shortly after that he began to have nose bleeds. According to the results of medical examinations, his lung- and kidney functions were weakening. By February, his doctors had diagnosed his illness as Wegener's Granulomatosis *(a rare disease, in which the blood vessels and other tissues become inflamed. This inflammation damages important organs of the body by limiting blood flow to those organs and destroying normal tissue. Although the disease can involve any organ system, Wegener's Granulomatosis mainly affects the respiratory tract--sinuses, nose, trachea [windpipe], and lungs--and kidneys.)* Our entire family remained hopeful as we watched Teddy bravely endure the changes and medical treatment in his life.

Since he couldn't attend school, anymore, one of his teachers tutored him so that he could graduate with the rest of his class in 1997. That Christmas, we took the entire family to Disneyland, one of Teddy's favorite places. Despite a trip to dialysis in a clinic in Riverside and frequent rests in the hotel, Teddy enjoyed himself immensely with his cousins until late into the night. The whole family took another trip to Disneyland on New Year's Eve 1999-2000. By then Teddy had weakened considerably. He was in a wheel-chair much of the time. Again, Grandpa took him to Riverside for his dialysis while the rest of us enjoyed the hubbub of Disneyland. We all admired Teddy's acceptance of his condition as he was unable to go on the more strenuous rides.

For four years, he endured dialysis three times a week. Any college and career plans had to be scuttled. He spent lots of time on the computer, dabbling with day-trading in the stock market and hoping to develop some employable skills. Despite the excellent medical care at Sutter Davis and enormous amounts of medication, his condition gradually deteriorated. Toward the end, the focus was on pain management. Our tears could not wash away the poison in his blood.

...and then Teddy was taken from us. While he did not have to serve in the type of war I railed against in the introductory poem, he had to fight a war which drained his blood three times a week and eventually claimed his soul. Rest in Peace, Teddy!

Underwear Drawers

"Marianne, did you know that you can tell a lot about people by the way they arrange their underwear drawers?" asked Lynne innocently one day. "There are linear concretes and randomly abstracts."

"Really? I wonder which one I am. I'll tell you my story. Then you decide."

Lynne nodded knowingly.

Dare I approach this maze? If I enter this labyrinth, will I emerge unscathed? I'm reminded of the warning, "Abandon all hope, oh ye who enter here." Perhaps a thorough examination of my dealings with underwear drawers will reveal the ebbs and flows of my personality more clearly than the perusal of any documentary evidence of my existence. Perhaps I'll find things I'd rather not have disclosed.

For the first few years of my life I was blissfully unaware of the wrappings of my nether regions. Surely there must have been a rectangular receptacle (called drawer) in the dresser for the freshly laundered, neatly folded evidence of a baby in the house—diapers. And just as surely, there must have been a circular receptacle (called pail) for the soiled evidence of said baby despite the incipient world war. As the political climate of the times heated up, and my mother had to drag our belongings from one bomb shelter to another, my underwear must have been the focus of her attention. I'm sure I would have noticed if no panties for me had popped out of the frantically packed suitcases whenever we had a moment to change clothes.

When I finally discovered that people usually wake up in the same place they fall asleep, I began to recognize certain material trappings as my own. My desire to keep them organized and available must have seemed obsessive to uninformed onlookers. Intimate items, such as the pink panty my grandmother knitted and the "body-guards" of soft flannel that wrapped themselves twice around my chest under sweaters on cold winter days, were neatly folded and tucked into the only drawer assigned to me in the tiny post-war apartment in Germany.

After I moved to America, unpacking, sorting, storing and fondling familiar things in my adopted country became a comforting ritual. I actually occupied three drawers in my house trailer bedroom. I would rearrange my unmentionables, which had in the meantime grown to include a brassiere and some nylony stuff, every day; sometimes twice. I inventoried the precious goodies as often as I could steal the time from my studies of a new language. While my brain was being washed of all things German, my underwear drawers safely stored my true identity and anchored my soul in reality.

A teenager on unfamiliar soil is an unpredictable creature, and my obsession with order soon vacillated with periods of total slovenliness. At times I had to search frantically through laundry baskets for a wearable item just before the school bus was due to arrive at my door. With cyclical regularity, I mended, labeled, folded and stored every bit of my lacy wardrobe for several weeks just to throw it pell mell all over the house again for as long as I was allowed to get away with it.

Which spirit would finally dominate? Was I going to become one of the randomly abstracts or the linear concretes? Due to circumstances, not completely beyond my control, I became the mother of three beautiful girls and a handsome little boy. Their underwear, along with their father's, symbolized my effectiveness as a wife and mother. Not only was I able to keep my own underwear neatly in line, but my expertise in judging just whose little bottom each bit of fluff would encase was known far and wide. I was the keeper of the family's treasures, six of them. I was determined to win first prize if there were ever a competition for having the largest ratio of clean-to-soiled swaddling cloths. I luxuriated in front of the dryer as I plucked each panty from the drum and filed it in its proper stack. I triumphed over the laundry basket as I folded matching socks into "store-style" pairs. Friends, who came to visit for a cup of coffee while I continued folding, remarked on the lack of unmatched socks in my home in comparison with the number of singletons they had accumulated over the years. I prided myself on keeping track of whose was what, and why it went where. No washer or dryer dared eat any of MY family's underwear!

Eventually, I succumbed to the inevitability of change. A long-repressed rebellious imp reared its head with the advent of my three daughters' menstrual cycles. Their underwear was no longer my concern. I adopted an attitude of aloofness toward laundry that could be envied by beggars in the black holes of Calcutta. My apparently impossible request that each person, especially female, was to take care of her own things was sometimes heeded, sometimes not. Anguished cries of "I can't find my bikinis" shrilled me awake on school mornings. New muscles developed on my shoulders from all the shrugging. There is only just so much effort a mother can put into the environment of her young, and I had reached a point beyond caring whether Viv wore flowers, Kathy wore hearts, or Lisa wore stars beneath their Levis.

My mind was beginning to travel the philosophical circuit. College seemed a more logical place for this brain of mine than the laundry room. Underwear became nothing more than a soft convenience separating me from rougher textures. In my dorm room, one drawer served as the catch-all for anything that might touch my person. Why waste time sorting lingerie when there was a classic literary treasure to be read or a new classic to be written? Only words, words, words strung together in clever ways were important to me then; all else was mere nuisance. Graduation day found me with a degree in English; there was no award for keeping the world's underpinnings in place.

Currently, a relaxed eclectic atmosphere pervades my bedroom. At times my chaotic underwear drawer runneth over, and at times the elastic is neatly aligned with the ruffles. I let my mood dictate my attitude toward my delicates. When I have too much on my mind and don't know where to start, I grab a pile of pantyhose and run my spread-out hand inside each leg to check for runs before placing them neatly folded in their designated spot: on the left side of the bottom right-hand drawer in the big dresser.....

Susie's Car Keys

"Carmelita, there's a phone call for you!" Marie called.

Carmelita was helping Marie Kostas set up a garage sale just down the street from where Patricia, one of Carmelita's daughters, lived. Patricia and Leo were the proud parents of Nicole and Maria, two precious little girls. Patricia was expecting another baby in about two months.

"Who could it be?" wondered Carmelita. "I just left the house, and my daughter Ann was alright. I hope nothing happened to her kids."

"Hello, this is Carmelita."

The caller was Susie, her prospective daughter-in-law. "Hey, Carmelita, have you seen your son, Harry?" Susie demanded. When Carmelita said no, Susie demanded, "You mean that he didn't spend the night with you?"

Carmelita said, "That's right, isn't he at his apartment?"

When Susie said no, Carmelita asked whether they had had a fight, and Susie said, "Sort of."

"Is there anything I should know about? I certainly want to know if my son is in trouble or something."

Susie briefly said, "No, it's okay," before she hung up.

Carmelita was still arranging stuff in the garage when the phone rang again. It was Ann. "Mom, Mrs. Norton called again. She's really mad!" Apparently, Mrs. Norton and Susie had driven around and found Harry's little green Toyota parked in front of Leo and Patricia's house. They suspected that Leo was concealing Harry, but nobody was answering the doorbell or the phone. They wanted Carmelita to run down there to see whether Harry was really there.

"Good Grief! What could have gotten into Harry? Okay, Ann I'll go check," Carmelita said. Harry had moved into his own apartment after

Ann and her three young children had come to live at home while her husband was deployed to Afghanistan. Harry and Susie had plans to get married later in the fall. "I guess I'll have to run down there. If you hear from Harry, let me know right away. Bye."

Leo was outside in his yard, and the Toyota was still parked at the curb. When Carmelita asked him about Harry, he denied that he knew anything. He said, "Harry isn't here, but if you don't believe me, you can go inside and check."

"I believe you." Carmelita's little granddaughter Nicole reached for Carmelita's hug. "Leo, I don't know what's going on, but tell Harry that I love him if he should show up. I've got to get back to Kostas's to help with the garage sale. See you later."

Pretty soon the phone at Kostas' rang again. This time Ann said that Mrs. Norton had had a long talk with her and that she was threatening to call off the wedding if they didn't get things settled within twenty-four hours. Carmelita just shook her head and wondered "What is going on?" and then went back down the street to Patricia's. This time she actually went inside the house to check. She hugged Patricia and then looked around. There was no sign of Harry. Patricia didn't mention till later that afternoon that Mrs. Norton had already called them several times on the phone. Patricia seemed upset, though, so Carmelita stayed a little while to chat.

A little later she walked back toward the garage sale. She had nearly reached the corner of the street when a familiar-looking car came careening around the corner and barreling down Canvasback Lane. Carmelita recognized Susie in the car and thought, "Oh, Oh!" She turned around and ran back toward Patricia's house where she could hear them screaming at each other in the kitchen.

Susie yelled, "I just want to know where he is!"

Patricia was screaming, "I don't know where he is!" Carmelita then yelled that Susie apparently didn't care who she hurt. "Can't you tell that Patricia is pregnant and likely to have a miscarriage if she gets too upset? Also my two other little grandchildren were playing outside when you drove your car like a maniac down this residential street. Don't you care whether you kill somebody?"

Susie stormed that she didn't have to stay there and get yelled at and turned to leave. Carmelita grabbed her by the arm and said, "You aren't going anywhere young lady! You're in no condition to drive a car." Susie struggled to get free and in the process she hit Carmelita in the face with her car keys. Susie sat down real hard on the stairs because Carmelita pushed her away. Both women were screaming and grabbing at each other, so Leo and Patricia came over to subdue them. Leo took the car keys out of Susie's hand.

Carmelita had put one hand over her eye. She gingerly lifted it away and asked Patricia whether it was damaged. She said, "Well, there is a little bit of blood."

"Don't you dare let her drive out of here unless you want to be responsible if she kills a little kid out there on the street," Carmelita told Leo, and then she went to the bathroom to inspect her eye and clean up the damage. The swipe with the car keys had left a mark from the center of the forehead down the left side of the nose ending in an open cut just under the left eye. There were a couple of lighter marks above the left eyebrow and on the lower cheek. Carmelita's right arm had several long fingernail scratches.

She came out of the bathroom yelling for Susie to look at her. By this time Susie was sitting at the dining room table. When they started yelling again with Patricia joining in, Leo suddenly shouted, "All of you, shut up!" That calmed the three women down considerably. Gradually they started talking about what the real problem was.

Susies' story: It seems that Harry had come home to his apartment from the ball game. Susie was waiting there for him. After being questioned, Harry admitted to having had a couple of beers. Susie got mad, and they sat in the apartment in silence for a while. Susie finally decided to go home and sleep it off. Then they had another small argument about which car she should take. The Camaro didn't have enough gas, but she didn't like to drive the Toyota pick-up. She decided to take the Camaro and buy some gas. She drove around for a while, and then doubled back to the apartment to check on Harry. The Toyota was gone, so she drove past Rico's Pizza where the rest of the ball team was still celebrating. Sure enough, there was the Toyota. She got mad and drove home to her parents' house.

She must have gotten Mrs. Norton upset, so they decided to drive around looking for Harry and his pick-up. They couldn't find it at Rico's Pizza, so they drove past Patricia's house. When they saw the Toyota, they assumed that Harry was there and that's when the all the telephoning began. "That's all there is to it," Susie said.

Carmelita's eye was hurting, and she was too embarrassed to go back to the Kostas's to get her purse. Patricia called to tell Marie Kostas that Carmelita wasn't coming back to the garage sale for a while. Then the three women sat around the table talking until three thirty. As the conversation got calmer and calmer, a lot of things came out in the open. For one thing, Susie was overly sensitive about Harry's drinking because of her background with a drinking father. For another, Susie was absolutely right to worry about his driving after he's been drinking. "I guess I nag him about it too much!" she admitted. Not wanting to hear all the talking, Leo stayed outside most of the afternoon watching his little daughters, Nicole and Maria.

Later when the kids came in to play in their room, Leo rode his bicycle around for a while, and he decided to ride over to his sister-in-law Debbie's house in the same neighborhood. On his way back, he saw Harry walking toward the house. Leo told him that three women were waiting for him inside and that he better go in and face the music before going home. It seemed that he was just going to hop into his Toyota and drive away.

Carmelita had just stepped into the back yard for a breath of fresh air and was petting the dog when she heard Harry's voice. She stepped inside just in time to see him leave through the garage as Susie was leaving out the front door. Carmelita called through the garage, "Harry, what's going on?"

Harry looked somewhat embarrassed and disheveled. "I spent the night in the park," he explained with his head down. Then he looked at Carmelita and asked, "What happened to your nose?"

"Battle scars," his mother answered.

What Am I? [6]

1985 I cannot let Patriotism be my emotion;
My person's not big enough to span an ocean.
When God comes to ask, "Where do you belong?"
I'll say "With you, Sir, please do me no wrong!
Wherever you are, that's where I am,
Though I secretly hope that you'll board a PanAm!"
If *I* left America, few people would care;
But **YOUR** leaving with me would create a **BIG** scare.
With you gone from the scene when the rhetoric starts,
They wouldn't know what they mean about such-and-so hearts.
Instead of looking for you in the sky or the sea,
There'd be sick, poor, and old people for them to see.
What is the reason for trying to determine
Whether my person has been American or German?
Did it matter whether Humphrey was Humpback or Gray?
People would have treated that whale the same either way.
As humans, they're wonderful, considerate and kind,
But as partisan politicians, they show their behind!"
Please, dearly beloved; don't ask me to prove,
Whether I'm Republican, Communist, Democrat or MOVE.

Facing a Monopoly

Simone was upset. "Ouch, you just pulled my hair, Vivi," Simone had become extremely irritable since her agent called.

"Sorry, Mom."

Simone shuffled nervously through her jewelry while her daughter was brushing her silky black hair. "You look beautiful, Mom. Will you be back soon?"

"Tonight's dinner meeting may take several hours, but I'm returning tomorrow. Do you really think I look okay? There'll be lots of people from throughout the galaxy. The Tri-Planet Independent Writers' Association (T-P IWA) is meeting about some very important issues," Simone was obviously anxious as she continued to scrutinize her jewelry box. "I can't decide whether I should wear these classic pearls from the Venus Oysterium or these vintage Baltic Amber beads."

"Well, which dress have you decided on? Your decision about the jewelry should depend on the dress. But Mom, why are you worried about such a trivial problem?"

"It's not the jewelry, or the dress or even my hair that's freaking me out. This is such an important meeting that I'm ready to jump out of my skin, that's all."

Vivi laughed, "Mom, be reasonable, you can't jump out of your skin, so let's concentrate on getting you ready." Her daughter was trying to keep things light even though she knew how important this meeting was to Simone.

Simone had been worried for weeks about her new book. The Venutian Publishing Monopoly was no longer considering any unsolicited manuscripts. Even her agent had complained that the VPM was not accepting any new work from writers. Unless an author had obtained fame in the entertainment industry, sports or politics, the VPM was not interested. Authors, even experienced ghostwriters and screenwriters, from the entire T-PIWA were meeting on Mars to discuss their options. Usually, the members of the subordinate branches of the T-PIWA met at their regional locations and stayed in touch with the association via the inter-planetary social networks, but a special convention had been called because of the intolerable restrictions recently imposed upon newer writers. Simone had talked with her agent about her invitation. Should she participate in the discussion or just stay home and hope for the best?

Her agent had promised, "If you want to fly out to Mars, I'll go with you. I know that only authors are voting members of the association, but I can spend some time at the sea-side resort while you're at the meeting. I hear that the Terrestra Sea is beautiful during the Martian autumn. You'll be busy at the conference, but there might be a little time for us to enjoy the colorful evening afterwards. We can discuss some of the options and strategies on the two-hour trip up to Mars." However, this morning her agent had called Simone with the bad news.

"I'll have to fly alone. Why did he have to get sick at the last moment?" Simone wailed. "I wish you could go with me, Vivi."

"Mom, I just couldn't adjust my schedule on such short notice. If you don't stop wiggling, I'll never get your hair done," Vivi scolded. "You've flown alone lots of times since Dad died. You can handle the helicar like a professional pilot. You've had your license for years. Stop fretting! Now let's check to see what you're going to wear."

Slowly Simone calmed down. Yes, she'd flown her helicar to Venus and Mars on vacations with her husband. She was quite familiar with the control panel, and the vehicle had recently been serviced. Vivi was right. Too bad she couldn't take a few days off from her job, but Vivi was ambitious. She wanted to become a doctor, so she was carrying a full load at the University while working full time at a hospital. It was not a matter of money; it was simple ambition that drove both women to excel at their chosen careers. For years Simone was content to work with her husband in their successful jewelry business, but his death changed her. She sold the business at a considerable profit and began to write. At first writing was just a therapeutic exercise, but then it became a passion. She was hoping to publish her third book, but recent policies of the Venutian Publishing Monopoly had upset her plans. Her colleagues wanted her to join in a serious discussion concerning the VPM. She looked at her reflection in the mirror. "Not bad," she smiled.

Vivi was at the closet taking a simple but classic black sheath off the hanger. "How about this one, Mom? The pearls Dad gave you will look lovely with this dress, and YOU will look stunning!"

"Okay, but I'd better try it on. Maybe I've gained some weight since the last time I wore it," laughed Simone. "Then I'll pack it in my overnight bag along with a few other items. I don't expect to stay more than one night, but I can't wear it during my flight. Wearing a space-pilot suit is mandatory on inter-planetary flights, and I sure wouldn't want to upset the Space Police with the wrong outfit," Simone had regained her usual sense of humor and was looking forward to do battle with the VPM.

The helicar, an interplanetary vehicle, in the garage that also housed a brand-new Cadillac, was one of Simone's most precious possessions. Her husband purchased it after he had made a particularly profitable jewelry deal. She was glad that he had lived long enough to enjoy several vacations to Venus and Mars. She didn't mind having to do the piloting as he grew weaker and weaker. He encouraged her to maintain her license and become truly proficient at the controls. Vivi helped her into the cockpit. "Mom, I'm sorry you have to go alone. I wish I could have adjusted my schedule to go with you, but I was so sure that your agent was going that I never gave it a thought."

"Don't worry, Vivi. I've calmed down, and I'm actually looking forward to the convention. There'll be lots of intelligent writers to brainstorm the problems we're having, and the discussions might bring about some changes. Besides, the seafood delicacies at Lai Hall's Shang Hai style restaurant are to die for!"

Once she was securely buckled into her helicar, Simone began the countdown. The colorful lights on the electronic control panel danced as the electric engine started to hum. She adjusted her breathing tube and watched Vivi go back into the house. The automatic garage door opened, and the helicar slowly made its way to the helipad for its last-minute analysis before take-off. After a few minutes of whirring and humming Simone felt the vehicle rise gently off the helipad. Within five minutes it achieved the speed needed to leave the atmosphere. "I hope Vivi doesn't forget to secure the house when she goes to work," Simone thought as she settled into her cruising speed free of the gravitational forces.

She programmed the on-board computer with the coordinates for her destination and made sure that the autopilot with its intermittent "Wake up, pilot!" feature was engaged. Simone had learned the hard way during her pilot training that the almost-silent spinning vehicle with its lightly humming engine could relax the pilot too much. There was little chance of her dozing off this time; she was too excited to meet some friends again and apprehensive about the discussions. Would anything productive come out of complaining about the conditions in the publishing world at this convention? Simone turned on the radio for some background music and the regular reports of Earth-Mars traveling conditions.

With all the "house-keeping" taken care of, the helicar began taking care of itself. Simone's thoughts turned to the people she might meet at the convention.

Her childhood friend Sue Ping, an avid writer about dolphins in the environmental genre had indicated that she'd be attending. There'll be fireworks when Sue Ping notices the Dolphin soup on the menu! Simone smiled. Yes, Sue Ping was a temperamental activist. She was not quite as tall as Simone, and she still had her girlish figure. Her favorite clothes were casual jeans and hoodies that looked sporty and accented her cropped curly brown hair. When the occasion called for being dressed in more formal attire, Sue Ping wore simple styles and no jewelry, yet managed to look ravishing. More importantly, Sue Ping had been a loyal and dependable friend when Simone's husband died. How would Sue Ping, the dolphin advocate, accept the easy-going attitude of Lai Hall, the owner of Lai's Amazing Seafood Delicacies, the enormous restaurant overlooking the Terrestra Sea? There were bound to be words! Simone and her husband had met Lai on their last vacation.

Lai, an elderly Los Angeles-born Chinese, "escaped" to Mars when his wife of twenty-five years decided she just had to attend a fancy University. She neglected Lai in favor of "getting an education," so Lai left. He established his restaurant when the settlement around the Terrestra Sea was just getting started. His scruffy beard had turned gray, and his forehead had gotten taller, but he was still an impressive figure. He spoke quietly but with an air of authority. His establishment had a large hard-working staff, but Lai maintained the records himself on his ten-year-old laptop. Simone's husband had teased Lai about that laptop, "You can afford the best state-of-the-art equipment! Why don't you modernize?" Lai had responded with some vague Confucian reference to being frugal. He smiled when he added, "It works. I can order my weekly deliveries of sauces and spices, and I keep accurate books. What more do I want?" Simone couldn't wait to see whether that old laptop was still in service.

Would Tom and Bill also attend the conference? Simone had never met them, but she felt that she knew these two Internet friends, one a publisher and one a market specialist. They had both been very favorable to newer authors, but as a result of the recent policy changes at VPM, both had become involved in the authors' protestations. They promised to do what they could to level the playing field.

As the helicar approached Mars, the lights on the control panel began to dance. Simone adjusted the instruments for a smooth landing and contacted the control tower at the Terrestra Settlement. Every settlement had its own helipad for easy access and a large parking/service/recharging garage for the two-seater helicars. Larger space vehicles had to land on a public airfield located near every city and use the shuttle services to the settlements. As the helicar quietly settled down onto the smooth tarmac, Simone noticed that the garage was filling up fast, but she found a hook-up for her vehicle. By the time she got ready to leave the next day, the helicar would be ready for another trip.

"It's good to see you again, Lai," Simone said as they embraced. "You have developed quite a reputation for your dolphin soup! I see that you've added a conference center since my husband and I visited."

Lai grinned impishly, "And guess what! I have a modern office with state-of-the art computers now."

"I'm proud of you, Lai. Tell me, have a lot of writers arrived yet? I only see a few people milling about," Simone was puzzled.

"Many are here, but they're down at the shore of the Terrestra Sea. It's quite spectacular at midday when the dolphins come to the surface to play. Why don't you go down there to join them?" Lai suggested.

Simone nodded, "As soon as I freshen up a little. First I need to change clothes." Simone accepted the cup of Oolong tea offered by an attractive young waitress. "I see that you've also modernized your staff. She's quite a beauty."

Lai smiled broadly. "A man of business must change with the times." He liked expressing his thoughts in platitudes. Simone let that one go.

"Are you still serving dolphin soup?" Simone asked with a worried look.

"It's one of our most popular dishes. People come from all over for our dolphin soup and the sushi. I remember that you wouldn't eat seafood, so why do you ask?" Lai was very observant.

Simone took on a warning tone, "One of the writers who will be at the conference is an avid environmentalist. She has taken on the cause of dolphin slaughter, and she is very outspoken. Lai, you just might have a fight on your hands. Especially at this conference. All of us are in a fighting mood and have come together to air out our grievances, so Sue Ping might take it out on you."

"Don't worry, I know how to handle a difficult woman," Lai gave Simone a sly look.

"Just thought I'd warn you. Well, I'm going to my room to freshen up, and then I'll walk down to the shore. Bye," Simone picked up her overnight bag and quickly escaped before Lai launched his speech about his former wife.

The dining room was quickly filling up. Because of the excellent acoustics, the voices of agitated writers blended into a soft murmuring. "Ah, yes, there are Tom and Bill," Simone thought just as Sue Ping ran up to her.

"Simone! I was hoping you'd be here. Why didn't you answer my e-mail?"

"Sorry, Sue. I got so upset about my agent that I completely forgot to check my communicator," Simone explained. "Let's sit together to catch up on the latest gossip."

Sue Ping agreed, "Ok, but I don't know whether we'll have much time to talk, I understand the speeches are going to start right away. There are a lot of very angry people here."

The ladies got settled at a round table of eight. Richard and Jean had already taken their seats. "I think Tom and Louis will be joining us. Bill will be on the panel of moderators. I haven't seen Jack yet, but David said he'd like to sit with us, too," Jean said to Simone and Sue Ping.

Richard greeted the two cordially, "Hi, I'm Richard. I'm practically a neighbor of the Venutian Publishing Monopoly. This is my first trip to Mars, and I'm glad to meet so many people of like mind here. Something needs to be done, but I don't know what options we have."

Just then Jack arrived. "Done about what, Richard?"

"The VPM, of course! Isn't that what we've come for?" Richard told his good friend and neighbor.

David sauntered up, "Would you mind if I sit with you? I promise I won't deliver any sermons about good and evil," The group of six nodded and started to make small talk.

Simone looked at Sue, "Sue, let me ask you a great favor. Please don't make a fuss about the dishes served here. We have more important issues to deal with."

"Simone, what could be more important than saving the living creatures, especially those intelligent sea mammals who are being senselessly slaughtered here and in several other places?"

"Good question! I'll tell you what's more important. Our ability to write and get our stories published and publicized. That's what's more important. Just arguing with Lai about his menu will get you nowhere. Writing a book about the issue of dolphins being slaughtered and getting it into the right hands may actually initiate some changes," Simone calmly assured her friend.

Sue Ping smiled, "I'll keep those good words in mind. Just poke me in the ribs with your elbow if I get out of control, OK?"

"I promise," Simone said as she picked up the menu.

Jean looked up at the two handsome men approaching the table. "Here they are! I think some of you may already know each other. Please, sit down gentlemen. Why don't we just introduce ourselves. Then we'll have time to chat a little before the speeches begin. My name is Jean, and I write serial killer mysteries."

Louis reached out to shake everyone's hands, "My name is Louis, and I'm here because I'm not happy about the way the marketing of books has been monopolized by the VPM."

"I'm Tom, and I've been pushed out of the small publishing business by the VPM. There must be a way to come to a compromise without hurting anyone." Everyone nodded.

On a slightly elevated stage, the panel of speakers was getting seated. Bill, a familiar face from the social networks waved to Sue and Simone. He had contacted them to ask for relevant talking points. Nine other panelists had been selected from the various branches of the Tri-Planet Independent Writers' Association. Tom remarked, "I see that Kevin and Robin have also been invited to be on the panel." Kevin, a independent author was the youngest panelist. He was also an expert in publishing technology, but he had been rebuffed by the VPM.

A hush of anticipation settled over the audience as youthful servers brought out the first course: thin slices of dolphin tongue on platters of crisp green iceberg lettuce. Simone elbowed Sue. "There'll be plenty of dishes you'll be able to eat. Please don't make a fuss!"

Sue smiled, "I'll do my best to remember the pertinent issue! Tomorrow I'll deal with Lai directly." Simone was puzzled, but she did not want to pursue this issue right now. The master of ceremonies had begun to speak and the audience fell silent.

"I hope you won't mind if we set aside about a half hour for dining before we officially begin the speeches and presentations." The audience clapped approvingly, and the emcee sat down.

The group at Simone's table had become curious about the murmured comments between Simone and Sue. Louis asked, "So, Simone tell us why you have been whispering to Sue."

"Nothing special, I know about Sue's special sensitivity about dolphins, so I focused her on the topic at hand: fighting the VPM," Simone explained.

"Ah yes, the VPM," Louis smiled. The others at the table nodded knowingly. "I wonder how we can persuade that monopoly to recognize the Independents."

David conceded, "There's not much we can actually accomplish without a meaningful compromise."

"It sounds like you have an idea, David," Sue looked up. She had been looking disapprovingly at the next dish being served. "What do you have in mind?"

"I've presented my idea to Bill. When it's his turn to speak, pay careful attention. There will be some unexpected reactions in the audience," David said.

Jean and Richard looked at each other. They had not expected much from David who usually monopolized conversations with good versus evil platitudes. Jack reminded them that he had not been introduced to the two elegant ladies from Earth.

"Oh sorry, Jack, may I present Simone, an author of mysteries, and Sue Ping, a non-fiction author who specializes in environmental issues," Jean quickly spoke up. "In fact, why don't we all briefly state our interest in this conference?"

Tom was next, "My name is Tom. I've edited a number of specialized cookbooks, and I own a small publishing company on Venus. Unfortunately, the VPM has made it difficult for anyone to do business with me. When

I heard that the T-PIWA was calling a conference, I invited myself along. How about you?" Tom had turned to Richard seated next to him.

Richard related his disappointment when his newest novel was sent back to him unread. "A simple note was pasted on the unopened package—We are no longer accepting unsolicited manuscripts. They published three of my books, and suddenly this? What is going on?"

"My name is Jean, and I live right here on Mars. I had a similar experience when I forwarded a manuscript electronically to VPM. It was returned as a mailer-daemon! They've gone completely underground! There must be some kind of government involvement, but no one is at war! What could possibly have caused such drastic changes in policy?"

David, Simone, Sue and Louis also briefly explained their interest in the conference as more courses of delicacies were served. Despite the publishing issues at hand, a mellow ambience had enveloped the table by the time Lai Hall, the owner came to pay his respects. "Well, Ladies and Gentlemen, how are you enjoying the dinner?"

Sue smiled guilelessly at Lai and gushed uncharacteristically, "I was just telling my friends here that I must personally speak with you about this exquisite dining experience."

Simone drew in her breath and pinched Sue's hand. Sue went on, "Will you have some time for me tomorrow, Mr. Hall?"

He nodded graciously, "A gentleman can always make time for a beautiful lady." Then he bowed and left just as someone at the dais tapped on the microphone.

Simone let out an audible sigh of relief. "Thank goodness, she's not going to make a fuss right now," she thought.

"May I have your attention? Please continue to enjoy your dinner while we make some preliminary announcements," the Emcee, a handsome writer from one of the Earth branches of T-PIWA, smiled at the audience. "You may have noticed that we have several representatives of the VPM. May I ask you to stand and be recognized?" A loud murmur and some desultory applause from the audience demonstrated the general animosity toward the VPM as the small group of men rose.

The Emcee went on to address the small group , "Thank you for coming. There will be some strong opinions expressed by our speakers. Please be assured that no personal attacks will be tolerated. The panel has asked you to be present at today's conference because we will request some concessions from you on several issues. We will not only clearly state our problems with the VPM but also present some possible solutions.

You, the representatives of the VPM, have assured the panel that you have the authority to negotiate with us, the members of the T-PIWA. We, the delegates of the various branches of the T-PIWA will have an opportunity to vote on what should be done." A great round of applause met this announcement. Several representatives stood up and yelled, "Hear, hear!"

Simone wondered what the panel had already discussed. Would there be a general writers' strike. As she was thinking about the possibility of a strike another speaker was introduced. Simone recognized him as Alan, a well-known screenwriter based on Venus. She thought, "Why in the world is Alan here. He's not having the kinds of problems we new authors are having."

"I'll make this brief. I've been given the authority by my union to support new authors, young and old," he smiled ever so condescendingly at Simone, "in their efforts to get published. We feel that new authors with their new ideas can only benefit the screenwriters. We feel that the process of selecting the best work of the best authors can be made fair, which, as I'm given to understand it is currently not." Alan acknowledged a hearty round of applause and sat down. Simone peeked at the VPM table and was surprised to see the representatives applauding.

"Well, that's interesting," she thought. "Surely, they don't care what the screenwriters think."

The Emcee was introducing the next speaker, Nancy, from the board of the Libraries Consortium. "Thank you, the members of T-PIWA, for inviting me to this conference. As you well know, libraries only purchase books published by the VPM. We have continued this policy for years, and it has served us well. Books from the VPM have undergone careful scrutiny, while books from independent writers may or may not meet our standards of quality. It's unfortunate that the arbitrary decision to refuse any new submissions has left particularly talented authors with no opportunity to shine. The Libraries Consortium has given me the authority to support new authors in their effort to get published. Thank you," she smiled charmingly toward the table of VPM representatives who smiled back. Another round of applause filled the room.

Tom remarked, "I wonder what the small publishing companies who have been put out of business by the VPM have to say."

"Do you have some representation on the panel?" Sue Ping asked him.

"There are a number of us who used to be competitors until the VPM put us out of business. We met last month to consolidate our ideas and came up with some solutions. Dan was chosen to present our ideas," Tom said.

"Here comes Dan now," Simone recognized Dan because he had published her first book.

"Ladies and Gentlemen," Dan's imposing voice startled several member of the audience to attention. "Once upon a time small publishing companies were a vital part of the publishing industry. We served specialized markets and gave new authors an opportunity to present their work. We have been put out of business!" Several boos rippled through the audience. "Even though, I feel angry and resentful, I'm not here to cause trouble. I'm here to offer some ideas that may not have been considered by the Venutian Publishing Monopoly." Dan deliberately emphasized the full name of the VPM and drew out the word monopoly. "When an entity becomes so large as to eliminate all competition, it becomes a danger to itself. Without the refreshing resources of new authors and the competition of small publishing companies, the VPM is in jeopardy of becoming a dinosaur!" Dan boomed to another round of boos and cheers.

"What could the small publishers possibly have to offer the VPM?" Jack wondered.

Tom whispered, "Expertise!"

Louis asked "Just how will the VPM benefit from that expertise?"

"That's what I was wondering about," Jack said.

The Emcee introduced Linton, the next speaker, as a member of the Ghostwriters' Association. "Good Evening, Ladies and Gentlemen. Thank you for inviting me to speak. I seldom have the opportunity to speak for myself or for our association, but the problems of the independent writers has come to our attention. I've been selected and authorized by the Ghostwriters' Association to support the independent writers of the T-PIWA." His short presentation was met with some curiosity and a friendly round of applause

"Even the ghostwriters have gotten involved?" Sue Ping was astonished.

"I know! This is even a bigger deal than I thought!" whispered Simone. Jean nodded.

"Bill is up next. I hope he can make the important marketing angle clear to those nasty VPM representatives!" Jean commented.

Simone said, "He will, and at least the VPM reps are here, and they've even clapped for some of the speakers. Let's give them some credit."

Jean nodded again. "Point well taken."

Bill got directly to the point, "Let's say that one hundred out of two or three thousand manuscripts by independent writers are worth a closer look. Let's say that out of that hundred, ten have some real potential of making money. Current VPM policies do not allow that potential to be realized. If we, and I mean all of us here in the room, the screenwriters, the ghostwriters, the small publishers, the librarians, and any other interested party, work together to bring truly talented independent writers into the industry, that potential will be realized. It's a win-win situation." The audience responded with a great roar of approval, and the VPM representatives rose to applaud Bill. They had been expecting a much more negative attitude from the panel, but so far they were surprised at the lack of acrimony. It seemed that everyone in the room realized that greater forces were at work, and that even the VPM had been pressured into recent negative changes. Now everyone had an opportunity to turn the tide.

The Emcee announced, "So there we have it. Each of us has different issue to deal with, yet we have a common goal. We want to continue writing and making our work available to readers. It seems that this room contains all the intelligence necessary to attain that goal."

"Talk about stating the obvious!" Louis said to Richard.

"I thought the consensus was leading toward a strike. What's happening?" Richard nodded.

David smiled, "I gave the panel some solutions, but they haven't been presented yet. I think someone will do that any minute now."

The Emcee continued, "Ladies and Gentlemen, we are now going to take a break from the speeches. We have a wonderful musical interlude for you while dessert is served. Please use the time to refresh yourselves. In one hour, the panel will reconvene to present you with some choices. We will then cast our ballots. And here for your listening pleasure, may I present the Martian Constellations!" The music began as the delegates and representatives of the various groups started to stretch their legs. A general hum settled over the assembly while the music added a warm atmosphere. The Emcee and the panel moved off the stage into the crowd which was mostly on their feet.

"Simone, so what do you think of my idea to buy Lai Hall's restaurant?" Sue Ping changed the subject so drastically that Simone let out a tiny scream.

"What? Have you lost your mind?"

"Not at all, Simone. I've been thinking while the rest of you were listening to the speeches. I know I can't change Lai Hall's way of doing business, but I CAN change things if I BUY his business. I'm going to approach him tomorrow morning," Sue Ping calmly explained.

"Do you really feel that strongly about saving the dolphins? I'm just so shocked because I was focused on the panel discussion. Suddenly you come up with a completely different topic." Simone still couldn't take it all in.

Sue Ping was serious, "I've spent years writing about the dolphins, and I've had some financial success in other areas of my life. I've never actually been able to do anything substantial that satisfies my desire to make a difference. Since VPM has not accepted any more of my books, and I have become bored with beating my head against the wall of apathy, I want to follow my dream of becoming my own boss. When I first saw this place, I was overwhelmed with a feeling of peace. I felt as if I'd come home. I can make a difference here. Do you think Lai Hall would consider selling this place to me?"

Simone had never seen Sue Ping so animated. She was absolutely glowing. "Well, you've already made a good impression on him, and he's willing to meet you tomorrow. I wouldn't be surprised at ANYTHING that comes out of this weekend. I'm already amazed at the conciliatory tone of the speeches and wonder how the vote will go, and now you come up with THIS life-changing idea. I can only watch in awe!

One of Lai Hall's beautiful young servers pushed a serving cart laden with all kinds of goodies toward Simone's table. Richard was the first to choose a crisp apple dumpling with vanilla sauce. The others followed by choosing from the large selection of scrumptious desserts. Simone's favorite was the buttercream torte with chocolate and pecan sprinkles. There were also some delicate petit-fours, jellied fruit slices, and almond cookies. Another gorgeous server brought coffee and tea. "Would anyone care for an after-dinner liqueur or an aquavit?" She asked, pointing to the beverage cart.

Several people nodded.

A number of people were on their feet visiting neighboring tables. It was difficult to make out isolated conversations in the subdued murmur of the crowd. Tom remarked, "It's amazing that there isn't more dissent among the people here. The publishing industry has always been known for its cut-throat competition, and now it seems that we're all buddy-buddy."

Louis offered, "Perhaps it's the idea of fighting a common enemy that has brought out the cooperative rather than the competitive spirit."

Richard agreed, and Jean said, "Not only a common enemy but a common goal seems to have united us. I can hardly wait to see the ballot. What choices could we possibly have? What compromise could the panel possibly propose?"

David smiled, "I think they'll propose a strike before they present the ideas I gave them."

"Come on, David, give us a hint," Sue Ping had set aside her own excitement and gotten back into the topic of the conference.

"A strike?" Louis asked, "Why would the screenwriters and ghostwriters support something that drastic?"

"I don't know, but the threat of a strike may serve as leverage. We must make it crystal clear to the VPM that we're serious and have the support of powerful allies," Richard stated matter-of-factly. "Jack, you haven't said much about the issues. How do you think this conference will affect the independent writers?"

Jack cleared his throat and said, "I was doing a lot of thinking about this while I was listening to the speakers. The T-PIWA obviously believes that its members are authors who deserve a chance at publication. That much is clear from this conference. The other organizations, such as the Libraries Consortium and the Ghostwriters Association appear to support the T-PIWA. I'm not surprised that the screenwriters support the independent authors because they have a lot to gain from the new ideas. Even the small publishers have come to support the independent authors, so I have a very optimistic view of the outcome."

Everyone around the table nodded in agreement, "I'm also optimistic, although the threat of a strike bothers me," Jean interjected. "What would ghostwriters have to gain by striking?"

Richard explained, "Many of the ghostwriters are also independent writers using pseudonyms."

Jean said, "Oh, I never realized that. Now it makes sense."

The background music stopped, and some chair-shuffling noises came from the stage. A kind of nervous hush came over the audience. Soon the panel would present the options. Bill, the chairman, was placing a box of ballots on the dais, and the Emcee took his place near the microphone.

"Ladies and Gentlemen, we are ready to commence with our meeting. I hope you enjoyed your desserts. How about another round of applause for the musicians, The Martian Constellations?" the Emcee waited for the applause to die down. "We've come to the moment of truth. The panel is ready to present its well-thought-out alternatives. Here is our chairman, Bill."

Bill, never at a loss for words, jumped right in, "In order to avoid a strike, the T-PIWA must work out a compromise with the VPM." A loud rumble went through the crowd. All eyes were on the VPM representatives at their table closest to the stage. The VPM reps looked somber. They had no way of knowing how the authors would vote.

Someone from the back of the room yelled, "Mr. Chairman, I move all writers go on strike."

Bill inquired, "Do I hear a second?"

Tom raised his hand, "I second the motion."

Bill opened the discussion, "Is there any discussion?" A dozen hands waved for recognition.

Simone groaned and whispered, "Oh God, Sue! Here we go. We could be here till midnight discussing whether to strike or not. Why did he have to bring that up first?"

"I think he wanted to show the VPM reps that we're serious about striking. We can discuss a strike and the alternatives. Then we can vote the strike down." Sue Ping assured Simone.

While the discussion went on, it became clear that the majority was ready to vote.

Sue Ping raised her hand to be recognized. "Mr. Chairman, only a few minutes ago, a compromise was mentioned as an alternative to a strike. Would it be possible to hear the terms of the compromise at this time?"

Bill gratefully smiled in her direction, "Yes, we are still discussing a strike, and all opposing viewpoints to a strike can be considered at this time. Let me distribute these handouts while I read the salient points of the compromise. After the membership has had an opportunity to review and discuss the compromise, the motion to strike will come to a vote. If the strike is defeated, we can offer our terms to the representatives of the Venutian Publishing Monopoly. Could I please get the members of the the panel to distribute the compromise handout. We will take a fifteen minute break after I've read the points. There's no need to rush into a decision. I'd like the membership to be well aware of this unique opportunity to influence the VPM. Thank you."

Simone elbowed Sue Ping, "Well done, Sue. Now we'll find out what the mystery was all about."

David's expression had changed to a satisfied smile. He was certain that the panel had taken his suggestions seriously. "I'm sure that the VPM will accept our terms," he whispered to Jean.

Bill began enumerating the point of the compromise.

1. All manuscripts submitted electronically or on paper by independent authors will be accepted at Level One and get at least one reading by trained college interns to qualify for a second reading. Manuscripts that don't qualify will be returned to the author with a brief explanation. VPM will be responsible for establishing and manning a Level One site in each major university within the Tri-Planet confederation.
2. All manuscripts qualified by level one will be advanced to Level Two and critiqued by experienced editors/reviewers for advancement to Level Three. Manuscripts that don't qualify will be returned to the author with a brief explanation. VPM shall be responsible for establishing and manning at least one Level Two site in each state/province on each planet, Venus, Earth and Mars.
3. All qualified manuscripts will be read at Level Three by a qualified editor. At this level, the editor may contact the author personally for critique and possible revisions. Again, VPM shall be responsible for establishing and manning one Level Three Editorial Board on each of the three planets.
4. The Level Three editors will then submit the polished and "ready to be published" manuscripts to the VPM management for final review.
5. VPM will then guarantee that at least fifty percent of the polished manuscripts will be integrated into their routine promotions, marketing services and advertising campaigns. The remaining fifty percent of manuscripts will be published if the author chooses to do his or her own promoting, marketing and advertising.
6. I accept the terms of this compromise_____
7. I vote to strike_____
8. My suggestions_____

The audience eagerly read the proposal along with Bill. At the end of his reading, Bill was met by a spontaneous clamor for recognition and random applause. He tapped on the microphone, "I know that all of you have comments and perhaps some objections. Remember, this is a compromise—a way of avoiding a general strike. There is no need to bring another motion to the table. We have a motion to strike on the table. I'm asking you to keep any further comments brief. Let's take a fifteen-minute break to absorb this compromise. You will then have an opportunity to vote on that motion. If you agree with the terms of the compromise, please vote against the strike. Mark number seven on the ballot with a NO. If you have any additional comments, please add them at the bottom of the handout." The audience had gone silent. Everyone was busy rereading the points of the compromise.

"Well, is that what you had in mind, David?" Simone looked up from her handout.

"Those points represent the essence of what I suggested. The panel did an outstanding job of presenting the entire issue. Look over there at the VPM representatives. They are busily engaged in studying handout. It looks promising!" David smiled.

"I wonder where that leaves us small publishers?" Tom wondered. Nothing in the compromise dealt with the dilemma of the small publishers having been forced out of business by the VPM.

Sue Ping offered, "Tom, perhaps this whole conference has opened the eyes of the VPM management. Why not benefit from all the manuscripts that will be rejected at each level? There are bound to be some manuscripts worth editing into a publishable book. This should provide enough work for the small specialized publishers. I have to believe that VPM couldn't possibly object to a small company that is not in direct competition with them."

"Also the small publishers have another thing to offer VPM: the skills to staff the Level Two and Level Three offices," suggested Jean.

Tom brightened up a bit. He had some good connections, and his business could survive if VPM doesn't interfere. A plan to garner the best of the rejections was beginning to take shape in his mind. "OK, I'll vote against the strike." He smiled.

When all the votes were counted, the strike was averted and the compromise accepted. The VPM representatives were smiling and shaking hands with the members of the panel. A general sense of relief settled over the crowded restaurant. The Martian Constellations were preparing to play another set of light-hearted songs as some of the guests called for more cocktails. A few were already leaving, but many remained to socialize.

Lai Hall made another appearance at every table. Ever the consummate host, he complimented the guests on coming to such a satisfactory conclusion. Then Lai sauntered over to Sue Ping who had moved toward the VPM table. "Miss Sue, I hope you haven't forgotten our appointment. Please join me for breakfast on the North Terrace. At nine o'clock we shall have a magnificent view of the dolphins playing in the Terrestra Sea." Knowing about Sue's concern about the dolphins, Lai enjoyed teasing her with his little joke.

====

Simone was enjoying a leisurely morning at the spa. She had gotten up early to check whether her helicar had been serviced for the trip back home this afternoon, and now she was lounging in a comfortable chaise, sipping a mint julep and watching the dolphins frolicking in the Terrestra Sea. Her curiosity about Sue Ping grew with every moment. Had she actually closed the deal with Lai? In the bright sunlight, she blinked as two figures approached her.

"Simone, I was hoping I'd find you here," Sue called out.

"Simone, your friend here drives a hard bargain," Lai smiled. "We have come to an agreement!"

"Well, don't just leave me out on a limb! What have you two cooked up?" Simone couldn't disguise her curiosity.

"You'll be happy to know that by three o'clock this afternoon, Lai's Amazing Seafood Delicacies will officially become Sue Ping's Amazing Delicacies. With a new menu, I might add." Sue announced. Lai nodded approvingly.

"I have seen the error of my ways," Lai acknowledged in his typically cryptic way. "I will leave my restaurant in the capable hands of your friend Sue Ping."

"Congratulations! Both of you! Shall we order some more mint juleps to celebrate?" An attractive server had already anticipated their mood and appeared with a tray of fresh drinks and some fruit and cheese. "What will you do now, Lai? Will you stay here and show Sue the ropes?"

"No, she has assured me that she will manage without my presence. The staff will support her, and I have developed a great desire to return to Earth, my home," Lai's eyes twinkled mischievously at Simone. "I understand you have a two-seater. I would love to be your passenger. How would you like some company on the way home? We could discuss your future as a successful author."

Simone's eyes twinkled back at Lai, "Of course, Lai."

Jumping Jacks

Our new baby, Vivienne, got her first firm shoes when she was only nine months old. She kept standing up and tried to walk every chance she had. The lady in the shoe store remarked that Vivi was a little young for walking, but the sale was made. As it turned out, Vivi didn't actually walk independently until she was just short of a year old, but the shoes had already shown signs of wear and tear. Soon they became too small for our cute little devil. It was time for a new pair of shoes.

For years I had admired a certain kind of baby shoe: the Jumping Jacks. The sole continued up the back of the heel and gave the shoe a look of firmness with plenty of support for the little angel's ankles. We somehow saved up enough money to buy a pair of these expensive shoes. Since babies' feet grow very fast, the Jumping Jacks were hardly worn before they became too small for Vivi. I put them away for any future children.

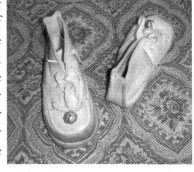

Our second baby, Kathryn, had delicate little feet. She didn't get to wear the Jumping Jacks until she was two years old and walking around outside. She wore the shoes for six months and put her own contours and plenty of scuff marks on the sturdy leather. Finally I cleaned them up and put them away for Lisa.

Our third daughter, Elizabeth, was our largest baby at birth. Before she was a year old, she fit into the Jumping Jacks for her first steps. Although the shoes had been used, they were so well preserved that Lisa was able to do her favorite dance in them. With one hand she held on to an awning post and walked round and round on the rough cement until she got dizzy. Then she let go and fell down on her well-padded bottom laughing. Within a month, the shoes got packed up. I had the idea to get them bronzed for posterity.

A few years later, our son, John, was born. Naturally, I couldn't resist letting him wear the Jumping Jacks for a couple of weeks. By now they had attained a sentimental value and history. John grew out of them quickly and got regular boy shoes before anyone could embarrass him about "hand-me-downs" from his sisters.

The Jumping Jacks, now a museum piece, remain a priceless treasure in our home!

It's Not Just a House

When my husband Lee was first transferred to Travis Air Force Base in northern California near the cities of Suisun and Fairfield, we were a family of five. Because we had three little daughters, I decided to stay with my mom and dad in southern California for a couple of weeks while Lee went ahead to find us a home.

Fairfield was a small but thriving town in 1963 with Suisun City a tiny shabby neighbor. Lee brought us to a rented three-bedroom apartment within a stone's throw of an oil storage- and shipping company in Suisun. Visions of explosions and rolling fireballs kept me from feeling secure in our new home. I was able to endure our cramped style less than a month. In Florida we had lived in a mobile home that was smaller than this apartment; however, there was a swimming pool, a playground, beautiful landscaping and plenty of open space in the Kingman Mobile Home Park. Here, in this ugly apartment, I was desperately unhappy, so we went house hunting.

Supporting a family on a limited military income was challenging but not impossible. With my home-making skills and Lee's frugal budgeting, our finances and credit allowed us to dream of owning a "real" (if not very fancy) house. We found a 980 square foot, two car garage house in a cul de sac near a school for $14,300. With a 5.35% mortgage we couldn't go wrong. In late August we moved into our future home.

We registered Vivi and Kathy in school that would start right after Labor Day. Lisa was not three years old yet, so my day was easy, and I was happy once again. We had a fenced-in back yard, a tree-lined street, a quiet cul de sac, nice neighbors and steady employment. What more could I want?

One day Lee told me he would be working on the night shift. My old insecurities gnawed at me. How would I be able to help my family if something happened while I was asleep? Through years of sleeping through all kinds of things that go bump in the night, I had learned to ignore noises and sleep like a log. I wanted a dog that would bark in case of an intruder. Lee agreed that a dog was a good idea.

"Happy" got his name because he was so happy to be adopted by a loving family with three little girls. All the way home from the animal shelter he seemed to smile while wagging his tail like mad. Happy moved around with us throughout our military years. I could go on and on about Happy in Colorado, Indiana, Maine, Germany, and North Carolina, but this is the story of our house, not of our dog.

Our house! Oh, the happiness! I made curtains. We fixed the landscaping. We scraped together furniture from thrift stores. We even bought a second-hand piano at a garage sale to give the girls a chance at music lessons. It was not difficult to fill the three small bedrooms to make us comfortable. By Christmas we were able to welcome my mom and dad for a nice vacation. Something else must have happened around Christmas that year because in September of the following year, we brought our newborn son John into our house.

We hardly had time to realize that our house was actually too small for our growing family. In early 1965 the Air Force transferred us to Colorado. I didn't want to leave my home, but a decision had to be made. Friends advised us to sell the house, but we didn't want to do that.

We rationalized that renting out a simple house built on a concrete slab was not risky business. Even if the house were completely wrecked by the time we came back, we could rebuild on the land. Besides, we had grown to love the location of our property. The weather was wonderful, we could see blue skies and NO SMOG, also it was between two beautiful cities, San Francisco and Sacramento, and so we decided to keep it. A real estate agent took over the rental management, and we were on the move once again.

After the training in Denver and an eighteen month stint at Dow Air Force Base near Bangor, Maine, we returned to Fairfield. Lee had orders again.

When Lee was transferred for one year to Thailand during the Vietnam conflict, I moved back into our house. My parents wanted me to live closer to them for that year, but I was sure I'd be more comfortable being my own boss in my own home. The girls went back to the same school they had already attended, and my neighbors welcomed me back. I was a wife raising a family of four while her husband was serving their country. Despite my patriotism, I gradually became an emotional basket case. The house patiently endured my anger and frustrations while I hammered on the piano or dug up the backyard. The walls bravely accepted paint and picture hangers, and the doors didn't mind being slammed. This was **MY** house, by golly, and I could do what I wanted!

I was hoping that Lee would return from Thailand for a tour of duty at Travis, but he was transferred to Indiana instead. However, he was able to return to the states for a short time in September for two weeks which helped to break up the loneliness for both of us. There was no question this time about keeping the house. We contacted the realtor again and moved our family to Bunker Hill Air Force Base in Indiana in early 1968. We didn't see our house again until August 1974.

In 1974 while stationed at Seymour Johnson Air Force Base in North Carolina, Lee decided to retire from the Air Force. He brought us back to our house early so the kids could start school. He would not be free to retire until November, so he had to return to North Carolina right away. That summer was particularly hot and called upon all my resources for survival without my husband.

Despite its welcoming embrace the house proved to be very restrictive for us. The girls were now teenagers, and John needed his own space. We had no air-conditioning, and the refrigerator broke down in the hottest part of that summer. Most of our stuff was still stored in the garage, so we felt like we were camping in our own house. For a little cool relief, Vivi and I dragged a heavy air conditioner from the garage into the kitchen doorway. The window installation would have to wait for Lee's expertise. We kept the broken refrigerator supplied with bags of ice. I told the kids this type of "indoor camping" was like the "olden days." We made plans for expanding the house when the head of the house came back.

With a very limited budget but plenty of heart, Lee began to transform our tiny house into his castle. First he got a building permit to convert the garage into a room. Then he had to build a carport that would not infringe on the easement between our property and the neighbor's property. Fine! Finally, he took the garage door down and built a wall with a window and front door. Many meals and many hours of sweat later, our house had a new living room. Lee put a temporary sliding room divider between the kitchen and the old living room to make a bedroom for Kathy and Lisa. Now we had plenty of space, and we were satisfied for a few years.

New ideas for remodeling kept nagging at me. I envisioned adding a playroom in place of our makeshift back porch. Even though our children were maturing and moving out, we had acquired a lot of stuff that needed more space. Walter, a close friend of ours, was a contractor who had added rooms to the homes of several other friends. We invited him to estimate the cost of adding a room and a laundry room. He came over one afternoon. After we had finished discussing the possibilities, we had a plan to build a two-story addition with a laundry room, a stairwell, an upstairs master bedroom, a dressing room and a full bathroom. We also took a second mortgage to pay for all of that.

Again, the sweat and energy of Lee and our friend Walt was cemented into our house. A mutual friend who was also a contractor, George, found a plumber who took care of the piping in the addition. Roofers and stucco experts were called. Little by little the house grew as I watched in amazement.

I made my contribution by keeping plenty of food and drink available to replenish the working men. By the time our fourth grandchild was born we had a large house with a new roof, central heat and air, and plenty of room to keep the babies comfortable.

Naturally, such a palace needs a modern kitchen. Our friend, George, employed his family in his local cabinet-making factory. We invited him to give us an estimate on remodeling our kitchen. A couple of months later Lee, George and Walt presented me with a brand-new kitchen. Our house was shining with pride.

In gratitude, the house provided sufficient equity to help finance my college education and the down payments on our children's homes. The house had turned into a gold mine. We rewarded the house with a doughboy swimming pool to make the hot summers more bearable for our grandchildren. Naturally, a covered deck had to be built. By this time, our son, John, and our son-in-law, Les, had matured into muscular helpers. Under Lee's supervision, they connected the swimming pool to the house with decking. Lee then finished the project with a patio roof.

It was 1985, and we had enough room to welcome Kathy with her two children, Teddy and Janine. Her husband Ted was in the Air Force and had been transferred to Turkey for a year, so they would live with us. One of the small bedrooms had become our office, and the other one was the children's room. Our former master bedroom offered Kathy a private space of her own while Lee and I had our privacy upstairs.

A couple of years after they moved out, we noticed a water-running noise in our downstairs bathroom. There was also a warm spot near the toilet. We called another friend, Gene, a retired plumber to give us a diagnosis and an estimate. The bad news was that the concrete floor would have to be opened up to repair the hot water pipe; the good news was that I could now have what I'd wanted for years: combining the two small downstairs bathrooms into a larger one. We had a second bathroom upstairs now, so remodeling downstairs would not cramp our style. Again, Lee poured his heart and soul into the building.

He dug a huge hole in the concrete to expose the broken pipe. Gene helped him install the plumbing for a new shower while I had the pleasure of choosing the tile and wallpaper to finish the project. That year we celebrated the complete amortization of our first mortgage. Our children had diligently paid off the loans we had extended to them, and our second mortgage was soon paid as well.

When we needed a new roof, we called another friend, Bruce, to give us an estimate. When we needed the outside painted, we called our son-in-law, Ted, to give us an estimate. Both men put their imprint on our house.

Lee retired, and I had a new career. Even though our happiness was tempered by the death of our beloved Teddy, and the divorce of our daughter Lisa, our family was doing well. We still had plenty to be thankful for. We rewarded the house with double-pane windows to keep the outside climate changes from harming the ambience of our home. After a new paint job, the house appeared to be content, but it was asking for another favor.

Our office was cramped and messy, and our hobby room was loaded with stuff. These two tiny former bedrooms were somehow incongruous with the nice guest room we made out of our former master bedroom. It was time to tear down the wall between the two small rooms and make a nice large "study" out of the space. We called George for an estimate. The plan was to put floor to ceiling cabinets on both facing sides and bookshelves along the entire window wall. Silently, George measured and calculated. Then he agreed to take the job.

His grandson, whom I had known since infancy, installed the cabinets. Another grandson came to install the doors. His daughter processed the paperwork. Who knew that George's family would become part of our house? Lee finished the project by installing a beautiful ceiling fan and hanging new doors on every downstairs room.

Our grandson Kimo helped me build a beautiful flowerbed to enhance our backyard landscaping. He was surprised how much effort and sweat had to go into such a project. I just smiled. Our grandson Keoki planted daffodil bulbs that still provide beautiful blossoms every year.

Our carport started looking shabby, and some of the wood had dry-rot. Kevin, our granddaughter Leilani's husband, had just been laid off, so we hired him to tear it down and replace it with a brand-new one. He also painted the woodwork on the rest of the house.

One day as I was relaxing in our hot tub that had replaced the doughboy. I was looking at the house and thinking of the things I've heard people say to rationalize when a natural disaster destroys their home, "It was just a house. At least we're all alive." I just can't bring myself to accept that. Considering all the elbow grease and sweat that has been cemented into these walls and listening to the echoes of the laughter and sweet voices of our grandchildren, Leilani, Teddy, Kaala, Janine, Keoki, Kimo Eric, Kelli and Leah reverberating from those walls, I insist: it's **not** just a house; it's a home with built-in humanity. It's a piece of God.

Memories of Della

We go back a long way, Della and I.

Back in 1964 when we both had children attending Anna Kyle Elementary School, we were members of the PTA. Della's husband George was the president of the PTA that year. In October, we both helped in a fund-raising carnival. Della and I ran the snow cone machine, a favorite concession on this hot day, and got all sticky. My little Johnny was 12 days old, and he sat in his little infant seat while both Della and I had a bunch of other little kids running around.

The following summer Lee and I moved to Denver. When we returned to Fairfield over ten years later, we joined the Elks. Della and I recognized each other and reminisced about our PTA days. We were still energetic and threw ourselves into Elks activities. I remember the salad luncheons, the White Elephant sale and a fashion show she organized. Della, the chairman, presented one of her creative ideas: We should have a "Dogpatch goes Elegant" fashion show.

She selected me to be Daisy Mae and wanted Lee (who happens to be Chinese) to be Li'l Abner. As she was cajoling, "Aw come on, Lee," Kaz Muto, a Japanese friend stepped up and volunteered to play Li'l Abner. In all seriousness, she looked at Kaz and said, "You can't be Li'l Abner because you're oriental!" Then she looked at Lee and screamed. The whole crowd around us burst into laughter.

Many happy moments were also generated at our Bingo games. One particular evening, Della and I were concentrating on our cards when Lee walked by. He leaned over to kiss me and then also gave Della a buss on the cheek. Just then her glasses fogged up. We had the whole table laughing. We used to have so much raucous fun at those Bingo games that people started to complain. Neither Della nor I took a care about the complaints, but we did tone it down enough to let people including ourselves win money. One day she had a new hand towel among her bingo supplies. It was a pretty design in pastel colors. When I told her that those were exactly the same colors of my new golf shoes, she said, "Oh, all right, you can have the towel for when you work up a sweat out there in the sun."

Suddenly we got it into our heads to start walking for physical fitness. We had heard that there was to be a March of Dimes Walkathon from Fairfield to Vacaville and back, so Josette, our mutual friend, Della and I started "training" for it by walking every day. We walked north on Dover. Now Paradise Valley Golf Course is located in the area, but in those days only agricultural fields and some horses were out there. We walked and talked and yelled at the horses every day. What a good time! On one occasion, we were way out on a back road when Della just had to "go." She couldn't wait, so we decided it would be okay for her to relieve herself in the field away from the road. Josette and I assured her that no one was around but a faraway bicycle. Just as she was hunkered down, I yelled, "Hurry up, Della, it's a motorcycle!!!"

Then came the day of the Walkathon. Betty Jo, Della's daughter, Josette, Della and I started out bright and early. We planned to walk all the way to Vacaville and back on the frontage road, a distance of approximately 18 miles. Lee and George Junior (Della's son) came driving by every so often to find out how we were doing and supply us with food and drink. Bravely, Della assured everyone that we were just fine even though her knees had started to hurt. She steadfastly refused to get in a car. All four of us managed to return to Fairfield High School under our own steam, but afterwards her knees gave Della lots of trouble. It was clear that when Della made up her mind to something, she was determined to see it through.

As our children grew up and got married, we attended each others' weddings and shared lots of good times. We rejoiced each time another grandchild joined our families and celebrated many events together. One such event was my twenty-fifth wedding anniversary. As Lee and I circulated among our guests, we came to Della's table. I showed off my newly reset diamond ring. Della took one look at it and exclaimed, "George, you never gave **me** a new ring!" The whole crowd laughed.

As our grandchildren were growing up, Della and I both spent many summer days with our respective families. One day I told Della that I planned to take my little group over to the Anna Kyle grassy field to practice golfing. She said she'd meet me over there with Gus, one of her grandsons who had expressed a desire to try some golf. Since our grandchildren were less than ten-year-old first-time golfers, most of their shots only went a few yards at a time. We were really enjoying ourselves. Then Gus lined a golf ball up and unexpectedly made contact. The ball sailed well over fifty yards! When we heard glass breaking on the other side of the fence, Gus quickly took refuge behind Della while the rest of cheered and laughed. That ended our golfing experiment with the grandchildren.

Gradually Della became less and less mobile. She gained a lot of weight and used a motorized wheelchair to get around.

One more poignant memory remains to be told. Lee and I were invited to one of her family birthday parties in the family business cabinet shop. George Junior and his band played Mexican music. Despite her obvious pain, Della couldn't resist. She got out of her wheelchair and grabbed her grandson Christopher, who himself had just recently recovered from surgery. My eyes filled with tears as the two of them danced joyfully to the live music.

Whether she knew it or not, Della has always been an inspiration in my life.

Betty Goldstein, Where Are You?

I suppose it would be easy to prove that Betty Goldstein actually existed once. There must be medical records, vital statistics, birth, marriage and death certificates with her name on them. Surely, some people remember her; I know I do.

I became acquainted with Betty after Governor Brown's 1976 plea for citizens to reach out to those in institutions, particularly those in community-based convalescent hospitals and nursing homes. Naively, I considered myself addressed. Was I not a free citizen who had plenty of spare time? Were there not several hundred captive souls just down the street from my home?

The first time I met Betty she sat in the lobby of the nursing home. A table had been set up to sell candy bars, gum, and other snacks every afternoon. Usually Betty was one of the two silver-haired ladies silently guarding the goodies. One day I stopped in just to say a quick hello to a couple of my friends before going home to fix dinner. I was a little hungry, so I was glad to see the "snack bar" still open for business. As I was choosing a snack, I mumbled something about not wanting one of those things with an artificial sweetener. Lo and behold, Betty smiled at me and said," That's right, if it doesn't have real sugar, it doesn't taste good."

I had been waiting for an opportunity to talk with those two silent ones, so we talked for a few more minutes. Apparently, Betty was equally pleased to have someone who actually responded, and our first conversation seemed very friendly. We soon established that I was to stop by to chat whenever possible. Since I had no regularly scheduled obligations after my children left for their schools, I promised to return often.

The very next time Betty recognized me, we barely had time to exchange friendly "Hellos" before she asked me to go buy her a hot dog somewhere in town. I inquired at the Nurses' Station about her diet and discovered that it was not restricted, so I was pleased to cooperate. Betty was eagerly waiting for me in the lobby and grabbed for the hot dog as if she hadn't eaten for some time. We walked back to her room where she got the correct change out of her purse to repay me. (That is significant because not many residents or patients there were able to talk, much less do complicated calculating.)

I was extremely puzzled. Why in the world was Betty a hospital patient? The answer came to me little by little. Of course, one of the things I did in search for the answer was to ask her this question directly. She told me stories about promises that had been made and broken by her son, stories about her heart attacks, stories about losing her husband while their only son served in the Korean conflict, and stories about the successful business she and her husband used to own in Philadelphia. Somewhere beneath that grayish-wrinkled complexion, somewhere inside that slightly hump-backed person, the memories of painful as well pleasurable experiences had interfered with her ability to enjoy her present surroundings. She was highly resentful and simply refused to participate in such recreational activities as guessing how many jelly beans are in a jar, attending weekly prayer meetings, listening to volunteers' renditions of "Home, Home on the Range", or assembling jigsaw puzzles.

I wasn't sure how I could help, so I asked her to let me know if I could ever do anything to brighten up her life. She seemed pleased but unable to think of anything for the moment.

During my next four or five visits, Betty and I became progressively more familiar, and we chatted and laughed easily. Her grip on my hand was always quite strong, and she walked proudly with me from her room to the lobby or through the hospital halls. I didn't particularly like her habit of smoking one cigarette after another, but I didn't really consider it my business since the staff didn't seem to mind. Occasionally, I even bought her some cigarettes upon her request.

I was quite pleased when Betty asked me to take her shopping one day. The staff nurse let me sign Betty out, mentioning that it was SO good for the patients to get out once in a while. Arm in arm, Betty and I started gingerly toward the door and a short while later we arrived rather effortlessly at my car. We cruised around town for a while, taking in a few sights and sounds before stopping at K-Mart. After Betty had made her purchases, we stopped at the lunch counter for a hot dog which we had no trouble putting away. Despite her protestations to the contrary, Betty seemed to have a terrific appetite. About an hour later, we returned to the hospital, safe and seemingly sound. After several such excursions, I noticed that Betty talked about the other patients as if they weren't worthy of her company. She seldom had a good word to say about anyone, nor was she interested in discussing anyone else's problems. Whenever I mentioned that I was pleased that so-and-so had gotten out of bed and walked around a bit after a long illness, Betty scoffed at the idea. She seemed totally uninterested in the welfare of her room-mates or of any of my other friends. She certainly enthused, however, when I mentioned that the Elks' Lodge was starting Sunday afternoon Bingo. She asked me to take her along. The staff encouraged such outings, so I stopped by the following Sunday to pick Betty up.

She was neatly dressed for the occasion. In fact, Betty was quite fastidious. Her grooming had always been of primary importance for her. Somewhere along the way, I had become a regular chauffeur for her "every other Wednesday" trips to the hair-dresser (right after lunch at an "all-you-can-eat-for-$2.50" Shakey's Pizza).

My other friends at Bingo welcomed her into our little crowd. Now every Sunday afternoon was Bingo, every other Wednesday was the hairdresser's, and several times in between were the luncheons. (Naturally, since lunch at the hospital was not very delicious on Sundays, I was persuaded to come by a little earlier to go have a bite to eat at Sambo's —yes, that was the restaurant was really called --before the Bingo game.)

I must admit that I really didn't mind. I had the time, and I enjoyed Betty's company; besides, it was very gratifying to watch her have a good time. Her whole appearance seemed to improve; even our mutual friends remarked about the change. Her demands on me, however, grew steadily, and she pouted whenever I found it necessary to refuse a favor.

In the meantime my welcome at the convalescent hospital was diminishing for reasons unrelated (I assume) to my friendship with Betty. She had obtained permission from her doctor to sign herself out for day-time outings, so our excursions continued. One day Betty surprised me and my husband with an invitation for dinner at her son's home. She had told me about her daughter-in-law's insistence on her remaining in The Butterfly Convalescent Hospital and her son's poor judgment in the matter. I had become eager to meet these monsters, so my husband and I accepted. Michael, his wife, and his three children seemed very friendly and hospitable. The subject of Betty's current residential arrangements was carefully circumvented, however. No one really wanted to discuss Betty's place of residence, her two roommates who had very conflicting idiosyncrasies, her refusal to eat hospital food, her unquestioning acceptance of medication and other treatment, nor her $900 monthly Medicare bill. After a few tentative remarks, In the interest of sociability, I decided to keep my mouth shut. I dropped the subject and settled down to enjoy the evening. Betty and her son seemed satisfied with the return for their tax-dollars. All in all, the evening passed very pleasantly.

I still had no idea that I was getting deeper and deeper involved.

When Betty nearly coughed her head off at Bingo one Sunday, and our mutual friends became alarmed, it occurred to me that I could be blamed if anything happened to Betty while she was with me. I had already realized that Betty didn't care whether anything happened to her, but I hadn't realized that she didn't care about the consequences to ME if she should die in my presence. I had no credentials or insurance to protect me from a lawsuit, nor even a scrap of paper to prove that her family approved of my taking Betty out of the nursing home at all. I began to wonder about the kind of rationalizing her doctor, her son, the staff (who were merely tolerant of my philosophy of free will), might engage in about my "allowing" a ninety-year-old woman to smoke herself to death on Bingo night at the Elks' Lodge. I was just beginning to wonder aloud about the wisdom of subjecting her to the strenuous outings when she regained her composure, stopped coughing and assured me that she was alright.

To reassure myself, I asked Betty to bring me a note from her son stating that her outings to various restaurants and other specified destinations in my company met with his approval. She was surprised but agreed. At first Michael refused, but after a serious family discussion, he grudgingly inked a memorandum "to whom it may concern."

Betty continued to convalesce, but her demands on others now extended even to her doctor. One day she was quite upset when I came by to pick her up. She told me that her doctor had visited her that morning. She had asked him, "When am I going to get out of here?" and he had simply stated, "Never."

After that day Betty became even more "crotchety" than she had been when we first met. One day I stopped by unexpectedly and found her lying on her bed. She weakly lifted her hands toward me and whimpered, "Oh, Marianne, I'm soooo glad you're here." She rose to hug me, and we chatted for a while. Before long, she seemed to feel much better and even walked around a bit.

I chided her gently for lying around so much and suggested, "Why don't you go around and cheer up some of the other patients?"

Her eyes flashed, and she blurted out, "I don't get paid to cheer anybody up!" I was stunned.

I could only reply sadly, "Neither do I, Betty." I felt as if someone had thrown a bucket of ice cold water at my face. I then muttered a quick good-bye and left. I thought of the tax dollars my husband and I were contributing to the government that was supporting her and the zero dollars I was getting for my time as a volunteer. I hated those thoughts.

The next day I went back to tell Betty that our Bingo, hairdresser, and luncheon days were over. She cried and asked me what she had done to me to deserve such punishment. I told her that she had done nothing to **me,** but I couldn't find the right words to tell her what she was doing to herself.

Sometime during the following year, I read her obituary in the local newspaper.

Sarah

Sarah was not a beautiful Negress with regal bearing or attractive appearance in the traditional sense, even though she may very well have been just that about seventy years earlier. When I met Sarah she was an unappetizing creature in a wheelchair. She was able to move only one hand voluntarily and her legs dangled uselessly from under her lap blanket. A towel draped around her neck and shoulders caught the dark juice of snuff that dribbled off her fleshy, drooping lower lip. Her face was a dry leathery mass of dark wrinkles surrounding two bloodshot eyes. She usually sat in her particular spot in the nursing home lobby near a main hallway where she surveyed the visitors and the staff as they scurried past her. When I first started visiting there, I noticed that most people, even other patients, either avoided her, looked at her with an expression of repulsion, or made comments about her dirtiness. She tried to be friendly and catch people's attention by waving her hand, but no one wanted to spend much time looking at such a sight.

One day I decided to stop and try to understand what Sarah had to say. I was sure she had some interesting tales to tell after having lived more than ninety years. Her voice was extremely strained and the words difficult to make out, but somehow we managed to communicate. I introduced myself, and when she told me, "My name is Sarah, and I come from Allibamy", I couldn't resist singing, "with a banjo on my knee!" That brought forth a genuine laugh from Sarah that cemented our friendship. After that, she enjoyed letting me push her to the dining room, help her get a clean bib, or put some fresh snuff under her tongue.

Usually I stopped to chat or bring her a Coke or a fresh can of snuff (she always paid me for these items) whenever I visited the nursing home.

One time she sneezed-just as I was about to put a spoon of snuff under her tongue. That brown puff of stinging powder all over my face made both of us burst into laughter.

If I had any doubt about Sarah's feelings about me, she dispelled it the time she introduced me to another visitor by saying, "This is Marianne. She's my brother." I was certainly moved! I couldn't remember ever being more complimented.

One day she seemed especially excited. Her son had taken her to church services the day before, and the minister had given her new hope! The old black minister had told her she would be cured if she could get two roosters (black, of course), draw their blood, and rub it all over her back and shoulders. It took a superhuman effort for her to make me understand all her words and to ask me to find two black roosters and bring them to her.

We finally got the story straight, and I told her I would try my best to make this wish come true but I wasn't making any promises. "Sarah, I don't think they'll let me bring roosters in here and kill them for the blood." She nodded sadly. We both knew that it would be impossible.

How I would have loved to make this ninety-some-odd-year old lady happy! What would have been the harm? The kind of food, care, and medication she was getting in that place certainly weren't curing her! Alas, the year was 1978. I was an intruder in an efficiently operated, state-regulated "Health Care Facility," and I had worn out my welcome--I was already in trouble over a couple of doughnuts! If I brought in two roosters, I'd be arrested!

The established methods of caring for Sarah prevailed, and a couple of months later, I read her obituary in the local newspaper. Now her story--nearly a century of living--will never be written and told to the world.

Hans Küppers

World History tells us that the "turn of the century" was a time of industrial growth. Many countries got involved with each other, building railroads to ship their products back and forth. Depending on the ideas, whims and beliefs of their leaders, countries became enemies or friends. By 1914, the world had gotten so mixed up that a terrible war started when Archduke Ferdinand was assassinated in Sarajevo. The German army in Serbia was fortunate to have one young soldier named Johannes Küppers, who served his country proudly.

Wounded in the arm, he returned home after the war. He found his young family alive and well despite the terrible conditions of the war. Gradually things improved, and he continued to work for the government-owned railroad driving locomotives (The railways had been nationalized after World War I). Hans (short for Johannes) and his family were fortunate to live on the ground floor in an apartment building owned by the railroad.

In his youth Hans had finished eight years of school and then started apprentice work with the railroad. He married young, but after his son, also named Hans, was born, his wife died. Because he worked on the railroad, Johannes traveled throughout Germany, leaving his little son to be raised by his parents. He met a young lady named Maria Hammes in Koblenz and fell in love with her. She had a little daughter, Martha, who lived in Macken with her grandparents. Hans eventually, married Maria. They had three more children, Leni, Tilli and Jupp.

As a result of the political unrest of the early 1920's in Germany and the railroad strikes, Hans and his young family were forced to move out of their apartment and evacuate. As "Ausgewiesene" (evacuees or refugees) they had to move to Blomberg, where they, with three young children, were not particularly welcome. Eventually, the family was allowed to return to the same apartment house in Koblenz, with the stipulation that they had to occupy a different apartment on the third floor. Because of the Inflation survival remained difficult. Workers were paid enormous sums of money, but a box of money would only buy a loaf of bread. The money had to be spent before the price went up so high that even a box of money wouldn't be enough. With a government job, however, Hans was somehow able to support his family even through those ridiculous months of Inflation.

One thing kept his family life from being perfect: He was becoming an alcoholic. Whenever he got drunk, he also got violent. He fought with other workers and beat his wife. Sometimes he was a superman who could show off in a bar. With one out-stretched hand grabbing a leg, he could lift the chair his wife was sitting on. Sometimes he was a gambler who won a piano in a card game, brought it home only to lose it again a few weeks later. Sometimes he was a mean drunk who gave his children's toys away to others. He brought home a mandolin and let his little daughter take lessons. Two months later he gambled the mandolin away. Strangely enough, he was also a good family man who grew vegetables in a garden and repaired broken furniture. In other words, his drinking made him unpredictable.

One day, after a particularly difficult drinking binge, he was fired from his railroad job. His young wife, afraid for her three children, went to the authorities and reminded them that he had served his country honorably and had only started drinking after the war. She begged to let him retire, so that she could receive a pension for her family. The railroad authorities relented. Although the pension, paid directly to her, was never very much money, it was enough to keep the family from being poverty-stricken.

Between the two wars, World War I and World War II, the German economy experienced a period of prosperity. Life was good, and Hans continued to live in the comfortable apartment in Koblenz with his family. He took odd jobs, such as boiler man (to heat the water) at a public swimming pool, and volunteer fire fighter. He leased a garden plot and grew fruit and vegetables for his family. He loved fishing in the Rhine and Mosel rivers with his "Angler's Club". On weekends he enjoyed playing his concertina. He was especially happy when his daughter, Tilli got married and brought him his first grandchild, Marianne.

This peaceful time did not last long. On the radio and in personal appearances Hitler was stirring up the German people, especially the workers, with national pride. Hitler railed against the Jewish people living in Germany and demanded that German people in other countries be repatriated. Some of the noisy fights between Hans and his wife had to do with the ideas brought up by Hitler. The drinking got even worse. By the time the serious bombings started, Hans had become an older man who volunteered his services in the civil patrol during air raids. His son, Jupp was drafted into the army, Leni lived (if running from one bomb shelter to another can be called living) in Berlin and Tilli had escaped to Austria with her little girl Marianne. Hans and his wife were left to survive alone in Koblenz.

Though the bombings stopped in 1945, hard times continued. Hans and Maria had to share their apartment with two other families because there were so few habitable buildings left. There was also a terrible shortage of food and water in the cities. Hans and Maria decided to move to a country village.

When Tilli and Marianne returned from Austria in July 1945, they found Hans and Maria Küppers in Macken instead of Koblenz. Instead of the beautiful modern apartment, a rickety little farmhouse had to be their home. Macken was the little mountain village where Maria had been born. An older sister still lived there with her husband Nikola, but they had not taken very good care of the old homestead. There was lots of work to be done. Fortunately, Hans was very talented. He and Nikola, a retired mason, restored the rooms as much as possible with the few tools at their disposal. Soon the ramshackle homestead took on the look of a well-tended home.

Hans fixed up a hayloft into a workshop. He had to build a ladder to climb up there, but he didn't mind. It was a place where he could be creative. He hadn't been able to bring very many tools with him, but he made good use of his hammer, pliers and soldering iron. Everything was recycled. Even bent nails were straightened and reused. The village farmers brought broken things to him. He earned food in exchange for his repair work. Sometimes he had time to make toys such as doll chairs, stilts, wagons, or spinning tops for his little granddaughter and her friends. With a big grindstone near his workshop he sharpened knives. He helped build barns and repaired furniture. He helped his wife plant a garden and took care of the fruit trees behind the house. He grew his own pipe tobacco and brewed schnapps from wormy apples, plums and cherries.

There were very few stores, so food had to be grown at home or gathered from the land. Hans took his wife and Marianne into the woods to gather beechnuts into large sacks that had to be dragged home on a makeshift wheelbarrow. After roasting and peeling the beechnuts, they took them to an oil mill to be processed into oil for baking and cooking. Other things that could be gathered in the woods were raspberries, hazelnuts, mushrooms, and blueberries. Chanterelle mushrooms were especially prized in Maria's special recipe. Then Hans and little Marianne smacked their lips in delight.

During the five years that Marianne lived with them, Hans and Maria was an energetic couple. Sometimes there were drinking bouts and terrible fights, but most of the time life was peaceful. On summer evenings Hans entertained the whole village when he sat at an open window and played his concertina.

When Marianne had to leave for America to be with her mother who had married an American service man, Hans tearfully wrote Marianne a poem as a going-away present.

Translation of the poem:

Remembrance
Here in our fatherland
Life is quite beautiful
You, my dear little Marianne
Must go to America to your mother

Wherever I would be
In the mountains or on the sea
I will think of you forever
And I will always write you

Always be happy and of good cheer
Then things will go well in your life
Always think of your loved ones
Who had to stay behind in Germany

Your Opa, Hans Küppers, Macken on Whitsunday

After Marianne left, his drinking got worse. One particularly bad night of drinking, Hans stumbled towards his home. He fell into a stairwell, breaking his skull on the sharp rocky wall. He was taken to a hospital, but never recovered. He suffered for six weeks before he died.

Raising a Son

Shortly after my husband Lee and I bought the house in Fairfield, we thought about increasing our family. We already had three daughters, so we had all kinds of dreams about a son.

I was quite excited when I discovered that I was pregnant, but unfortunately it was not an easy pregnancy. Perhaps the combination of trying to be a good military wife, a mother of three little girls, promoter of the arts, seamstress, baker, knitter, housekeeper, cook, homemaker, and gardener all at once, proved to be too much for me. When I was about four months pregnant, I started to have terrible nightmares. Before long, I couldn't breathe without pain and finally ended up in the hospital with pneumonia. For two long weeks I stayed there and worried myself even sicker about my unborn baby and my children that I was not allowed to see. Eventually, I began to get better. Finally I was released and gradually brought myself back to health.

Friends of ours, Scotty and Frankie, gave me a surprise baby shower, and my health improved by leaps and bounds. In September I felt the familiar pains that mean a new life is about to enter the world. Lee took me out to the hospital, and a neighbor watched the girls. False alarm! I went back home and started to watch television. No good. The pains persisted, we called the babysitter back, and the hospital let me stay for the night. Lee left to let the baby-sitter go home. He kissed me and said, "See you in the morning."

At two-thirty in the morning I called him on the phone, "We have a son!"

In all seriousness he answered, "Great, I'll see you both in the morning!"

I was crushed. Sure, I could understand his practicality. We had already disturbed the neighbors twice in the same evening about baby-sitting, but I felt that getting a son was worth waking the whole world up for. Despite my disappointment, Lee and I were thrilled to take a wonderfully healthy little boy home a few days later.

My mom and dad, who were traveling throughout the Northwest, stopped by for a few days to admire the new arrival. A month later Lee's mom and dad, left Los Angeles for the first time in twenty-eight years to come see their first grandson. They had arranged a typical Chinese welcoming called a "Red Egg and Ginger party," in a San Francisco restaurant. We met a number of their old friends and family members who presented little Johnny with silver dollars and other presents.

As Johnny was peacefully lying in his bassinette in the restaurant, Mom Tong leaned over to put something on top of the blanket. I was always very suspicious of anyone who went near my little boy, so I hurried to see what was going on. Mom had placed a beautiful pendant with a gold chain on Johnny's chest. It was a Chinese jade "ring of life". I stood there and looked at her. For the first time we understood each other even though we didn't speak the same language. I picked up the necklace and admired it. Then I promised her that I would keep it safe until this boy grew into a man, at which time I would give the piece to his bride. I have worn the necklace occasionally with the express intention that it belonged to John's future wife. In keeping my promise, I eventually gave it to Katie as a wedding present.

A couple of months after John was born, Lee came home with the news that he had an opportunity to retrain from missile maintenance to precision measuring equipment maintenance. This would entail a nine month school in Denver, Colorado. He was excited about the chance to get away from missiles. Since the family could travel with him, I consented. Although we had a few friends, we didn't really have any stable relationships with anyone in Fairfield, so it was easy to make the move.

Children being children, however, they got the chicken pox just about the time we were supposed to travel to Colorado. By the time we hit the road, Vivi and Kathy had gotten over them already, but Lisa still had a few spots, and baby John had a full-blown case of the chicken pox as we made our trip. Going into restaurants, I felt guilty about hiding our spotted little boy under a blanket. Waitresses wanted to see the baby, but I was embarrassed to let them. I was afraid to get thrown out, but it never happened. People were kind, and we made it to Colorado without a hitch.

We lived on a nice street in Aurora near Denver with lots of kids. Several of the bigger boys loved little Johnny because he was never a crybaby. They taught him to walk and played with him in our front yard throughout the summer. Naturally, I kept a watchful eye on all four of my little ones. We celebrated his first birthday there, and then we had to move on.

Our next assignment was Bangor, Maine. We arrived there in November 1965 on a cold day. Our military sponsor welcomed us and helped us to find temporary quarters while we waited for base housing. It snowed, and we were far from home, but I was happy: I had a good husband, three daughters, and a son!

Before Christmas, we had hidden the toys in the garage and through the house. On Christmas Eve, we took everything out and set it up for Santa Claus to bring to the kids. We had a nice holiday, and we soon resumed our routine. About four days later, we opened one of the bins in the garage and found the plastic motor bike I had hidden for Johnny. Since he was only fifteen months old, he didn't mind. The girls were old enough to laugh at me, so I was embarrassed.

In the spring, all the kids and I got the mumps. We were a mess. Our necks had swollen up and we couldn't eat. I was glad that Johnny was only a little boy and could build up his immunity to the disease early in life.

Then there was the time he fell down the stairs. Our bedrooms were upstairs. Usually on Saturday and Sunday mornings, we slept a little late and let the kids play in their room. Since the house had a steep stairwell of fourteen steps, we had a gate across the top. One morning, we were just lying in bed enjoying the sounds of our family when we suddenly heard the most soul-shattering thumping and the girls screaming, "Johnny fell down the stairs!" I almost fainted, but Lee flew out of bed and got to the foot of the stairs about the same time as Johnny. The baby was alright, but Lee had moved so fast that he burned his palm on the handrail as he was going down.

We had met some very nice people, including a Guamanian couple across the street. Because they were Catholic, we asked them to be John's godparents. It was decided that John should be baptized because his three sisters had already been baptized earlier. Jesse and Cecilia proudly consented to stand up with us at the Dow Air Force Base Chapel.

We lived contentedly through the summer and into the winter. Our friends and neighbors helped to pass the time with card games. The girls went to school and practiced their piano. Johnny was my pride and joy. With our wonderful neighbors we celebrated life by going sightseeing, picking apples and keeping the family growing. For Thanksgiving, we had the Mullineaux and Roberts families at our home. There were ten children and six adults.

Then one day Lee called me and asked me how I'd like to spend Christmas with my folks in California. A shock wave went through me. The United States was at war in Southeast Asia, and lots of other servicemen had been transferred there leaving their families to fend for themselves in their home states. I started to cry, but it was too late. Lee had orders for U-Tapau, Thailand, but I was not allowed to accompany him on this assignment. I decided to return to our home in Fairfield, about four hundred miles away from my folks and his. The children would have a chance to get reacquainted with their permanent home, and I would have my own piece of land to keep me from going crazy. On December 17, 1965 we left Bangor, Maine and headed for California. On Christmas Eve we arrived at my folks' home. Johnny was too young to know what was going on, but my heart broke for him. A little boy should have a father, especially one who loved him as much as was humanly possible.

We moved back to Fairfield, and I tried my best to hold the family together. The children continued to grow. The girls went to school. In Maine, Lisa had entered Kindergarten; however, in Fairfield I was informed that there wasn't any room in Anna Kyle Kindergarten. I asked to have her tested because she was already reading the other girls' books. They called me back to let me know that she would be welcome in first grade. It meant that Johnny and I would be alone at home during the school day, but we didn't mind. There were lots of ways for us to pass the time.

For his birthday that year, I bought him a little red car he could pedal. It had doors that opened, a steering wheel that turned the front wheels, and a trunk that could hold his little treasures. He got into it and wheeled all around the circle as if he were born to drive. That night he parked the car next to his bed. After everyone had gone to sleep, I relaxed in front of the TV and concentrated on writing my hubby a letter. All of a sudden I heard a noise in the hallway. I got up to look and had to laugh out loud. There was my cute little son, driving his car down the hall with his eyes almost closed. He was so tired, he could hardly hold up his head. I gave him a big hug and assured him that his car would still be there in the morning. Then he smiled and slept through the rest of the night.

After Lee's tour of duty in Thailand was done, we hoped to be assigned to Travis Air Force Base, but his orders said "Bunker Hill, Indiana". In February 1967, we said good-bye to our families in California and traveled in our big blue station wagon to Indiana. Even our dog, Happy, enjoyed our new home. It didn't have a fence, so he ran away frequently returning at dinner time. I also remember some special things about Johnny during that time.

It was in Indiana where he had his worst illness. To this day, I can't imagine what caused him to become so ill, but I suspect it was something he ingested. He lost all desire to eat, play or do anything. His little grey face just stared into nothingness day after day. Naturally, I took him to the doctor. Some medicine was prescribed, but he wasn't hospitalized. I took him home and worried, prayed, and stayed by his bedside day and night. This went on for an incredible three weeks. Now and then I forced a little gelatin or some broth into him, but nothing helped. He became very weak. Then one day, he vomited something into the toilet that looked like a sponge. It might have been dried blood or whatever. Shortly afterwards, he began to ask for food. The nightmare was over.

I had joined the NCO Wives Club at Bunker Hill. We befriended Joan, the social chairman of the club. Her little boy, Christopher, was just a couple of months younger than Johnny. The two of them became good friends and loved going to the Child Care Center together. We also planned quite a few family events, such as picnics, card parties, and outings.

It was at one such outing to a lake that I really grew in stature in John's eyes. We were at Indiana Beach, and I was standing at the edge of the water, watching the two little boys play. Not too far away a group of young guys, maybe high school age, were playing with a football. They were playing pretty rough, but they weren't bothering anything. Suddenly the ball got away from them, and one big guy lunged after it. He nearly knocked one of my little boys over, and headed straight toward me. In reflex, I raised my right hand and chopped him a good one on his neck. I also yelled something about being careful around little kids. The guy fell at my feet. His friends laughed as they pointed in my direction. Our friends who had been watching from a shaded area were laughing and calling me their karate hero. John thought it was great. Luckily, I've never had to prove my Karate skill in a repeat performance.

We had only lived in Indiana for about eighteen months when we got new orders to move. We were going to Germany!

Once we were in Germany, I looked up my father whom I hadn't seen in nineteen years. He immediately fell in love with his "Jungche", John. We frequently went to his home-office combination, and John played with the typewriter. Großvater (my father) also came to our home a lot, and we often made day trips to Luxembourg, Bernkastel, Vianden, or other places around the area with him and his wife. The kids called her Tante Lotti.

The four years in Germany were filled with activity, yet the memories of that time seem to have a holistic feeling. I hardly know where to start in regard to John's development because I usually thought of terms of my whole family. There were ski trips, sight-seeing tours, baseball tournaments, pig roasts, skating parties, and teen club events. John always fitted in despite his age. He gave me practically no trouble. Whatever was in the family plan, his good sportsmanship and cheerful disposition could be depended upon.

When we went skiing in Berchtesgaden, he was only six years old. On the slopes he acted as if he knew what it was all about. He kept up with his big sisters even though he was quite a bit younger than they. A couple of years later, in 1972, we took the Trier Teen Club on a ski trip to Garmish, a resort in the Alps. John came along and felt at home with all the teen-agers.

John joined the WEBELOS, the youngest level of the Boy Scouts. He proudly wore his uniform to meetings, and carried his official wallet wherever he went. One day he came home from the playground. Suddenly he noticed that his wallet was gone and got upset. I asked him where he might have lost it. He explained that he had it in his pants pocket just a little while ago. I said something about being a little more careful with things in his back pocket. All his frustration was expressed in his loud outburst, "Next time buy me some BIG pockets!" I couldn't help but laugh as I hugged him and promised to sew some huge pockets on the inside of his coat.

This was also the time that John became interested in baseball. Our housing area had a solitary baseball diamond that was used for men's and women's softball, teen club games, major and minor Little League games and all the practices. We signed John up in the Peewee League. His first team was called the Pirates. We were incredibly proud of our little slugger. He graduated from hitting the ball off a tee to hitting home runs off pitched balls in a very short time.

Just before leaving Germany, we went to say good-bye to Großvater and Tante Lotti. There was picture-taking and small talk, and then it was over. In November 1973 we flew back to the United States.

Our first assignment in the continental U.S. was at Seymour-Johnson Air Force Base in Goldsboro, North Carolina. We only stayed in North Carolina until August 1974, but in that time we did quite a few interesting things. We viewed the U.S.S. North Carolina Battleship Memorial in Wilmington. We also took a short vacation to Washington, D.C. to show our children the Nation's Capital. Since we had bought a camping trailer we spent some time in at a camp site near Manassas, Virginia to view the battle field where the First and Second Battles of Bull Run were fought during the Civil War.

There was school, softball, Sunday afternoon Kiddie bingo at the NCO Club, and golfing to keep everyone entertained. John joined a Little League baseball team and soon found that he had been taught well in Germany. We had a nice house in base housing, and we should have been very happy. Unfortunately, we (or at least Lee and I) were not happy there. We were far away from any other part of the family, and were suddenly notified that Grandpa Tong had died. We didn't even know he was sick, and his death was quite a shock to us. Also, all our other relatives were in California, and we had hoped to get transferred to one of the many bases there. So in November 1974 Lee retired from the Air Force!

With our travel trailer we enjoyed a leisurely trip back home in August 1974. In our tiny trailer it got very hot at night. Johnny decided that he and Happy, our dog, would sleep better in the car than in the crowded hot trailer. That's how we made our way across the United States. Our first stop was San Diego, where Johnny had a chance to get acquainted with his Uncle Gene and Aunt Cindee. Grandma Tong was living with them, and we were surprised to see how much the cousins Leighton and Alicia had grown. They had only been little babies the last time we saw them. One night we went Grunion running on one of the San Diego beaches. The cousins John and Leighton had a great time, but I spent the time in the truck keeping Alicia warm.

We also stopped at my parents' home in LaVerne. Oma and Opa had a beautiful house with a swimming pool. Uncle Jerry and Aunt Riz came to visit, so we had a wonderful time getting reacquainted with our families.

In the summer of 1975 Gene and Cindee took a tour to Asia. While they visited Japan, Korea and Hong Kong, we took care of Leighton and Alicia. It was our pleasure to have them with us, but John and Leighton seemed incredibly ready to have wrestling matches at every opportunity. I had to pry them off each other constantly. I was a nervous wreck because

I just wasn't used to having TWO little boys in the house. We made it, though, and everyone survived.

In July we let John go to visit Oma and Opa. This was going to be his first time away from home for a whole week. Leighton and Alicia were going to spend some time with their maternal grandparents near Los Angeles, so all three of them took off on the same airplane. A week later he proudly returned unaccompanied.

Back home, John made friends with the other boys in the neighborhood. He went to Anna Kyle Elementary, Crystal Middle and eventually graduated from Armijo High School. He stayed active in baseball and played the trumpet in middle and high school marching bands.

In the meantime, I found that I had the time to take some college classes. Johnny was very supportive and proud when I told him about a good grade I had earned on a test. He noticed that I really enjoyed studying, and we often did our homework together. For a time I became frustrated with my seeming powerlessness in the face of world events and started to write letters. One day Johnny found me crying over the typewriter. He wondered what the matter was.

I sobbed, "I'm trying to type this important letter, but I keep making mistakes! This is already the third piece of paper I've messed up!"

Calmly Johnny asked, "Mom, why don't you just write it?"

Immediately I felt better and gave him a great big hug.

John's one brush with the law came shortly after he got his first car, a Toyota Corolla. One weekend evening he went cruising with his friend, George. Since we had had no problems with John, we retired calmly as usual even though John hadn't returned yet.

Around midnight the phone rang, "Mrs. Tong, do you own a rust-colored Toyota?"

My heart pounded as I said, "Yes, what's the problem?"

The voice woke me up with the jolt, "Your car has been found on Woolner Avenue as an abandoned vehicle."

I said, "We'll be right there" and jumped out of bed yelling at Lee to get dressed. We had to get the car and find our son!

Lee grabbed the extra car key, and we drove toward the street where the car was supposed to have been abandoned. As we were driving on one of the nearby streets, who should we see but John and George walking calmly back toward town. We told them to get in the car, "Do you realize that the police called us?" I demanded.

They explained that a couple of guys from school had cut them off, so to teach them a lesson they decided to egg their house. When the "egging" started, the parents yelled out the window that they had called the cops. The boys left the car behind, hid in the nearby field for a while, and finally ran away. We told them that we were going to face the police and the people whose house had been egged. They weren't exactly happy about having to face the music, but we gave them no choice.

Outside, the police and the parents of the other boys were waiting for us. The guy started yelling at us about his young daughter being scared to death when the eggs hit their house.

When the man started yelling that I was lucky that he didn't get a hold of my son because the last guy he hit had blood coming out of his ears, I got very angry. I yelled at him, "I was a child in World War II and I'm not about to be intimidated by your talk about stuff coming out of people's ears."

The cop tried to calm us down, but I still had a few things to tell him about their sons cutting off my son's car in fast traffic. When the lady yelled about all the things she was going to do to her sons for playing dangerous games in traffic, I told her, "If you know so much about how to control people, you ought to run for Congress." By this time the cop saw the humor of the situation and calmly tried to get us to come to some kind of agreement.

John and George promised to clean off the mess they had made if they could just go home without being booked. The people agreed not to press charges of vandalism, so the cops agreed to let them go with a firm lecture and a stern warning this time. Lee, John, and George used the people's garden hose to clean off the side of the house where the eggs had been tossed.

Lee and I drove the cars home and dropped George off at home. John got quite a lecture and was grounded for a couple of weeks. For the rest of his teenage years John didn't have any more trouble with the law.

Four years after graduating from high school, John married his high-school sweetheart.

Tante Katt

During the time I lived in Macken with my grandmother, I got to know her sister, Tante Katt, (Aunt Katherine) a unique character.

When I first met her she was around sixty years old. I liked her right away. She was a little old woman with an explosive temper. From among the seven siblings born to Moritz and Barbara Hammes, she alone had remained in the old Macken homestead.

After the war, my grandmother moved back there and Tante Katt gladly made room in the rather large but dilapidated house. Her husband Nikolas had been a bricklayer by trade, so he and my grandfather, who was handy in all kinds of things, fixed the upstairs rooms for us while Tante Katt kept her living quarters downstairs. There was plenty of room for all of us.

I had come to live with my grandparents in the country because my mother could not support me in the post-war city of Koblenz. The country village of Macken was the perfect place for a child. Despite very primitive conditions, we enjoyed our five years together.

Both Tante Katt and I especially loved the early evening hours when my Opa (grandfather) would play his concertina. Lyrical strains of "Waldeslust," a well-known folksong would come wafting from the corner windows. We knew all was well with the world when we heard the music. Both of us had already experienced hard times, and we were grateful for every peaceful minute of every day.

As a young woman, she had to have a hysterectomy, so she and her young husband never had any children. He became a heavy drinker, and the two of them did not seem to have a happy marriage. He had some peculiar habits, such as rolling up home-grown tobacco in bits of a newspaper margin to make a cigarette. Even in his later years he drank everything he could find and did very little farm or gardening work, yet she tolerated him.

Tante Katt puttered around in her garden the best she could, but her flowers and vegetables were sad stepchildren next to my grandmother's colorful produce. Tante Katt depended mostly on the goodness of her friends and neighbors for support. She was delighted that my grandparents moved in and was willing to share her space in exchange for food and companionship.

One of the things that bothered me was the way the children of the village mistreated her. She had become the butt of many practical jokes because of her temper. Raising a broom above her head, she would threaten any boy or girl who "scared" her chickens or pulled her cat's tail.

In retribution, some of the meaner boys found the perfect trick to play during the annual village pig-slaughter just before winter. Several times a Tante Katt fell for the trick of a naughty boy who brought her a nicely wrapped sausage from Farmer So-and-so. She'd be all excited, but upon unwrapping the package, she'd find a pig's tail instead of a tasty sausage. Then she'd grab her broom and chase the laughing boy out of her yard.

One of the things I remember best is her generosity when my mother or some other relative came to visit. She brought some concoction she had cooked and offered to share her bed. I was always chosen for this honor. Sleeping with Tante Katt was an adventure. Her narrow bed did not have a flat mattress. Instead it had moguls of straw-stuffed ticking like a deeply rutted road. During winter months she kept several wrapped, warmed bricks and hot water bottles under the covers. These had to be left in place while we squirmed around to find a comfortable spot among the stuff she considered necessary in the nest she called her bed.

In those days, I begged my grandmother not to make me sleep with Tante Katt. Now the memories of that horrid bed and that sweet but explosive old lady bring a nostalgic smile to my face.

During one of her visits to Germany, my mother had an opportunity to visit Tante Katt in a nursing home. She was clean and well-fed. When my mother asked whether she was happy, she told my mother, "Tillche, I've never had it so good!"

TIME OF GIVING

by Vivienne Tong, age 16, December 15, 1973

A mother and father as poor as can be,
Lived with their poor little children three,
Christmas was coming and closer it grew,
But they were too poor to get anything new.

Their stockings were hung by the chimney with care
But still they knew nothing would ever be there.
But still they had hopes that someone would come
With presents and candy and cookies and gum.

They were even too poor to eat three meals a day
But for Santa milk and cookies were there for his stay.
And wishing as hard as their little hearts could
They went to bed hoping Santa saw them good

But they knew no one loved them, for they were still cold,
No one would ever buy things that they sold.
Their mother and father were in bed asleep,
And later at night for the stockings they'll creep,

And put in some candy and small things to eat
A weeks worth of supper for a very small treat.
Then long in the night after nothing was happenin'
Outside one could hear a whip out there crackin'.

A jolly, bold man jumped out of a sled
With a big, fat belly and all dressed in red.
He jumped on the roof and down thru the chimney
Tho' the door didn't even have a key.

He looked around and saw the tree,
And knew he was the only hope for these three.
He saw three stockings within arms reach,
Then put in a couple more things for them each.

Then three big presents he put under the tree,
Right in front where all could see.
He jumped out the chimney, and slid down the roof,
And accidentally landed under a reindeers hoof.

Then he got up and into his sled,
He was just about ready to fall into bed.
When, in the morning the children awoke
They saw those presents and none of them spoke.

Their mother and father were both so surprised
Neither of them could believe their eyes.
As they stood they felt a warm breeze
Then all fell down to their knees,

And said, "Thank you, dear God, that we're living,
For now we know Christmas is the time for giving!"

Thank you, Viv

1981

Just think how poor I'd be
If you had never been born.
How could "Claire de Lune" stir my soul if you hadn't
Played it for me a jillion times?

How could the pain of motherhood have been a pleasure for me
If you had never made me weep and laugh,
Swell with pride and burn with anger?
And healed me with a smile?

If you're ever fortunate enough to have a daughter
Who can kill you with a word, rip you apart with a glance
And bring you back to life with a touch of her finger,
You will know me.

Who would have thought so long ago
That my little "love-baby"
(That's what I called you then)
Would become such a welcome and pleasant part of my life?

Happy Birthday, Dear Lisa

As you finish out twenty-seven years of life, I thought I'd like to congratulate you on some of your accomplishments which make me particularly proud to be your mother.

First of all, you were a quiet and cheerful little baby. You loved to stand on the couch and watch your slightly older sisters play before you decided to get into the act. As you grew bigger and were able to defend yourself against their rough-housing, you easily took your rightful place as one of my three active little girls.

That little girl, you, gradually showed just how smart and easy-to-get along with she was. You learned to swim, read and play the piano with very little effort. Since you had a January birthday, you got very impatient about going to school. You finally got to go to Kindergarten in Maine, but then we had to move back to California where they didn't have a place for you at Anna Kyle. I asked to have you tested for first grade, and you were accepted. I remember how thrilled we both were. You did not want to spend that time until September at home, and I couldn't blame you. School is fun—I still love it!

Throughout your school years you always brought home fantastic grades. As we moved from place to place, you adjusted to every new situation with grace and a mature attitude that I found hard to understand in such a young person. I finally realized that this is you, and I love you for it. When we moved to Germany you made Dad and me proud in your participation in the cultural programs. I'll never forget the speech you made in the German language at the Volksfest in Trier. After our return to California, your marching in the Rose Parade at the head of the Armijo Superband was also a highlight in our lives. You have often pumped new life into our aging bodies with your performances. There were piano recitals, singing with the choir, badminton championships, tennis tournaments, and softball games for us to watch and enjoy.

Naturally, there were those anxious moments of pain when I could only hope that I'd do the right thing to help you. Your broken toe and smashed finger in the early years were nothing compared to your confused heart in your senior year in high school. I prayed and prayed that you would somehow find a solution.

You did. Because of you we have memories of a beautiful wedding, beautiful grand-children and a beautiful young woman in our life. That woman is you. You are really something. In many powerful ways, you remind me of myself, but I know that you are your own person. Without ever giving up, you have accomplished things that others don't even dream of.

Now I ask you, where could I have found a birthday card with all this information in the verse?

Happy Birthday! Lots of Love! Your Mom

A Letter to the Hospital Commander When Kathy was Sick

April 8, 1986

Dear Sir,

I need help!

When I visited my daughter (Kathy, Ward D-3) this afternoon, I became even more distraught than I have been in the past week or so. Her complexion was brightly mottled red. She complained of having been subjected to six different attempts to insert an IV needle into her arms the night before. She told me that one of those attempts resulted in a bubbling up of one of her veins. She told me that she had been crying a lot since her admission into the hospital. Her arms were so weak that she couldn't unwrap the sandwich on her lunch tray. At the moment she still sounds relatively coherent, but I wonder just how much more experimentation with different substances she can take before she loses all concept of herself. She told me that she had been trying to tell the doctors that she feels well enough to come home (she makes her residence with my husband and me at the present time, due to her military husband's tour of duty in Turkey), but that they don't believe her. She keeps getting vague promises of "Well, maybe tomorrow," whenever she asks about her release.

I'm fed up with it!

What do you think this is? A movie named "Annie?" "Tomorrow" is a cop-out when it used to shut up a patient who wants the truth. If my daughter is so ill that she requires further hospitalization, I demand that her husband be notified of that fact! Not tomorrow, but today: April 8, 1986!

The following is a general release of my emotions written a few days ago. I hadn't intended to send it to anyone, but now I need to let someone know how I feel. If I am truly expected to remain poised and lady-like in this situation, then please read it and place it into Kathy's records:

"I think I'd better make a journal entry into my computer before I blow a gasket. Today is Saturday, April 5, 1986 Things are going from bad to worse around here, and maybe I can at least help myself to think clearly about them. My mom and step-dad arrived on March 24 for a visit. Considering my mother's state of health, she did great. We went to the BX once and we even went looking at model homes one afternoon. She got around amazingly well despite her rheumatoid arthritis and colostomy. My dad is still very overweight. His knees gave him quite a problem, and he even fell while he was trying to take some pictures of the kids outside.

The worst part of the week was Kathy's illness. The week before, the kids had snot-noses, and I also got the twenty-four hour flu. I had a lot of phlegm and coughed for a couple of days. Kathy also got sick. We all had fever, too, but it went away before my folks arrived. Kathy didn't seem to get well, though. She lost her appetite, and went out to the hospital. In her weakened condition, she had her IUD removed. I don't know whether she was experiencing pain in the general area of her female organs, or whether she just got the idea to have it removed for general principles.

Nevertheless, she had it done, and was taking medication to prevent possible infection. She moped around for a few days and just couldn't get in the spirit of my folks' visit or anything else. She canceled her planned visit with her in-laws in Mt. Shasta and lay around complaining of a pain in her abdomen and leg. She seemed to have increasing pain, so I finally suggested she at least call the doctor who had removed the IUD. On Thursday morning, she finally called the nurse practitioner who had attended her. She immediately suggested Kathy come back to office hours.

My mother and I drove Kathy out to the hospital around 1:30 for a 2:00 appointment. We dropped her off and went to the BX to nose around for a while. We returned to the hospital around 3:00. Kathy was still in OB-GYN and told me she had to go get some blood work done. The nurse practitioner came out and told me that she was thinking of admitting Kathy to the hospital overnight. OK, what could I do to help? She said I could take Kathy over to the main hospital in the car. My mother had to wait in the car while I took Kathy up to Ward D-3 as I was instructed to do. I thought all this time that the arrangements had already been made, but when we arrived on the ward with the admission form, they asked Kathy whether she could go downstairs to register. I replied very shortly that if she were well enough to walk all over the hospital she didn't need to be admitted. They then asked me to take care of the registering. At first I agreed, but when the corpsman told me that it would "only" take about a half hour or so, I hit the ceiling. First of all, I had a very sick mother sitting in the car, and second, I remembered all the trouble I got myself involved in as a volunteer in a convalescent hospital a few years ago. I handed the form and Kathy's ID card back to the nurse and asked them to take care of it themselves. I kissed Kathy good-bye and left to take my mother home.

When Lee, my husband, came home from work, we went out to visit Kathy. He was very surprised to see her getting a blood transfusion. We found out that the kids could visit, too. At home we called Viv and Lisa and Les, as well as Mildred and Marguerite, Ted's grandmothers. Kathy had already called Ted's mother and the Red Cross to notify Ted of the recent development.

So now what, coach? Kathy and I have been attending Solano College this semester, but at the moment we were on Spring break from school, so we weren't missing any classes. We went along for a few days with talk about her temperature. She was getting intravenous antibiotics. I asked about calling Ted to let him know that his wife was hospitalized. I was told that the Red Cross was attempting to locate him. He did call a couple of days later and sent some flowers.

My folks left, as scheduled, on Monday, March 31. That afternoon, when Lee and I visited Kathy, the doctor came by; I asked him what was going on. Why was she still in the hospital? He told us that she has a couple of abscesses on her pelvis (I think he said pelvis, but it might have been some other word, like cervix) He said that they were attempting to treat her with antibiotics, but that there was a possibility of a complete hysterectomy. Well, needless to say, I did not take that bit of information very lightly. The whole idea of womankind suffering for the pleasure of mankind is abhorrent to me, anyway. We women, as a group, represent at least one half of humanity. We have borne the brunt of birthing, have been infected with all manner of man-made disease, have had our children snatched out of our arms in the national interest, and had our homes destroyed by rage of every kind. I have, personally, endured enough to make the angels weep.

As a little girl, I saw my home destroyed, my parents' marriage destroyed, my health destroyed, my opportunities of an education destroyed, and my homeland yanked out from under my feet. Before I had attained the age of reason, I had been persuaded that my future lay on a continent where language, customs, food, and even the people themselves were completely different from mine. When I adjusted and accepted al*l that was offered (especially a husband in the form of a young Chinese from Los Angeles) I was chastised and rejected by the very ones who had brought me to this strange America.*

As a result of my constant attempt to remain pleasant in the face of adversity, my personal health has fluctuated between excellent and critical ever since I was born. Apparently, my liaison with my husband healed my wounds, as I gave birth to four healthy children who have survived into adulthood. When I chose not to have more children, however, I became victim to the Dalkon shield. My body has been subjected to so many atrocities throughout my life that heaven should cry out. My person has done just that: cried out. In recent years, I have learned to empty my thoughts onto a piece of paper or into the computer. This habit has made life a bit easier for me, but nothing has essentially changed. Women are still being used. And now it seems to be my daughter's turn.

My services as caretaker of a military man's family are being taken completely for granted. Although my grandmother-heart loves the two little ones produced from the union of my daughter with a young man who entered the U.S. Air Force because he couldn't hold a civilian job, I resent my role in the greater scheme of things. I am, in effect, subsidizing the military-industrial complex of the United States of America every time I cook a meal, wash the clothes, correct the children's behavior, sacrifice the time I should spend on my belated and well-deserved education, or otherwise lend, GRATIS, my expertise to military dependents. I think about and resent the fact that my husband and I had to work hard and long to build up our home that is now under siege. If my daughter is indeed so ill that she must be hospitalized extensively, then her husband should be called to tend to his responsibilities toward his young family. My job was done on the day they married!

Yesterday, I had to attend classes, so I had to pay for the children at a baby-sitter's. Later, when my husband and I visited their mother, I became quite upset. The scene we encountered upon entry into the ward did not please me. Here was my attractive married daughter sitting side by side with an attractive corpsman on her hospital bed! I was distraught that her husband had not been sent to be with her at this time of illness! Why was a stranger comforting her? My daughter introduced me," This is my mom." When the corpsman shook my hand and said, "Hi Mom!" I snapped back, "I'm not YOUR mother!" He quickly left the room.

Last night my husband I had company at our home. His obligations as Exalted Ruler-elect of the Fairfield Elks require occasional officers' meetings in our home. I prepared the children for the event. Our little granddaughter became ill and vomited three times while my company was present. I remained as poised as possible, cleaned up the mess, and delayed my nervous breakdown until after all the guests had left. My husband had to go to work at 6:00 AM, so we dropped into our bed early. We are both exhausted from the emotions that this entire episode has forced upon us. I, for one, cannot be expected to smile bravely while this holocaust continues. If nothing else, the world must know that I am ANGRY!"

Sincerely,
Marianne Tong

P.S. Around 10 AM this morning, my husband came home from work unexpectedly with diarrhea and feelings of total defeat. It is now six o'clock in the evening, and I can't take it anymore!

I printed out the letter, placed it in an envelope and wondered whether I should actually send it to the Hospital Commander. Just typing out my frustrations had already given me some relief, but **my** relief wouldn't make any significant difference in Kathy's condition.

"Love, I'm going to drive out to the hospital and slip this letter under the Hospital Commander's door. I don't want some secretary to short-stop it," I called out to Lee.

"Okay, drive carefully, it's already getting darker outside," he admonished me as I jumped into the car.

When I visited Kathy the next morning, she had already been moved to a much brighter room. Her face was still brightly mottled, and she expressed worry about her children and her college classes, but she appeared more spirited.

"Kathy, try not to worry about anything except to get well. Don't make any drastic decisions about surgery without talking it over with Ted. I'm going to make sure that Ted gets here soon. I've already written to the Hospital Commander," I tried to be as reassuring as I could be. My emotions no longer surfaced unpredictably. After delivering the letter and enjoying a good night's sleep, I had regained the ability to remain calm.

"So you're the lady who wrote that letter!" smiled one high-ranking military doctor, as the group of five or six white-robed people approached Kathy's hospital bed.

"Yes, and I'm not at all happy with her treatment," I stated matter-of-factly.

"Ma'm?" he looked at me as if he expected some explanation.

"Since no one seems to be sure whether something has gone internally wrong with my daughter, or whether the Russians have scattered some biological weapon over this base, I want her to be examined properly and treated accordingly. I also want her husband here to help make any important decisions before his wife is cut into pieces!" I was calm. The entire group of doctors and interns looked at me with surprised faces.

"We are not at war this year! There is no reason her husband can't be brought home for this emergency!" I added for emphasis before I gracefully made my exit.

Ted was, indeed, brought home for a thirty-day leave, and Kathy was released. She recovered quickly without drastic surgery, and our family life returned to normal.

July 22, 1980 Letter to U. S. President Jimmy Carter[7]

Jimmy Carter, President of the United States
The White House, Washington, D. C.

> *Dear Mr. President,*
>
> *Now that you have established the procedure to make government property out of 19 and 20 year-old men, you ought to make plans to compensate their creators.*
>
> *I've calculated the following guidelines to facilitate the disbursement of funds:*
>
> *In the nineteen years it took to create a young man, his mother will have spent at least 13880 hours in his direct maintenance. The following will show how I derived that figure*
>
> *Of her twenty-four per day, a mother of four will have slept 8 hours; tended to her own affairs 8 hours; and taken care of the children's food, laundry, etc. 8 hours. The figures average out to two (2) hours per day per child. Hence: 13880 hours in 19 years (incl. 5 leap years).*
>
> *Even the lowest minimum wage during the period of 1961 to 1980 of $2 per hour will amount to $27,760.00 in retro-active pay for services rendered to each draftee: due and payable on induction day.*

The sum of $27,760.00 represents straight time and does not take into consideration the intensity of personal feelings, such as the pain of the birth process, the terror during illnesses, the anxieties of school recitals, or the anguish of lost Little League games. Even the U.S. Treasury wouldn't have enough money to repay that.

Sincerely, Marianne Tong

In Search of GPA

(A letter to my counselor at UCB)

When I first arrived at the University of California at Berkeley in the fall of 1979, I had such a wonderfully positive attitude that I was certain nothing could depress me or discourage me, but something happened to me there.

It wasn't exactly blind faith or a Pollyanna attitude that sustained me. But because I had already experienced the realities of life, death and illness during my childhood in Germany and my adult life in the United States, I knew myself. I had given birth to four children who are now grown, had major surgery, directed a club for teenagers, volunteered in a convalescent hospital and tutored adults who couldn't speak English. In other words, I had learned to navigate through life. It was, however, made clear to me in recent years that I had to have "credentials" in order to continue to be useful to American society.

The recent influx of new immigrants who would need to learn the American way (as well as various other elements of stress on the American institutions) has guided me toward a decision. Should I remain a homemaker and unappreciated volunteer, or should I attempt to enter the job force in the capacity which will make effective use of my proven talents? I chose the latter: to come to Berkeley to study my alternatives, get a degree in English and enter the job force.

My husband and my counselor at Solano College, encouraged me to apply for a Regents Scholarship, and I was selected. Even though I didn't qualify for financial aid and had to pay my own way, I was elated to accept the opportunity to get degree from the University of California. I had no idea of the inhumanity and apathy that awaited me here.

Throughout my life I have already had enough hardships to keep me humble for a thousand years, but, unfortunately, my scars don't show. Since I've come here, nearly every professor has made it his or her business to keep me from getting a swelled head. I have been insulted with snide remarks about joining the cheerleader team, suggestions that my home-life must be unsatisfactory, and worst of all, undeserved bad grades. Most insults pass through my ears without hurting me too much, but my grades definitely reflect my deteriorating state of mind. My attitude is no longer optimistic or even pleasant. The grades I have accumulated will remain on my record and either prevent me from successfully completing my major or force me to spend more time and money than is fair; worse, the grades will eventually force me to quit.

A recent incident, which is just one more in a series of bureaucratic run-arounds, sent me to the Student Services Department for emotional support in coping with my anger. I certainly don't want to disturb my family and friends unduly with my UC-related emotional outbursts. Here is what caused my latest crisis: In my grade reports for the Fall '81 quarter, an expected "B" had erroneously been recorded as a "C+." I returned to the teacher during the first week of the Winter '82 quarter. After examining his records, he discovered his mistake and promised to rectify the error at the earliest convenience.

In the meanwhile, I was notified by the Letters and Science dean that I was on probation, so I made an appointment with one of the counselors there. I explained the expected grade change and also another change. A low grade from another class was expected to be changed to a "C+" after a lengthy appeal through the ombudsman office. The L & S counselor advised me to make sure that the two changes are recorded and brought to her attention **this quarter** so that she could adjust my Grade Point Average (GPA) and take me off probation.

I wasted considerable time and effort running back and forth between Campbell Hall, Sproul Hall and Wheeler Hall in order to get this administrative mix-up cleared from my record. The "C+" was changed in a timely manner, but the other grade remained unchanged. I returned to the professor for a third time to remind him of the grade change. His unfriendly manner in hurrying me out of his office on the pretext that other students have a more pressing claim on his time than I did, changed my typically cheerful mood into a monstrous anger. I was barely able to remain civil as I reminded him that my time is just as valuable as anyone else's.

As I left his office and stormed down the three flights of stairs, my fist was so tightly balled that I thought I could single-handedly knock down the Campanile Tower on campus. I walked straight to the Student Services Department to speak with a counselor there. I was advised to go to the mental health clinic in order to be calmed down.

I have become extremely wary of people telling me to come back some other time. I, too, have stacks of reading and other academic matters to attend to within deadlines and can hardly afford to waste my time and money in chasing down the difference between "C+'s" and "B's." I resent the insinuation that my efforts are futile and cannot tolerate the disrespectful attitude of the professors toward the grading system. There is no need for them to remind me that grades don't matter. **I** know that grades don't really matter in "real life;" **they** know that grades don't really matter in "real life;" but **we** know that students cannot graduate or qualify for certain careers without a passing GPA.

I doubt very seriously that there is a concerted effort to keep me, specifically, from graduating, or to destroy my health; however, unnecessary things keep happening. I am very puzzled. I would like to have someone explain to me exactly what to do next.

Please don't bother to tell me to go to hell; I've already been there. Just give me an honest evaluation of my potential to graduate. As a simple undergraduate, I don't expect any exceptional assistance in building my yellow brick road; however, I would appreciate fewer bricks randomly thrown in my way. I've paid an enormously large amount of money for an education. The professors are paid well, so why must I struggle with them? My positive attitude and respect for them is rapidly disappearing.

Sincerely,

A Sampling of Journal Entries While I Studied at UCBerkeley

Spring 82

Sociolinguistics is an extremely difficult area of study because it forces the linguist to preoccupy him- or herself with everything in the world including with what is in a language. Bolinger and Sears believe that an uncontrollable flood of issues, questions and controversies come pouring in to complicate the basic study of a language specific to a social group once the subject is opened to discussion. Huh?

They seem especially sensitive to the identification of language with self. Forcing an adult to conform to the "language of the day" can cause a severe handicap in that adult. It may even destroy his- or her hold on reality and undermine physical well-being as well as job performance.

What is even more unfortunate is that this handicap is less apparent and more vulnerable to ridicule than blindness or lameness. An internal culture-shock, so to speak, can occur which may leave the speaker permanently disabled.

I agree with them. My particular experience with the English language has already caused me so much pain and cost me so much money, that I can not and will not discuss this subject unless I am quite certain that my listener is indeed interested in my welfare rather than my demise. I simply don't have the time this quarter to tell it all.

April, 1982   Stern Hall

I am so upset tonight I could jump right out of my skin. I don't know exactly why, or what's wrong with me. I'm getting too fat and I have a pain in my left side and I guess I'm afraid that something is going wrong with my heart. Or maybe I have an ulcer or who knows--who cares?

I'm just so low and unhappy that I can hardly stand it anymore. I feel so unloved; probably it's that I just don't like myself anymore. I'm such a bitch! Here I am at school and my husband and son are at home.

My husband! Sometimes I get so mad at him I don't know what to do. He's so demanding! He doesn't help me where and when I need help the most. But I guess he couldn't possibly know how terrible it in this country to be a middle-aged German woman who is stuck with all kinds of bad childhood memories and who has to somehow face the day despite all the stereo-typical ideas in people.

I guess I really carry a big grudge about him not ever facing anybody to ask them why they think I've done the wrong thing, etc. It really bothers me that he always thinks everybody else has a right to their opinions and that it's their world, tacitly implying that if they want to hurt his wife that's OK with him. It makes me feel so worthless too, when I'm the one who has to give up and try again some other time, some other place. I probably AM that worthless. I'm nothing but a sob-sister looking for help, and I'm so sensitive. People can hurt me so easily. My sense of hearing is so painful sometimes that I get all constricted when I have to listen to the low-bass voices of some of the professors, even if WHAT they say is pretty interesting. And I hear so many unpleasant sounds that make me feel all stimulated without feeling human or alive. But most of all, I feel homesick. I'm homesick for my husband's warm loving embrace. I'm homesick for my kitchen and the comfort I felt in my home before I was so rudely awakened to the outside world. I feel like I'm being punished for whatever I may have done wrong without knowing what it was and with the apprehension that I may accidentally do it again and get punished all the more the next time.

It really wasn't MY own idea to be born in Germany in 1937. So I'm now too old and too German to fit into the American society of the 1980's, even though I was good enough to serve this country as a law-abiding, tax-paying citizen for over thirty years. Even though I supported my U.S. Air Force husband for fifteen years, I'm not welcome here. I have to keep hearing about how barbarian the Germans are and how awful women in general are and all kinds of other words that really cause me all kinds of tension because I'm not able to really argue the issues without confirming all my listeners' opinions that I'm insane, stupid, domineering, unpleasant or who knows what else. And then people keep away from me, including

131

my own family, and pretend that everything is all right when I know darn well that is isn't.

Other people keep sucking off my money, but I'm not allowed to appear in the places where my money is welcome! Bullshit! I guess I really resent having it all laid to ME! It seems I have to GIVE UP my family life voluntarily in order to keep it from being destroyed by society because of me. That's really the HELL of it!

THE IRONIC, TERRIBLE HELL OF IT!

So THAT'S what's bothering me so much! I resent having to give up my family life voluntarily in order to keep it from being taken away from me. But I'm forced (?) or chosen (?), or I don't know what--to tell all the members of my generation or older that they aren't worth risking my children's lives for. If they want to keep on screwing up their own lives with all kinds of pollutants and make their planet an uninhabitable world, fine! But they'd better not expect me and my family to die for them or to keep on financing all the crap they think up! I'm tired of breathing all the shit they put out and I'd like to feel like a human being again instead of a computer that's been badly programmed!

October 15, 1982

My head hurts so much I can hardly stand it. Lynn's talking about convection currents while I'm picturing a King Alfonse drink. And then this morning's Ling 20 lecture almost made me crazy. The three TA's took twenty minutes each for the Review, and it was a mess! They were nervous and their tension passed on to me.

I wish I didn't care so much about other people's feelings, but I just can't help it. Remembering that they're working for a living and getting paid doesn't seem to help. I know that they are human, sentient creatures, too, and that passes on to me, as well. I just can't seem to get the nerve to stand up in class and say, "This is giving me a headache!" Everybody else in the class is trying to survive and that's not easy in this high energy world. I'm really exhausted already, and I'd like to go to sleep, but I don't want to take the time because I have so much work to do.

November 1982

Damn, I can't sleep! My poor head is again going round and round. All kinds of facts and figures are arguing among themselves, and confusing thoughts are torturing my brain. I have a stomachache. I think it is hunger, but it's only 4 AM, and I ate dinner last night, so I shouldn't be hungry yet. I should be nicely sleeping. I have two classes tomorrow and I really can't afford to be all bleary-eyed. What is really my problem is that I miss my husband! I'm so accustomed to sleeping next to him that a vital part of me is missing. I'm so afraid of surviving him some day that I make my own life miserable.

Somehow, I'm becoming the kind of person I really disrespect. I cry so much and seem to have no courage to face the people down who make me feel so bad. I don't know what to say to clear up the misunderstandings with my TA's. I'm really threatened by their callous attitudes toward women of my age. Do they hate their mothers and grandmothers so much that they feel resentment toward me? Is that what is carried over? I suppose, that's possible. Being understanding doesn't help ME, though. I am scared to death that I won't pass all my classes. I doubt that I'll finish my degree if I don't get all the units this time.

Fucket! Dammit, why did I ever get involved? I was a happy person with an occasional temper tantrum before I started college. Now I spend far too much time crying and self-analyzing. It seems like nobody here is satisfied with their own country, or the system or whatever. I am not coming back if I fail this quarter. If my hubby doesn't like it, he can damn well lump it—even if I made him promise not to let me quit once I started!

I think I'll give Rita (the TA in History 17A) a copy of my paper about Sarah. Do I really want or need to convince her of anything? No. I'll just do my work and let it go at that. Who the hell gives a shit about me or Sarah, anyway? Life has become completely worthless and only the language counts. If I say the right words in the right order, everything is fine and I get a smiley face from the teacher. If I goof and maybe use the wrong tone of voice, or put an accent where it doesn't belong, I get gonged. One thing that all these people forget is that I pay them to teach me. I don't remember asking them to punish me if I can't reproduce exactly what they can do. It seems that they ought to be satisfied just to get their salaries-- never mind getting me to spout forth all kinds of "right" answers. Well, tomorrow's class will probably be interesting. I'll give Mr. Skolnick my paper for the midterm. He did, after all, promise to read my work. It's too bad that they've driven me so far that I have to jeopardize my United States Citizenship as well as my health in the process of being a good citizen and living human person, but I guess that's the paradox of life. At a time when one is most fatigued, one is also the most incapable of resting calmly. Now I'm going to lie in my bed and sleep until I wake up naturally. My class is not until 12:30 and nothing is so important that I have to get sick over it. I guess, I just can't get some people out of my mind--like Bill B., Ann B., Tess M., Betty R. and all the others that have already opted out of life.

Having my father on the verge of death from lung cancer doesn't help, either. Maybe it's HIS spirit that's making me so unsettled. Well, Vati, you'd better get back into your own person and visit us as a living member of the family instead of haunting MY dreams. I'm tired of having all kinds of dead people waste my time.

Please stay away, all you ghosts! Either take a break and float around heaven, or occupy somebody else for a while. You're crowding out MY soul! Only Shelley's ghost and Calhoun's can have access to me this week. Shelley, you'll get your chance to help me write a paper about you. That way you can make sure I only say things you want me to say. Calhoun, I don't know whether you were represented very well by Prof. H., but I'll try to tell the class a little about you next Monday. Wow, by Tuesday I have to have the Shelley paper all written and ready to hand in. A part of me says I can do it, but another part of me doesn't want to get started. Damn, I hope I can hang in there!

Prosody

The rhyme in prosody
Is great for melody

To be less terse
Use free verse.

How to Earn an F at a University

"The Augustan Age" was a small class in the English Department at UC Berkeley and only offered every other year. I had always liked Jonathan Swift's *Gulliver's Travels*, which was on the reading list, so I thought I might as well check it out. Selected works of Alexander Pope, John Dryden, and David Hume among others would be discussed three times a week. As an undergraduate attempting to earn a degree in English (not, by the way my native language), I diligently studied the intriguing required books. The professor was knowledgeable, the students friendly, and the classroom bright and cheerful. I thought I was doing fine, and I was ready to pass the "Take-home" midterm exam. One of the choices was to write an essay dealing with Dryden's *Religio Laici* and Hume's *Of Miracles.* The question "How might Dryden and Hume review each other's work?" was posed, so this was to be my focus.

Since Hume wrote in supercilious Prose with all nouns starting in Capital letters, I thought the following would be acceptable to the professor:

Hume might have reviewed Dryden's Religio Laici in the following manner:

Dryden's Religio Laici is an Example of Violation of the Laws of Nature; tho' Experience has establish'd that it is impossible for a Layman, a Member of the deluded Multitude, to be erudite and incisive, this particular Layman has proved himself to be miraculously so. His Skill of producing a literary Masterpiece in the English Language belies his disingenuously humble Identification as a Layman who, in the Light of his own weakness and want of Learning confesses to combat Irreligion. It seems that a Man of Sense has finally reasoned his way out of Membership in the deluded Multitude and exposed weakness in the Delusions of Religion.

While Dryden must have had his Reasons for continuing to attend the weekly Services and participate in their Rites and Customs, he also had the Wit (one might call it Foolishness) to criticize certain Doctrines. Throughout his poem, Dryden objects to the Reasoning that those who have not heard of the Merits of the Son to Man will not attain Salvation. Charitably he pontificates:

> Most righteous doom! Because a rule reveal'd
> Is none to those, from whom it was conceal'd
> Then those who follow'd reasons dictates right;
> Liv'd up, and lifted high their natural light.

Yet, he displays an unreasonable Need for reveal'd Religion and Subservience to a Master in these Words:

> With Christian faith and virtues, we shall find
> None answ'ring the great ends of human kind,
> But this one rule of life: that shows us best
> How God may be appeas'd, and mortals blest.

One Example of faulty Reasoning is brought to Mind in Dryden's Assertion in the Preface of his Poem:

> They who wou'd prove Religion by Reason, do but weaken the cause which they endeavour to support: 'tis to take away the Pillars from our Faith, and prop it onely with a twig: 'tis to design a Tower like that of Babel, which if it were possible (as it is not) to reach Heaven, would come to nothing by the confusion of the Workmen.

As a reasonable Man, Dryden shou'd have known that true Faith requires neither Pillars nor Twigs. The Cause of proving Religion by Reason is redundant because both Religion and Reason are mental Activities based on Words and Concepts learned and memorized in one's Infancy. Had Dryden employ'd both Reason and Religion in his Analogy, he might have avoided the Tower of Babel as an Example of his Assertion. His Statement is neither religious nor reasonable: it is as meaningless as stating that it is not possible to reach one's big Toe or any other integral Part of one's own Person. After all, the Planet Earth is an integral Part of Heaven, is it not?

Despite the Unreasonableness of Dryden's Reasoning, he offers delightful and refreshing Hope and Reason in these lines:

> Yet, since th'effects of providence, we find
> Are variously dispens'd to human kind
> That vice triumphs, and virtue suffers here,
> (A brand that sovereign justice cannot bear;)
> Our reason prompts us to a future state:
> The last appeal from fortune, and from fate:
> Where God's all-righteous ways will be declar'd;
> The bad meet punishment, the good, reward.

Dryden, a poet who wrote lengthy poems, might have styled his views of Hume's work in the following manner:

> Bright as the Moon among the other Lights of Night,
> Shines Hume's Enquiry Concerning Human Sight,
> So reasonable a thesis he expounds,
> That he miraculously us confounds;
> In theoretical and expository prose
> This prodigy his reasonableness shows.
> Before our admiration carries us away,
> There are two things we ought to say.
> Hume makes assumptions two in his treatise,
> About which we may state, the opinion is his.
> First, he allows that a reasonable man
> Wou'd expect better weather in June than
> In months as December or other such seasons,
> Without thinking that one may for various reasons,
> Prefer, or consider winter weather better,
> Thus I take exception to this subjective letter.
> Another assumption is brought to light
> In the paragraph that deals with a dead man's plight,
> Again it is a subjective call
> Whether man be alive, sick or dead, at all.
> Tho' these assumptions do not from the whole detract,
> 'Tis my habit to notice such matters of fact.
> Of maxims he speaks with an elegant flair,
> His erudition, religion, and reason to air.

To quote Hume:
"The Objects, of which we have no Experience, resemble those, of which we have. The most Usual is always most Probable."

> Which is to say that Men often use
> An analogy in matters that them confuse,
> In short, men who had an experience,
> Will understand others' in a deeper sense.
> His second maxim follows here
> His prose in my poetry must appear:

"No human Testimony can have such force as to prove a Miracle, and make it a just Foundation for any such System of Religion."

> He thinks that tho' language is human life,
> Its falsehood can frequently lead to terrible strife.
> To blindly accept the words in profusion
> Can plunge entire nations into confusion
> One must not forget the example he gives
> Of the Paphlagonians that Alexander deceives.
> The Pentateuch with its fabulous stories,
> Has oft been the basis of religious Glories,
> Tho' skeptick of the Testimonies therein,
> To deny its miracle wou'd be a sin.
> He warns that religions on Delusions are found,
> Yet leaves us the hope that reason abound.
> His wide use of abstracts and conceptual nouns,
> Lend tone to his work of miraculous sounds.
> While none of his offerings are edible,
> I feel satisfied; it's incredible!

Thinking that the professor would enjoy my neatly typed essay (imitating the styles of Hume and Dryden), I presented it on time. Although I wasn't necessarily expecting an A, I was highly disappointed with the D when the professor returned our papers a few days later. Lots of little notes in the margin led me to believe that I could correct any unsatisfactory spots and resubmit the essay for an improved grade. Consequently, I wasted no time in going to his office hours. Naively, I expected to discuss my essay and started by asking when I could resubmit the edited paper. The short answer was no, he would not accept an edited version later. He continued to criticize my writing. I tried to focus on my current dilemma of having a D on a paper; he deflected the discussion to other arguments.

Finally, in desperation, I asked, "Professor X, just what **do** you want?"

Looking me over from top to bottom with a smirk, his answer, "If you don't know that, you'll have a hard time in my class," made me very self-conscious.

"Thank you, Professor X. Good-bye!" was all I could stammer as I headed for the door. What could I do? The deadline for withdrawal from the class had passed. I didn't want to risk a penalty, so I determined to do my very best on the Final Exam. We were to compare and contrast Gulliver's behavior in Books II and IV of the Travels. We were also to consider our responses to him, our sense of Swift's presence in the work, and our sense of Swift's purpose. One of the questions on the exam even asked us to explain the role we take on as we observe our surrogate in the stressful environments of Books II and IV.

I somehow managed to attend the classes and did all the required reading in the hope that I would at least earn a C for the course. I participated in discussions and felt comfortable enough in the presence of the other students although I remained leery of the professor. Finally, we had to present our Final Exam papers. I submitted the following:

$E=mc^2$ or *Was Jonathan Swift the Father of Einstein?*

In Books II and IV of Gulliver's Travels, Swift takes the reader on an excursion into the never-never land of relativity. The very first word of the Travels, "My," Swift establishes the fused consciousness of himself, Gulliver and the reader that moves inexorably through space and time, interacting with creatures that are larger, smaller, more or less reasonable, powerful, smelly, or otherwise unequal to itself.

Swift is the absolute presence throughout the entire work just as is the reader. One knows that the "author" is Swift thinly disguised as Gulliver. However, because of the intensity of Swift's style, one becomes progressively less conscious of the activity of reading and more conscious of the activities that Gulliver is engaged in.

Interest is aroused immediately, and by the time Gulliver arrives at Brogdingnag, the reader has become Gulliver.

In Brogdingnag, the land of physical or quantitative relativity, the inhabitants are much larger than Gulliver, and Swift accounts for details of measurement in various ways; for example,

At length he ventured to take me up behind by the middle between his forefinger and thumb, and brought me within three yards of his eyes, that he might behold my shape more perfectly. I guessed his meaning, and my good fortune gave me so much presence of mind, that I resolved not to struggle in the least as he held me in the air above sixty foot from the ground, although he grievously pinched my sides, for fear I should slip through his fingers.

"Within three yards of his eyes" and "above sixty foot from the ground" establishes the concept of known measurements, and "I should slip through his fingers" demonstrates the relative sizes of Gulliver and the giant King. Again and again, the reader is reminded of the quantitative differences between himself and his imaginary environment. One gets to walk on a dining table, sleep in a baby doll's cradle, and ride in a box small enough to fit on a child's lap. Except for the size differential, however, the inhabitants of Brogdingnag appear to have much the same physical characteristics and engage in the same activities of Swift's human society.

The Country of the Houyhnhnms presents the spiritual or qualitative relativity of life. The creatures encountered in Book IV are more or less reasonable, more or less civil, or more or less pleasant to be with than Gulliver but not appreciably different in size. Intelligible language, reason, tolerance and good manners appear in the shape of horses while completely uncouth behavior takes on the human shape. Along with Gulliver, Swift and the reader are horrified to discover that humans are shaped just like the yahoos. The horror is gradually replaced by a calm realization that humans must be members of the reasonable species as well; otherwise, we wouldn't be able to read and/or be horrified by our reading.

As one emerges from a reading of Gulliver's Travels, one no longer feels the need to be just exactly like someone else because Swift has made the relativity of all things and processes obvious for us. One is, however, left with the vague sense that Swift had not met his match, quantitative and qualitative, until he met his reader. Though quite different in important ways, we are two of a kind, Swift and I: we are both human, imaginative and as we share the experiences of Gulliver, we react in much the same manner. Neither of us can forget the political realities of the times while we indulge our fancies in fictitious affairs.

When Gulliver is carefully scrutinized by the Master horse and his servant and realizes that he shares the physical characteristics of a yahoo, he is in a state of horror and astonishment. He gradually becomes familiar with the horses, learns their language and answers their questions about his country. Gulliver gladly tells them all that he knows but soon realizes that his stories would be believed only in the concepts which were familiar to the horses. During the questioning, however, Gulliver fades and Swift's voice comes through loud and clear. He gets carried away with a catalogue of the foolish arguments with which his countrymen regularly destroy each other. Gulliver and Swift are interchangeable as they take a kind of fiendish pleasure in listing the weapons people use in their own destruction, and

Swift finally gets completely caught up in a gloating, almost bragging, description of the worst side of life in Europe. It's a wonder that humanity is still thriving in the twentieth century!

Seeing himself through the Houyhnhnms' eyes, Gulliver becomes hateful of his own species, and the reader becomes uneasy with the sense that Swift has forgotten that he's the one who is doing **all** the seeing and reporting. Why would Swift want to immortalize so many evils of his own society in a work of art?

In Book II, when Gulliver's questioned by the giant King, he wanted "the tongue of Demosthenes or Cicero, that might have enabled me to celebrate the praise of my own dear native country in a style equal to its merits and felicity." Swift exaggerates and lavishes praises on every facet of the European social scene until, in the giant King's words, he made "a most admirable panegyric" upon his country. The satire, however, appears as Swift, in the voice of the King, criticizes his country:

"But, by what I have gathered from your own relation, and the answers I have with much pains wringed and extorted from you, I cannot but conclude the bulk of your natives to be the most pernicious race of little odious vermin that nature ever suffered to crawl upon the surface of the earth."

Gulliver reacts to this criticism with the apology that he had to "rest with patience" while his noble and most beloved country was so injuriously treated. It is absolutely astonishing that the reader is expected to read this straight; however, that is exactly what happens: one believes it momentarily, and then does a double-take, "Hey, wait a minute!" Isn't Swift the one who is doing **all** the commentary here?

One can well imagine Swift never batting an eye as he lets Gulliver grovel humbly before the King, artfully eluding many of his questions and placing the virtues and beauties of his "political mother" in the most "advantageous light." No matter which character had criticized his country, Swift has made his point.

Swift's attack on European civilization in both Books II and IV is breath-taking and vicious. An audience that sees itself represented in such satirical terms is certain to enjoy the joke. One can almost visualize the learned heads of England nodding assent and chuckling over their own foibles, exploits, and weaknesses represented in print. What possible harm could laughing and bragging about one's own societal ills do? No one could possibly mistake Swift's blanket attack on European civilization as an attack only England, could one? No, of course not! No enemy of

England could possibly identify with the Brogdingnagian King or with the Houyhnhnm Master. Surely, all Europeans were smart enough to realize that Swift was making a generalization about the entire species.

The question, "What do you think of the giant King and the Houyhnhnm Master as authorities?" causes me to make the shift from identifying with Gulliver to my own identity as a twentieth-century survivor of historical realities. I have recognized for some time that those who occupy a territory are the authorities, and those who enter their realm are subjected to whatever forms that authority takes.

The giant King ruled Brogdingnag before Gulliver ever appeared. It is not only his size that demands the respect and subservience of Gulliver who strives to learn the language, blend into the culture and otherwise ingratiate himself in order to survive in the presence of this giant authoritative force. Swift continually reinforces the King's authority by having Gulliver compare his own dimensions with those of his captor, thereby emphasizing the King's power. As a newcomer to the world, I occasionally find it difficult to remember that Aristotle, Jesus Christ, Hitler and various other imposing figures were roughly the same physical size as myself. Even present world leaders are actually very near my size although they **seem** to loom large over me. With such perceptional distortions, it is not very difficult to assign authority to those who already occupy a territory be it actual or conceptual, be it a white house or a university.

The Houyhnhnm Master represents the type of authority that seems to be innate in those creatures who are at ease with the rest of the universe. Gulliver perceives him to be completely in control of his own nature as well as the nature of his environment. He need merely exist in order to maintain his position of authority because there is no reason for anyone to challenge such a reasonable, inoffensive creature.

Neither the King nor the Houyhnhnm Master has strengths or limitations because they are fictional characters invented by Swift. He can have them do anything he wishes—including an attack on European society. A reader could identify with the giant King and despise Europeans as vermin, or he could identify with the horse Master and compare Europeans with the vile Yahoos. How this could possibly enhance **anything**, I don't know. Rather, it fosters hate.

In answering the question about the roles I take on, I must state that I have read <u>Gulliver's Travels</u> twice: once, years ago, as recreational reading. I thoroughly enjoyed it for its narrative value because I was reading without the pressure of grades or analysis. I simply accepted the story. The second reading was more recent when I read the book as a class assignment under very hurried conditions and as part of an enormous amount of reading material from other coursework as well.

I remember that during my first reading I **was** Gulliver. I felt what he felt, saw what he saw and never really thought about the possibility of taking on any other role. I was enchanted by the flight into fantasyland in the comfortable smugness of my immediate surroundings. The satire did not entirely escape me, but I was not affected by it.

In the more recent reading I deliberately became a critical observer of all the characters and remained aware of the historical implications of literary works in general and this work in particular. Knowing that nearly every man, woman and child in Europe had read Gulliver's Travels before the two world wars, my consciousness was clouded with unpleasant thoughts, such as "Did Swift's satire give birth to the hatefulness of world wars?" I tried to remain in the eighteenth century long enough to travel with Gulliver; however, the reality of the twentieth century is no longer comfortable enough for me to enjoy guided tours into my own psyche. None of the characters played a role that could tempt me to abandon the role I play at the moment: that of critical reader who would gladly give a King's ransom to regain her former ability to enjoy the thrills and spills of fictional characters. Alas, Babylon! How was Swift to know that $E=mc^2$ would someday become an absolute and that the never-never land of relativity would someday become the nuclear age?

Lest this essay become too didactic, it should end on an uplifting note:

Question: How does Swift conceal and reveal himself in this text?

Answer: Not at all, but he does it so well!

Having invested a lot of time and effort into the above essay, I expected a passing grade. Perhaps it wouldn't deserve an A for this Final Exam, but surely, the professor must find **some** value in it. We students were to pick up our graded papers in his office two weeks later.

Apprehensively, I climbed the stairs to his office on the fourth floor and waited my turn to enter. When I noticed an F at the bottom of my paper, I became angry but controlled my temper. Because I was conscious of the other students in the hallway, I remained silent. The professor explained, "You just didn't get on top of the material."

I tossed my paper on the floor, stepped on it and quietly said, "There!

Now I'm on top of the material!" Then I picked it up and left. My grade point average had received quite a blow because I would not be able to make up this grade. This particular professor was the only one who taught this particular course every other year. Even though I tried to fight this unjust grade through the Ombudsman's office and even spoke with a counselor regarding sexual harassment, I could never prove that my work in "The Augustan Age" deserved anything other than an F.

A Letter to God

Oh, please dear God, give me the strength to write this fucking paper about Yeats' stupid poetry. I have no idea what he was trying to say, but I'm obligated to read his shit just because the English Department at UC Berkeley considers it required reading.

How can you expect me to do your work if you don't help me at all? I'm just a person who has always tried to do the right thing, haven't I? I've always done all the things that you and everybody else expected me to do, such as **live** through experiences when it would have been **so** much easier to die, or work to the point of exhaustion when I could have slept in my nice warm bed. I've done my best to learn the language of this land since I came to America. I've been a good citizen, I've tried to help old people in convalescent hospitals, I've done all I could and I'm still doing all I can to keep peace in the world by working against the proliferation of nuclear arms. I've kept a smile on my face even though I'd much rather lash out and kill the sons-of-bitches who make life so difficult for everybody. Oh, dear god, what more do you want from me? Please tell me what Yeats was trying to say so I can tell Ms Walker, the professor. I'll never make it through the English Department, but that doesn't matter. I can find a job somewhere, I'm sure. There must be plenty of restaurants that need waitresses or dishwashers. Or maybe, I could just walk the streets while my husband and kids are at **their** jobs. Or maybe I won't have to worry about it (my extra time) at all, because you plan to let that long-awaited apocalypse destroy everything I've worked so hard to build up.

Oh please, please let me know soon. I can't carry on much longer. It's hard enough to see all the bad things on this planet and read in **plain** English all the bad things that people do without having to rack my brain trying to figure out the stupid symbolism that Yeats invented. He had no consideration for his readers. Did he really think that human beings could read the shit he wrote? In fact, did he care even one little bit that people would fail in school and a whole nation would lose the potential of intelligent people just because they couldn't cope with the crap he wrote? No, the son-of-a-bitch wrote his stupid poems and the rest of us fail in school because, after all, his poetry is "English Literature" and therefore worth more than real live human beings. Well, I think his poetry is a lot of shit.

Oh, dear God, what am I saying? Has it come to this? Must I use obscenities to express my opinions? Maybe I should give a few examples of what bothers me the most about Yeats' poetry.

For one thing he keeps talking about Troy. In <u>The Rose of the World</u>, he doesn't make any sense at all when he says, "Troy passed away in one high funereal gleam, and Usna's children died." What is that supposed to mean to me? America is on the verge of one high funereal gleam and my children are about to die, and I'm sorry to say that I couldn't care less about Troy and Usna. Oh God, I'm so tired of crying. Please, please give me some hope. Okay, okay, I've regained my composure!

Then there is his <u>No Second Troy.</u> he writes about a woman who supposedly filled his days with misery. Good! I'm glad she did! He deserves to have his days filled with misery; he's filling **my** days with misery. He hints that she is an anachronism because her type of nationalism and "high and solitary and most stern" beauty is not natural in an "age like this." Well, what "age" was it? Just when **is** her type of beauty natural? And what's more, **she** didn't burn Troy in the first place; a bunch of stupid men did. But the dirty son-of-a-bitch hints that **she** did it: "Was there another Troy for her to burn?" Chalk another one up for the innocence of mankind. It's all a woman's fault!

Well, God, I'm just about fed up with the guilt trip that has been laid on me since I was born. I've been trying to make up for anything other women **may** have done wrong, but apparently my efforts haven't made one bit of difference to you. You keep letting men write untrue statements about women in prose and poetry. You keep letting men build more and more machines that threaten to engulf this entire planet with a living hell, and you keep letting them have the power to deny women any kind of authority about matters of life and death.

Women are branded too ambitious when they get politically involved. They are branded too apathetic when they **don't** get involved. If I'm active, I'm likely to get assassinated, and if I'm inactive, I'm likely to die of boredom, In any case, I'll be destroyed just like "Eve" or "Helen" or who knows who else.

If I stay home and tend to my own personal affairs, I'm considered too lazy to do something about the things I know to be wrong. When I criticize too much, I'm told I'm ungrateful to this country and I should go back to Germany where I came from. When I don't criticize enough, or in the expected form of "papers," I'm given bad grades and denied a degree from a system I've supported financially for many years.

Well, God, I've calmed down a little, and the tears have stopped flowing, but that doesn't mean I'm not in a terrible dilemma anymore. Nothing has changed! The missile factories are still grinding them out, old people are still dying, young people are still robbing and killing each other, and the chance of my ever graduating is just as remote as Peace on Earth by Christmas.

I'm leaving it up to you. Show me that life is worth living. I've done all I could.

(Submitted as a paper for a UC Berkeley English class in 1980)

A Bump on the Head in Ashland

Ouch!

On Wednesday, Aug. 1, 2001, my husband Lee and I were in Ashland, Oregon to watch Shakespeare plays with some friends. Lorraine and Dave , Kathy and Mark and we had gone to watch <u>The Merry Wives of Windsor</u> that evening. It had been so enjoyable that we weren't ready to go back to our motel in Medford yet. Instead we went to a bar called Maxi's. It was nearly empty, so they were glad to have us come in. Three lonely musicians played just for us for about a half hour. We had great fun and even danced a little. Around midnight we left in our van.

Mark, the tallest in our group, had folded himself into the back space because there was only seating for five. When we got to the motel, Lee opened the back hatch so Mark could climb out. As we were piling out of the van, I asked Lee to get my jacket out of the back. I was standing close by and peeked in to make sure he was taking the jacket out. Just as I leaned over, Mark pulled the hatch down. Bang! I received a glancing blow at the top right side of my head. A bump developed right away, and I thought my skull had been split open. No blood was coming out, though. Dave ran to get ice, and Mark apologized profusely. I stayed on my feet and walked around talking to myself. I wanted to make sure nothing bad had happened. Lorraine thought I should go to the "Urgent Care" facility she had visited the day before. I wasn't sure I needed to do that in the middle of the night. Dave arrived with the ice, and Lee wrapped it in a washcloth for me.

I sat on my bed for about two hours with the ice on my head. They all told me not to go to sleep. The lump gradually went down, and the pain subsided. I did some embroidering and recited some German poetry to check my coordination and mental abilities. Everything seemed to be okay, so I took a Tylenol and went to sleep. Dave teased me the next morning, "You know, Marianne, reciting German poetry is a sign that something is wrong with your brain." I had to laugh!

Now it's Tuesday morning on August 7. I still feel the tenderness when I touch my head, but there is no severe pain. Two symptoms, however, have come up since that head bump. For one thing, since Thursday morning I have had a twitch in my <u>left</u> eyelid that comes and goes. I can feel it right now. For another thing, this morning I noticed a tiny bruise next to my right eye. There is no pain associated with this, and my vision doesn't seem to be affected.

P.S. It is now January 2010, and I'm still okay.

An open letter to President Bush and Governor Schwarzenegger[8]

May 7, 2006

Let's get this straight: I'm an immigrant and naturalized U.S. Citizen; my husband is a natural-born U.S. Citizen, son of an illegal immigrant (long since deceased). Together we have been law-abiding citizens and tax-payers for over a hundred years (over fifty each).

It's not easy for me to observe the current hullabaloo and sort out the media hubbub regarding immigration. Considering my history how can *I* possibly choose sides? Well, let me try!

Rather than getting crazy about millions of people who've come legally or illegally to the United States **to work**, I'd like to focus on those who've come or will come across our southern border **to commit serious felonies.**

If I'm to believe some of the media hype and Dept. of Justice figures, I'd have to agree that our prisons house a large percentage of illegal immigrant **convicted felons.** These are the individuals nobody needs in America. I believe that even the current protesters and most liberal judges would agree with my proposal.

Deporting felons to their country of origin upon conviction would be my first choice, but I realize that the appeals process makes immediate deportation impossible. I won't lobby for that idea, but I'm offering an alternative:

Let's construct prisons along the southern border of the United States. At intervals of approximately 200 miles, ten good strong prisons with back gates opening directly into Mexico should be sufficient to house the convicted (and illegal) felons until their release.

Any immigrant from south of the border convicted of a felony that requires incarceration should be sent immediately to one of the border prisons to serve their time and await the appeals process. (Surely, even the most liberal judge could not object to such a policy.) Release through the back gates guarded by armed observation towers should assure the proper direction that the freed individual will take in the future.

The guard towers surrounding each prison can serve a dual purpose: Keeping prisoners inside the walls, and keeping "wanderers" outside the U.S. borders.

My ideas haven't necessarily always solved problems, but they certainly have a history of ameliorating them. While I am a person who thinks of this planet as a whole and enjoys the benefits of free trade and unfettered travel, I strongly believe in the integrity of national borders until such time when all human beings can be trusted to possess personal integrity.

Respectfully submitted, Marianne Tong

Getting and Losing a Job [9]

Another chapter in my life. After much stress and strain, I finally got the education I always thought I needed so badly. It was 1955 when I graduated from high school, and for most purposes of that time, a high school diploma was enough. Although I passed the Overseas Cambridge Entrance examination that would have gotten me into Cambridge University in England, there wasn't enough money for me to go to college. Besides, my step-father said, "Women should stay at home and make a man happy!" So after graduation, I got a job selling stationery and newspapers in an airport terminal and met my husband-to-be.

Moving around with a military husband was very exciting and adventurous despite the many sacrifices. Military dependents seldom had a chance to develop careers of their own. Consequently, the wife of a military man had to find other ways of filling the hours between wars. Some became alcohol dependent; others volunteered their services; and others prepared themselves for eventual future careers.

I was among the latter two. Wherever we went, I joined the Squadron Wives' Club, the NCO Wives' Club, or whatever else was available. I studied the cities we visited while we were stationed in Germany and led American youth groups on sight-seeing trips throughout Europe. I read books and helped my children with their schoolwork. I hoped and hoped that one day I would have the opportunity and the money to do something academic with the intelligence my former teachers had been so sure of. In short, I wanted to go back to school once my husband retired from the military.

By the time that opportunity finally arrived, I was, at age forty, sadly "over the hill." School is supposedly for the young. Against the advice of well-meaning friends and family members (however with the encouragement of my community college counselor and my loving husband), I tortured myself with book learning. The buckets of tears generated by the college courses that ridiculed the very principles I had lived by, did not deter me from achieving my goal: a degree in English. In the process, I endured what I now recognize as harassment. A Physics professor who blamed all the trouble of the world on housewives who should stay home to take care of their children; a counselor who suggested I become a cheerleader; a Journalism professor who labeled my idealistic paper an "elaborate cop-out;" and English professor who looked my person over from head to toe rather than find some value in my writing and flatly stated that I'd have a difficult time in his course; a Chicano professor and his TA who expected me to concur with their anti-Americanism and put it into writing; a department chairman who refused to review my writings as proof of passing work and challenged me to prove that I was being harassed; a professor who took several young male students out of the office hours line even though I was ahead of them—were part and parcel of my education. None of the offensive incidents were grievable. I just had to chalk them up as experience.

Finally in 1983, with bittersweet pride in having accomplished my goal of learning the English language, I received a BA degree in English from the prestigious University of California, Berkeley. I had been made to believe that I needed this to prove my opinions, and now I felt my worth as a valued member of the community.

In the intervening years I had never lost sight of the things that are most important to me: my home and my ever-expanding family. There were weddings, christenings, and funerals. There were also alarming newspaper articles about teacher shortages and problems in the school system, but I was reluctant to obligate myself to a full-time career. When Bob, our life insurance agent, suggested I take the CBEST (California Basic Educational Skills Test) and become a substitute teacher, I laughed at him. I had never in my wildest dreams thought about teaching in public schools. I was using my newly-acquired skills to write letters and chapters of my life story. Besides, I had read in the newspaper that the dead-line for applying to take the CBEST had just passed. As a member of the County Board of Education, Bob made a couple of phone calls and Bingo! I was taking the test!

After one year as a substitute in a great variety of classes, I was asked to take a long-term substitute assignment for a vacancy at Fairfield High. The position for three sections of General Math 9 and two different sections of English was being advertised, and I would only be there until a credentialed teacher could be hired. I accepted the offer knowing that I could only be sure of one week at a time. There was no empty classroom available, so I would have to teach in five different classrooms in separated building wings during other teachers' "prep times" (each high school teacher has one student-free class period for preparation of materials, etc). The English department chairman gave me a set of books with short stories for the tenth graders and a set of literature texts for the eleventh graders—no lesson plans, study guides or other supporting materials. Furthermore, there was only one class set of math books, so I would have to move them on a tiny-wheeled projector cart from one class to another across concrete walkways—rain or shine. I also had to make up hand-outs for homework because the students couldn't take the books home. I had practically no other help. There were no lesson plans (and I had never made any before) and no indication that some of my students were resource students (a branch of Special Education). I found out later that some of the students in the math classes lived in group homes and had already been to Juvenile hall. Discipline and classroom management proved to be a challenge! Talk about being blind-sighted! However, I rose to the occasion. I spent a lot of time at home each night preparing for the next day, but it was something I liked to do, so I did it. Eventually, the principal put all my afternoon classes in the Agriculture building, a small portable on the other side of the parking lot serving the "Ag" classes in the mornings. The good thing about this move was that I could spend all three afternoon classes in the same classroom. The down-side was that now I had to drag my projector cart across a large bumpy parking lot twice a day. Besides, despite a telephone, I was isolated from any immediate assistance from the main office in case of an emergency.

As each day went by, I became more comfortable. For five weeks, I was making lessons plans one week at a time, giving quizzes on Fridays and recording the grades. Other teachers accepted me as a colleague. Even though I knew that the district was still looking for a fully credentialed teacher, there was no indication that one had been found. Then one Monday morning I found a different name on my mailbox. I asked the secretary about this, but she had simply done what she was told. I asked the principal whether this meant that I didn't need to stay for the rest of the day. He said that he was sorry I had to find out this way. He told me that a teacher with a Doctorate in Education had been hired. Then he told me that I could stay for a couple of days to "show her the ropes." I was floored! What could I—a non-credentialed substitute who had been given a projector cart and not much else in starting out the year—possibly impart to a Doctor! I went home and calculated the students' grades for the past five weeks, and then I took the grade book to the school office. As far as I was concerned, I was finished, but I was wrong. Some of the students, especially those who had made a special effort to work with me, were quite upset that their work for me was not going to be averaged into their grades, and so was I. I had to go back and fight for my students. Finally the "Doctor" relented and decided to average the grades earned with me into their total grades.

I'm sure my abrupt refusal to be helpful at that time and my subsequent fight for grades were remembered a few years later during an interview by the same principal for a part-time German language position at the same high school. I did not get that job!

In 1986 I served another long-term stint for six weeks in the English department at Armijo high school and loved it. I was requested because of the reputation as a no-nonsense disciplinarian that I had built up over my three years of subbing. The teacher who requested me had left plenty of materials, and I had a classroom in the English department wing. By this time, there was little question as to my calling. I was obviously born to teach, and lots of students and teachers kept telling me to become a "real" teacher. I made up my mind to try getting a teaching credential. With several letters of recommendation in hand, I was accepted at Sac State (California State University, Sacramento). Because I hated the idea of commuting, my husband and I started thinking about renting an apartment in Sacramento or purchasing a second home there. Thank goodness, this was not necessary. Coincidentally, Chapman College was offering the first teaching credential program in Solano County that same year.

At a social event one Wednesday evening I was talking with a friend about my plans to go to Sac State to earn a teaching credential. She said that her neighbor had just enrolled in the credential program at Chapman on Travis Air Force Base. She was starting classes the next day! I couldn't believe my luck! Perhaps I wouldn't have to go Sacramento after all.

First thing on Thursday morning I went to the Chapman office, and that evening I attended my first class in the credential program. Because my degree from UC Berkeley had not required a course in the U.S. Constitution, I had never taken this course. Now I would still have to complete this required unit before I could obtain full graduate status in a teaching credential program. Naturally, I hustled right over to Solano Community College to enroll in the PoliSci (Political Science) course that would satisfy this requirement. Those were the days when I was sickeningly eager to comply. I felt that I needed to raise my GPA (my Grade Point Average was barely adequate because of the two F's I had to absorb at UCB), so I also enrolled in two German classes at SCC. Unfortunately, this new need for education meant that I would not have time for subbing, and I would have to suspend earning money. Again, my husband encouraged me to go on with my education. He was sure that I would eventually make up for our financial losses. I also talked with my mother who responded with moral support in this new venture. For a couple of days I was actually enrolled in three colleges at once. Naturally, I withdrew from the program at Sac State on the following Monday.

At considerable financial cost, I succeeded at Solano College and Chapman and eventually got ready to do my student teaching. Because all four of my children had graduated from Armijo, I had a sentimental reason for wanting to do my student teaching there. It was arranged for me to have two master teachers. I would be working with Charlene for Remedial English 10 and the Jr./Sr. Great Reading and Writing class; with Winnie (my former college counselor's wife) for College Prep English 11. For eight weeks I was in heaven; then my world fell apart. It was March 1987.

After the Spring break I was to start at Sullivan Junior High School with Karen, my master teacher. Before starting there, I went to visit my mother who was living in Azusa. Her health which had been steadily declining for twenty years had reached a crisis point. It was a very sad visit, but I could not stay because of my student teaching schedule. Both my mother and dad wished me luck and promised to spend more time together in the summer; however, the stress kept piling up!

Since German was my native language and I had also taken a number of college classes in German grammar and literature, I decided to take the NTE (National Teacher's Examination) test in German. Passing the test would enable me to add German as a single subject to my Teaching Credential in English. There were also some social obligations my husband as Exalted Ruler of the Elks wanted me to attend with him. One of those obligations was a bus trip to Reno. Because I had acquired a reputation of knowing lots of things including the lyrics of most folk songs, a friend suckered me into leading the bus riders in song. I also had a briefcase full of papers I still had to grade for my college prep students at Armijo and felt very guilty about letting them wait another day. Feeling pressured, my throat got tighter and tighter. By the time we got home, I was so sick I couldn't start my student teaching at the Junior High on time. I was no longer sure I could actually complete the program. I called my Chapman advisor who told me she'd notify the school. I was to let her know when I was ready to start again. After a long cry, I slept for two days.

Within a few days I had regained my composure and finished grading the Armijo papers. Also, my mother assured me that she was doing much better and told me not to quit. My husband encouraged me to continue with the student teaching and promised to be less demanding about the social obligations. I called my Chapman advisor who made new arrangements at Sullivan Middle School.

At Armijo I had had two master teachers who worked together and made me feel confident, competent and important. At Sullivan, I was assigned to two master teachers who disagreed in their basic educational approaches, who kept interrupting each other when they were instructing me. They acted immaturely in the lunch room (throwing wadded-up napkins back and forth across my nose as if they were naughty students), gave me no cubby hole for my things, wanted me to teach about the atom bomb on Hiroshima (a theme that I, as an experienced WWII survivor but inexperienced teacher, felt unprepared and unwilling to tackle) and made me feel miserable and generally in the way. When I called my Chapman advisor about my concerns, she told me that my stress might be age-related and hormonal. I asked her to set up an informal meeting with my two master teachers. She suggested I go to see a doctor first. I told her I was quitting. Then I threw myself on the bed and cried.

Between sleeping fitfully and crying pitifully for three days and nights, I caused my husband considerable grief. He empathized and nursed me back to health. He also reminded me of the huge investment we had already made and potential rewards my hard work could yield. I called my mother and told her that I couldn't go on. She begged me not to give up. I told her it was too late. I had already quit. She pleaded with me to go back to Chapman and see whether I could start again in September.

When I called my mother back and told her that I had called Chapman, and that they would let me register in August, she made me promise to give it one more try. She wanted me to finish and become a real teacher.

For the next couple of months I let life take care of itself. Every time I phoned my mother, she asked me about my plans for August, and I had to assure her that I was not giving up. In July we visited her for week. She had become so frail! An incident between my mother and my dad nearly unnerved me, but she insisted that it was an accident and he usually took good care of her. Above all, she wanted me to go back to school and fulfill my dream. She reminded me that she had given up on her childhood dreams and that now it was too late for her. She did not want the same thing to happen to me. On August 13 she died.

My new student teaching assignment was arranged. Considering my problems at Sullivan a few months earlier and my mother's recent passing, my counselor at Chapman may have been a bit nervous about assigning full-time work for eight weeks, so she offered me sixteen weeks of part-time student teaching at Willis Jepson in Vacaville. I would be working mornings only. Lynne would be my master teacher for a college prep ninth grade English class, and Lily would be my master teacher for Exploratory German. I accepted these conditions and set aside the fact that I was losing a great deal of time in paid employment because of the scheduling at Chapman. According to the manual, an informal meeting should have been arranged with the master teacher to resolve problems; instead, they had sent me to a doctor. I was resentful but also grateful for the opportunity to undo the damage. Despite my grief over my mother, I was happy as a lark at Willis Jepson. I was healthy and life was good. Indeed, I was doing what my mother hoped I would do. I finished the student teaching with letters of recommendation in hand.

Although I sent out my resume and application to every district in Solano County, I received only a couple of interviews. All my bright-eyed hopes were being dashed on the harsh reality of my situation. The story was always the same: I did not fill the school's needs. (translation: I was too old.)

In September 1988 I placed my name on the Travis and Fairfield-Suisun School district substitute lists. Subbing this time was not the same, though. Before I had suffered through the credential program, I didn't mind the abuse a substitute sometimes has to endure at the hands and mouths of obnoxious students. As a credentialed but unemployed teacher, I minded very much, indeed! One particularly bad day at Fairfield High convinced me to take my name off the sub list. Instead, I accepted assignments as a home/hospital teacher, a part-time position with the school district.

In the meantime someone asked me to try subbing at the McGrath School in Napa State Hospital. I was surprised to learn that there were children and a special school in that institution. For a few days I gave the application some serious thought because I had enjoyed working with not-so-perfect individuals throughout my life. In order to be placed on their official payroll, I had to obligate myself to obtain an additional credential: Mild to Moderate Learning Disabilities. Fortunately, that very same year, Chapman had begun a brand new program: credentials in Special Education. I enrolled in the first class (at $149 a unit) and signed on at Napa State Hospital as a "permanent intermittent employee" in November.

For a year and a half, I enjoyed the intermittent subbing at Napa State Hospital mixed with home teaching for the Fairfield-Suisun Unified School District. Then that naughty Lady Luck decided to get involved again. Three events happened within one month that made me so mad I could have chewed nails and spit out thumbtacks.

First, my former master teacher at Armijo called to ask me whether I could sub for her for the last six weeks of school. She was having elective surgery and would love to have me take over her classes: college prep English, including an advanced placement class in which I would cover Existentialism. She had confidence in me! I felt on the top of the world; after all, she had observed me for eight straight weeks in the classroom. She needed to know whether I would place my name on the sub list again, so she could make her plans. I promised I would.

When I contacted the sub desk the following day, I was told that they would be glad to place my name back on the sub list. When I mentioned that I was only interested in the subbing assignment for Mrs. P., the lady told me that she could not guarantee that. I told her that this was a teacher's special request and please to check it out with the personnel director. After a few minutes, I was told that they were sorry but that someone else had already been assigned to that long-term job, and that Winnie couldn't always get what she wanted! I wondered what kind of hornet's nest I had stumbled upon now. Naturally, I was disappointed, but I had not sustained a loss. I still had my intermittent job at Napa State Hospital and my home students.

Second, a memo circulated at McGrath indicated that a recently hired permanent aide would substitute for a teacher for a month. When I asked why an aide rather than I, a credentialed teacher, was given that assignment, I was told that they were now going to be able to save money by letting aides sub for teachers. Besides, I had not always been "on-call" available on short-term notice because of my home teaching. I tried to remind my supervisor that he had approved my home teaching and had indicated that I would get called for the monthly sub assignments in plenty of time to adjust my schedule. Two other teachers showed me the section of the Education Code covering substitutes (who were to be credentialed teachers) for Special Education teachers. When I drew the supervisor's attention to this Code, he stated that a precedent had been set at another State institution due to budget constraints. I soon sensed that my services were no longer welcome at McGrath.

The shop steward of the Teacher's Union tried to help me for a while, but she was released from her teaching position for an unrelated incident. Bummer! At least my home teaching was a success! Parents, students and my supervisors complimented me frequently.

Then the third bombshell hit. My home teaching supervisor told me that the District had approved home teaching as a full-time position. She was sure that I would get an interview and probably the job if I filled out an application. She would be on the interview panel and make a favorable recommendation. I was never called for that interview. A couple of weeks went by, so I called my supervisor out of curiosity. She was very embarrassed. It turned out that they had only interviewed "Indistrict" applicants. A person who taught evening school had been hired. My supervisor tried to assure me that I would be called if there were ever too much work for the new teacher to handle. Remembering that she had been on my side, I excused myself and crawled out of her office like a whipped puppy.

Life goes on. I continued taking classes at Chapman for the Learning Handicapped Credential that seemed nothing but a useless piece of paper now. However, I was so deeply invested, financially and emotionally, that I continued in the hope of future success and getting a place to do my required field work.

My counselor at Chapman arranged for me to call the Director of Special Education at Travis Unified School District. The Director asked me to come meet my new master teacher, the high school Resource teacher. There would be some direct classroom instruction and some consultation with the teachers of the students on our caseload. I would observe for the first two weeks and then take the full responsibility, including attending IEP (Individualized Educational Plan) meetings with parents and teachers. Both the director and the master teacher seemed very friendly, and I was looking forward to this eight-week assignment. Deep in my heart, I resented the fact that only one other student in my Chapman credential program and I were paying over a $1000 for the privilege of working while the other ten students in the program were able to use their full-time (working on emergency credentials) employment in place of the Special Education field work. I did not allow this resentment to show and remained friendly and professional in my contact with the students and teachers at Vanden High School. At home I had another good cry on my husband's shoulder.

The students and I were getting acquainted, and I had already begun to take over some of the direct instruction when I got a cryptic phone call from the District Office. Would I be willing to come and discuss a possible change in my program? When I looked puzzled, my master teacher explained that I might have to change schools. There was another Special Education class that was having problems, and they needed some help. I remarked that if they needed help, they should hire someone. Inwardly, I wondered what I had done wrong now. I figured that when so many problems keep happening to a person, that person must be causing them. I fully expected to be sent packing.

At the District Office I was treated very friendly, so I became totally curious. The new Director of Personnel took me into her office and closed the door behind me. What in the world? She could read the puzzled look on my face and said, "If you want to finish your field work in the Travis District, you will not ask any questions and simply accept the change as an administrative adjustment." She had already called Chapman to authorize the transfer. I tried to tell her that I was very sensitive to my own personal shortcomings and was wondering whether I had done anything to precipitate this sudden change. She repeated that it would be better all the way around for me to accept things without questions. I nodded, and then she walked over to Golden West Middle School with me. On the way she briefly explained that I would be working in a Special Day Class (SDC) instead of the Resource Specialist Program (RSP). I learned that a student's placement in one of these programs depends on a formula derived from the severity of the disability and the amount of modification needed. In other words, the students I would be working with in the SDC had more severe learning disabilities. When we arrived she introduced me to the teacher who appeared genuinely surprised. She had only been told that very morning that she would have a student teacher.

More than a year later, long after I had successfully finished my field work, I learned about the political quagmire I had accidentally stumbled into: the situation with my master teacher at Vanden High had been building up long before I arrived on the scene. My transfer to the Golden

West Middle School was partly for my own protection and partly to prevent my former master teacher from using the assignment of a student teacher as validation of her expertise. The District had been working on releasing her from her duties for some time.

The new assignment at Golden West Middle School turned out to be a pleasant surprise. For seven weeks, the SDC teacher, her teaching assistant and I worked as a team of three. We joked about having the students "surrounded." I soon took over the direct instruction, and our fourteen very difficult students with special needs responded well. Dealing with their problems certainly prepared me to work with Special Education students in other middle schools.

After I finished my field work at Golden West, I yearned to get my own classroom. I was hopeful when the director of Chapman sent me an announcement from the Winters Unified School District. I submitted my resume and application. A few days later I got an interview and the job as Resource Specialist at the Winters Middle School.

In September, I felt confident about my ability to serve effectively despite my inexperience in a full-time position. It didn't take me long to work with the students in the "Learning Lab" and get them to work for their mainstream teachers. I got along well with my instructional aide, a woman with fifteen years of experience in Special Education.

Storm clouds began to gather in October. The principal called me into the office and let know that he was not satisfied with my performance at the three IEP meetings we had held so far. I accepted this criticism without comment and tried to follow his suggestions for improvement. By my first evaluation I had apparently not yet met his expectations, I received a "Not Satisfactory" in the area of preparation for IEP meetings. My classroom management was also called into question. At this time, I felt that my evaluation had not been completely accurate, so I wrote a response:

November 6, 1991

> *To: Xxxxx Xxxxxx, Principal*
>
> *From: Marianne Tong*
>
> *Re: Evaluation*
>
> *Please attach this response to the recent evaluation which indicates that I walk into IEP meetings unprepared and therefore negligent of my duties. This comment is not strictly accurate.*

For the past six meetings, I have spent time preparing myself conscientiously in the following manner:

1. *I have sent out notices to parents and other involved parties, and I have prepared the schedule of annual reviews for 91-92.*

2. *I have assessed the students' achievement with the Woodcock-Johnson Revised Achievement Test provided by the District and obtained scores to be used in the decision-making at each meeting.*

3. *I have studied the existing IEP files to discover the Special Education history of the students.*

4. *I have given the appropriate classroom teacher a timely opportunity to make comments on a prepared form.*

5. *I have coordinated with the school psychologist, the counselor, the English as a Second Language teacher, the SDC teacher and the school nurse whenever necessary.*

6. *I have made sure that an interpreter (Spanish) was available whenever necessary.*

7. *I have invited regular education teachers to the meetings when appropriate.*

8. *I have studied the Special Education Handbook of the Winters Unified School District to familiarize myself with eligibility criteria and other pertinent information.*

9. *I have made every possible effort to become acquainted the RSP students themselves—within the classroom setting as well as informally on campus.*

10. *I have brought each meeting to its proper closure by getting signatures, distributing the forms as appropriate and bringing the cum files (the accumulated records of each student) and IEP files up-to-date.*

I attribute any perception that I may be unprepared at meetings to my natural desire to be discreet. It has been my life-long reluctance to be an aggressive, assertive participant, especially in meetings where other individuals are more qualified or have more authority and seniority to make decisions than I, Marianne Tong.

A second evaluation in March 1992 caught me by surprise. I had not expected to be so harshly judged. My students were succeeding in their classes, and I was keeping up with the testing and the IEP meetings. There were no indications that the teachers were dissatisfied with my efforts. There **had** been problems of unscheduled meetings called by the District office to dismiss students on very short notice and problems of non-communication by the counselor regarding pertinent information of RSP students. In the interest of keeping the peace, I accepted blame for the mistakes of others.

In response to having my short-comings laid out in the unjust evaluation, I composed a poem:

> If there's one thing that fills me with consternation,
> It's absorbing a negative evaluation.
>
> Today's observations called for rebuttal
> My career I was tempted to scuttle
>
> But because of numerous smiling faces
> I realized I must have some saving graces
>
> So rather than fight with the principal,
> I offer these palabras invincible
>
> In matters of management, it's true,
> Sometimes I don't give a culprit his due
>
> Though I'd like to have every student behave,
> It's a fight to be firm in the effort to save.
>
> When a student is absent three days out of eight,
> How can I insist that he never come late?
>
> When recalcitrant students finally make a contribution,
> Should I counter with "raise your hand" in retribution?

When an underachiever finally gets on the track,
Must I dampen enthusiasm and perhaps push him back?

On a day when a special boy wants to shine,
Should I dampen his spirits to keep him in line?

Should someone feel a bit under the weather?
Can I force her to write...bent for leather?

While management may not be a strong suit of mine,
Motivational skills are a bit more my line.

"What!" said a student, "Do a book report? Not me!"
"Okay, then," said I, "We'll have to do three!"

He thought I was crazy, and tried to take cover,
But three book reviews were done before the period was over.

A girl who couldn't spell three words without errors,
Now takes Spanish and Science without feeling terrors.

A free spirit who used to forget all he had,
Now carries his instrument, bag, pencils and pad.

One guy who used to be too obnoxious for Core
Now works and helps others without making them sore.

As I go through the day making umpteen decisions,
I know that some of them will invite derisions.

While I try to remember the ways of the Team,
I'm aware of the children and their low self-esteem.

Their problems are varied and their choices are few.
IEP's are important, but the children are, too.

Marianne Tong, March 13, 1992

The principal responded verbally with bemused denial. He read this effort as a philosophical difference and possible disrespect for his opinions.

As a result of the negative evaluations from the principal and the superintendent despite the support from my mentor teacher and others, a team gathered to formulate an "Improvement Plan." I was retained for an additional year.

In good faith, I accepted this "Improvement Plan." I took the time to respond to it point for point on June 7, 1992 despite demands of the end of school week and the finals for the two classes I was still enrolled in at Chapman.

From: Marianne Tong, RSP

Re: Response to Instructional Improvement Plan

I. *Improvement areas:*

a. *Communications:*

i. *I have had conferences with the school psychologist, principal, and counselor regarding the RSP Program, specifically the scheduling for the coming school year and the disciplinary problems which have arisen. I have communicated with the Speech and Language Specialist regarding several of my students, and I have contacted the school nurse regarding a student's glasses and another student's arm injuries.*

ii. *I have closely monitored a new resource student and collaborated with his teacher as to expectations. I have worked closely with my mentor teacher, as well five regular education teachers, in setting expectations for our RSP students enrolled in their Core classes.*

iii. *I have closely monitored my instructional aide as she supports our RSP students in the mainstream classes. We consult daily as to effective ways to help our students succeed.*

iv. *I have worked with every member of the Staff in the common cause of educating the RSP students in the mainstream.*

v. *I have brought irregularities to the attention of the Director of Special Education in regard to legalities I was unsure of.*

vi. *I have facilitated a meeting of my high school counterpart with all of the rising eighth-graders who will be in her program in the coming school year.*

b. *Discipline:*

i. *I have contacted parents whenever I encountered problems with students that parents should be aware of*

ii. *I have conferred with the counselor, regarding a particular student I had problems with.*

iii. *I have enforced and monitored detentions which I had assigned.*

c. *Instructional Strategies:*

i. *I have analyzed the student's IEP's and made a listing of student needs which should enable the counselor to schedule students appropriately.*

ii. *I have attended the Sheltered English Workshops offered by WMS.*

iii. *I am currently enrolled in a Consulting and Collaboration Services course at Chapman. There we discuss a variety of teaching techniques.*

iv. *I have taken students who have not met with success in mainstream math out of their regular math classes for direct small group instruction in the Learning Lab.*

v. *I have developed a simplified lesson plan for*

The Iliad which I presented to my students with great success. Those students who wrote projects for the Writer's Fair under my tutelage won Merit or Honors awards. I developed a strategy for generating lengthy compound and complex sentences which my students readily accepted and utilized.

vi. I developed a social studies contract with a teacher for a student who was unable to attend a mainstream Core 8. This student completed his contract in the Learning Lab under my supervision and passed his class.

d. *Professional Development:*

i. I am currently attending two classes related to my credential: Health in Education for Teachers, and Consultation Skills (for Resource Teachers)

ii. I have attended a "Goals and Objectives" Inservice at the District level Special Education Office.

iii. I have received a list of possible sites for visits/ observations.

e. *The IEP Process:*

i. I have conferred with the high school Resource Specialists, and the elementary Resource Specialists regarding IEP's. I have also collaborated with the Special Day Class teacher at WMS (Winters Middle School).

ii. I have begun to write goals and objectives as recommended by the school psychologist at the Inservice.

iii. I have attended the IEP meetings of fifth-graders who will be in my program in the coming school year.

Shortly after the end of the 1991-92 school year in June, I received the following letter from the principal in the mail.

Dear Marianne,

Thank you for being a part of our school and helping to make Winters Middle School exceptional!

Every year as various members of our staff visit other schools, we come to realize more and more that our school is unmistakably superior. I say this not from vanity, but as a matter of fact. We have a great community, great kids and an incredible staff! Every custodian, secretary, teacher, aide, and the principal, all of us truly care about our school and our students. We all work hard to make the school the best it can be.

Your work, your caring attitude and your willingness to periodically put aside your own needs and desires to help this great adventure be a success is irreplaceable; and that's what you are.

Have a great summer!

On September 23, 1992, I received the following letter:

Dear WMS Teachers and Staff!

I felt extremely proud of our school at our Back-to-School Night last evening. The classrooms looked super, presentations to parents were excellent, and all your preparation was evident.

Parents kept telling me all evening how impressed they were with the school and teachers. We had over 210 parents and adults here, which is the best turnout to date. They come because you all make WMS a place worth coming to see and hear about!

I sincerely appreciate all your efforts. You all work extremely hard and our school shows it. Congratulations on a job well done!

Sincerely,

There was not one word in either of those letters hinting that my work might be the exception.

The day before the above letter, I had already received the following note in my classroom:

> *Marianne, The superintendent of Winters USD) is planning to be in your classroom on 9/28, Monday, for a formal observation. I would like to meet with you during first period on Friday, 9/25 for a pre-conference. Please let me know ASAP if either of these dates will present a problem. Thanks,*

The meetings took place as scheduled. For the observation there were five students of various mathematical strengths in my group. I planned a short review of a new concept learned during the previous week and a short quiz for feedback.

The Evaluation was severe: Three sections were marked "not satisfactory"; two, "needs improvement."

I prepared a rebuttal and submitted it on October 4, 1992 to Dr. X:

From: Marianne Tong, RS

Re: Evaluation
> *Dear Dr. X,*

> *Please attach the enclosed response to my evaluation of September 28, 1992.*

> *First of all, I want to let you know that I appreciate your taking the time to observe my classroom for an entire period and to follow up the observation with an explanation of your findings.*

> *If I have understood your observations correctly, your primary concern is that I may not have familiarized myself with each student's specific learning disability and the goals and objectives of his or her Individualized Education Plan. Another area of concern appears to be that other professional staff members who are responsible for assisting in the delivery of services to special education lack confidence in my grasp of my job responsibilities. It also seems that you feel group instruction with five students who have IEP's is not an effective use of time, and that individualized assignments will produce a greater volume of instruction for students.*

> *As a result of your observations, I'd like to take this opportunity to let you know that I feel somewhat confused now. There seems to be a discrepancy between what I have accomplished and what*

I am credited with. Several points, therefore, need to be clarified. Toward that effort, I'll address the points made in your observation one by one:

1. *Group instruction versus independent assignments:*

   a. *When I was evaluated on November 5 last year, a great deal of emphasis was put on my developing group instruction. I was advised to take over the class (in regular classrooms) for various lessons and consult with the classroom teacher about my effectiveness. I got the idea that I should use more direct instruction of entire groups while keeping individualizing and ongoing assessment in mind but at a minimum.*

   b. *Then on November 19, my technique of getting a small group of students to work independently was evaluated as effective, although the appropriateness of copying a paragraph for daily homework versus doing original writing was questioned. We discussed this concept at the debriefing, and the validity of this strategy has since then been borne out; that particular group of students is now succeeding in regular 7th grade core classes. All have improved their written expression of original thought. Throughout the year, I used a spectrum of modalities to engage the students and build their confidence as well as their skills.*

   c. *In March 1992, another evaluation emphasized small group instruction and having all students responsible for certain problems. Wanting to comply with suggestions yet knowing that each has exceptional strengths and needs, I continued to provide the materials and environment with a balance of group instruction and individualization throughout the year. The only student who failed to thrive was absent the majority of the time due to suspensions not related to his specific learning disability.*

   d. *At a recent visitation of an out-of-district resource program recommended by my supervisors at WMS for its quality, the resource teacher presented direct group instruction (non-individualized) exclusively throughout my entire visit. Again, the implicit message I received was that group instruction was a desired mode of delivery.*

e. *One of the skills most noticeably lacking in many students with exceptional needs is the ability to follow the activities of a group and act appropriately within that group. I would like to think that practicing this skill of cooperation in the Learning Lab will enhance the students' ability to succeed in mainstream classes.*

2. *Familiarity with each student's specific learning disability and delivery of individualized services:*

a. *In planning for the 92-93 school year, I did the following: Studied each student's psychological report; researched each student's exceptional needs; observed an Elementary School Resource Room for several hours; attended several IEP meetings of fifth-graders who would come to WMS; participated in several meetings with WMS staff to plan the optimal placement for each new sixth-grader; re-familiarized myself with the district's GLE's (grade level expectations); studied the IEP's goals and objectives of each student and adjusted the placements accordingly; prepared a general lesson plan which addresses the GLE's and includes a variety of learning strategies to address the special needs of every student; obtained the mainstream materials for individualization: 2 seventh grade texts, 4 sixth grade texts, 1 Spanish sixth grade text, workbooks for review and reinforcement of previously acquired skills, and laminated timed tests of adding, subtraction, multiplication and division problems for attaining automaticity with speed and accuracy.*

b. *On a continuing basis I am doing the following: working closely with my instructional aide who goes into classrooms to deliver services to resource students; collaborating with the teachers who serve resource students in the mainstream; presenting a variety of lessons to students for skill development and progress toward meeting the GLE's within the scope of each student's abilities; and assessing reflectively to determine levels of difficulty which each student can attempt and attain.*

3. *Confidence in one another:*

    a. *Toward the end of last year, I received an "Improvement Plan" which gave me the impression that my colleagues and supervisors perceived me to be a potential embarrassment. Accepting this document in good faith, I have already accomplished the following:*

        i. *Scheduled students according to the stipulations on the IEP and submitted the schedule in writing*

        ii. *Submitted the schedule for my instructional aide's time*

        iii. *Submitted the schedule for my time in the mainstream as well as in the Learning Lab*

        iv. *Sent appropriate communications home with students*

        v. *Collaborated with a number of classroom teachers*

        vi. *Observed a recommended RSP in Sacramento*

        vii. *Made reservations for the Fred Jones workshops*

        viii. *Established a consistent behavior management system which has resulted in greater student compliance*

        ix. *Posted clear expectations in the classroom*

        x. *Passed two courses toward the full Resource Certificate (with A's)*

        xi. *Enrolled in the final course (currently in progress)*

        xii. *And, most importantly, rolled with the punches:*

1. *5 Interims (new students, placement pending) 2 meeting already held*

2. *1 Referral for assessment*

3. *2 Annual Reviews: 1 dismissal and 1 absent parent already contacted and satisfied*

4. *1 unexpected and unsuccessful placement (against my better judgment and over my objections) in independent study with subsequent readmission to Special Education*

5. *Between 10 and 15 phone calls home regarding resource students*

6. *Several last-minute cancelled or postponed (by administration) meetings even though I was prepared*

Please do not construe item number 6 as a complaint. It is simply a statement of fact. I am more than willing to go with the flow and understand that the unexpected is always just around the corner. With the clear understanding that others will perceive me as they perceive me, I am willing to do my utmost for the children's sake.

Finally I want to thank you for giving me this opportunity to explain my efforts more fully.

Respectfully,

In addition to writing rebuttals and explanations, I also prepared lists of the students on my caseload with their specific learning disabilities and suggested remediation for each teacher. I contacted each teacher in person to discuss the RSP students and handed each teacher a pertinent list with a request to keep the information confidential and safe.

As a result of the mixed messages I was receiving from students (cooperative and progressing), teachers (supportive and positive), the principal (sometimes negative, sometimes positive, publicly pleased with the entire faculty and privately displeased with me), classified staff (accepting, friendly) and the superintendent (negative, critical and not satisfied) my confidence was shaken. I became self-critical and alert to the slightest thing that might interfere with the Resource Program's success.

Among the stipulations in my Improvement Plan was my District-financed attendance at the Fred Jones Positive Classroom Discipline Workshops on October 6 and 7 and November 17 and 18, 1992. I attended all four sessions and incorporated the methods into my instructions.

My contract included attending mandatory meetings at the Special Education office. All the Special Education teachers at the meeting received a caseload list of their students. We were to correlate the list to our own files. When I noticed that one student's status appeared as RSP but he had not been assigned to me, I asked the Special Education secretary about him. She told me not to worry about him as he was designated Psych-DIS (designated instructional service). I confirmed this with the District Psychologist. I was satisfied and thought no more about it.

In preparation for the State Compliance Review, the Special Education Office conducted several such meetings. We teachers were instructed to review the files for correctness and completeness. The box of files was delivered one afternoon with instructions to return them after a thorough examination for compliance.

The file of the afore-mentioned student (Psych-DIS) was delivered to me, the RSP teacher. I read through the file briefly and discovered that he had indeed been a Special Education student at another school, and a letter to the Special Education teacher at the new school (that would be me) was still in his file. Because this letter contained information which would have been extremely useful to his mainstream teacher, who, by the way, had had lots of problems with this student, I contacted my mentor teacher. Together we approached the principal with this discovery. He simply responded by placing this student with another teacher in the mainstream. No consultation or IEP meeting had occurred to change his Special Education status from RSP to Psych-DIS. I knew that this was out of compliance and expressed my concern to my mentor teacher who suggested I contact the Special Education Director with my concerns. The main point I wanted to make was that I should not have been left out of the information loop. I could have forestalled problems if I had known this student's status. Receiving this file out of the blue, when my status was already on shaky ground, made me very uneasy. In this sensitive case I wanted my responsibilities clearly defined by my superiors.

On November 12, I received the following communication re: Student X from the Director of Special Education:

I thank you for having brought your concerns to me regarding student X's case. I have continued to investigate this case and wish to share some observations with you. It is my understanding that the counselor knew from the initial enrollment that Student X was special ed (DIS only). Because of the very delicate nature of his history, she may have chosen not to share this special ed history with the principal. I don't know. You have stated that he did not know. I would suggest that in cases such as Student X's, only a very limited number of persons should have access to his records. Even his classroom teacher might be given only limited access. We are dealing with mental health issues here, not learning issues.

Neither RSP nor SDC services should have been an issue in this case. Neither RSP nor SDC teacher nor staff should have had access to or consulted regarding his file. I understand that both the District Psychologist and the secretary shared with you that you did not need to concern yourself regarding the case, that he was DIS only. They were correct in stating that. If any consultation needed to be made regarding this case, it should have been from the DIS provider, the principal or the counselor with the regular classroom teacher.

I do apologize for having sent you his file with your RSP files. That must have been very confusing for you. I appreciate the fact that both you and your mentor teacher decided that it would be a good idea to contact me regarding this case.

In one of the later conferences with the principal, this case was alluded to as an example of my bad work judgments. He questioned why I had made such a fuss. I told him my reason had to do with me having the sense of being against the wall and that I had to protect myself. I felt that I would be blamed if anything went wrong with this case. He made no comment to that.

In early November, at the principal's request, the other Special Education teacher, (SDC) and I presented an Inservice at the monthly teachers' meeting on Special Education issues. Since the State is moving toward full inclusion, a presentation on the collaboration model was well received. The principal responded with the following note:

> *Dear Marianne, I would like to thank you for the presentation you made yesterday during our Inservice time regarding the Special Education Consultation Model. Making a presentation to peers is always a bit stressful, and your time and effort is appreciated.*
>
> *Sincerely,*

The phrase "a bit stressful" made me wonder what I had done wrong now. My level of sensitivity to his criticism was rising.

On November 16, the principal scheduled an observation of my performance in a sixth grade classroom. The observation took place on November 23, the Monday after Thanksgiving, and the post-observation conference took place on December 15, three days before the Christmas break when the students are already all stimulated about the impending holidays.

In the intervening three weeks, my level of anxiety became nearly intolerable. Unable to sleep at night, and not wanting to disturb my husband who had to be at work by 6 AM every day, I used a headset to listen to the radio until early in the mornings. Sometimes I fell asleep with the earphone still at my ear. Eventually, my health suffered. On Thursday, December 10, the day I was to be observed by my RSP counterpart at the high school, I woke up with the left side of my face paralyzed. Since I was able to think, talk and move about, I did not suspect a stroke and thought that I would be okay by the time I got to school. When I arrived at Winters Middle School, I went directly to the secretary and asked her to call the high school to postpone the observation and to arrange for a substitute. The secretary got frightened by my face which still hadn't awakened and immediately called the principal and the counselor. The principal drove me to the hospital and the counselor called my husband to meet us there. I was diagnosed with Bell's Palsy, a dysfunction of the facial nerve that travels through the skull in a narrow bone canal beneath the ear that results in inability to control facial muscles on the affected side. Bell's Palsy is defined as an idiopathic unilateral facial nerve paralysis, usually self-limiting. The trademark is rapid onset of partial or complete palsy, usually in a single day. I told the doctor that I had fallen asleep several times with my headphones still on. He told me never to do that again.

A substitute took my classes until Tuesday, December 15 although I returned to school several times to prepare for the IEP's still scheduled for the Beginning of January. The students accepted my appearance and were concerned about pain. Except for the embarrassing paralysis of one side of my face, I was functioning normally.

On December 16, my post-observation conference took place with another teacher present. (By this time, I had become leery of being called into the principal's office without a third party present) the Evaluation was confusing: two categories "effective;" two, "needs improvement;"and two, "not satisfactory." I was shocked and wrote a rebuttal as soon as I got home that evening.

During the few days remaining before Christmas vacation, I shared this rebuttal with my mentor teacher and the principal:

To: WAEA (Winters Area Education Association, the Union)

This is an official rebuttal to at least one component of my evaluation received December 16, 1992.

While the collaborative mode, under my direction, has been effective in the progress of students toward grade level expectations and adherence to curricular objectives, much criticism has been leveled at my methodology. Since some perceptions are strictly judgment calls, I won't engage in quibbling about management, etc.

I am always willing to accept my share of the responsibility for the success of the overall mission and probably far too eager to accept my share of the blame when things don't go just right; however, I am not willing to stand by when outright lies are being documented as facts.

In particular, item number 6, "Professional duties and responsibilities" as cited in the collective bargaining agreement and the job description: is now called into question and open to discussion.

Considering that a psychological disorder with its accompanying specific learning disabilities is not a temporary condition that changes from day to day, the information I provided in early October 1992 to each collaborative Core teacher in regard to the Resource students they serve, should still be valid and pertinent. The statement in the Evaluation is untrue and patently insulting. There has been ongoing personal communication in regard to each

179

student's problems and progress as well as access to up-to-date IEP documentation in the cum files available to the faculty any time. In addition, another Special Education teacher who publicly credited me with providing important information about disabilities, and I have presented an Inservice at administration's request. I have also submitted semi-annual updates on each student's status and placement to the administrator. I have attempted, as gently and diplomatically as possible, to remind some teachers of my students' sensitivities and encouraged my instructional assistant to provide all the moral support and personal guidance needed by those students who don't immediately respond well to the command, "All right, sit down, be quiet and get out your notebooks!"

In the interest of fair play, better morale, and open communication among the faculty at Winters Middle School, I grieve the untruth, "Teachers, even collaborating teachers, have virtually no knowledge of RSP students (sic) disabilities," written in my evaluation and herewith I request mediation.

Sincerely submitted,

Although my mentor teacher was very sympathetic and called the Union Grievance Chairman, she suggested I wait before taking any official action. She and the high school RSP teacher would try to contract Dr. X on my behalf unofficially. I left a copy of this rebuttal in the principal's mailbox on the last day before the Christmas vacation. One the first day back to school in January, the principal, with the rebuttal in hand, approached me in my classroom with an attempt to point out my shortcomings and defend his comments on the evaluation. He refused to name the teachers that had complained and remained adamant that I had been remiss in my duties to keep them informed. When I showed him copies of the lists I had submitted to the teachers, he began to defend his opinion with analogies. He averred that teachers don't read all the things they are given and stated that they were much like Special Education students. He drew the parallel between trying to teach a particular sixth-grade Special Education student that 2 plus 2 equals 4 and telling a teacher about the learning disabilities of a student, He told me that I would have to repeat and repeat and repeat. At that point, I answered that a college educated professional is not at all like a learning disabled sixth-grader and that if he could not bring the conversation to an acceptable level, we had nothing further to say to each other. With the comment, "So you're going to submit this?" he left.

I conferred with my mentor teacher concerning my current discussions with the principal. At her request, I continued to withhold contact with the WAEA. My face was still embarrassingly disfigured, and my mentor teacher's family had health problems. This was a very vulnerable time for both of us. We were hoping to resolve this dispute by informal means.

In the middle of January, I began to be uneasy about time limits concerning my grievance. My mentor teacher tried to reassure me but suggested I send Dr. X a copy of my rebuttal to be attached to my evaluation. I did so on or about January 19. I heard nothing further until I got a reminder that my improvement plan had not yet been completed:

I just wanted to give you a reminder regarding your Improvement Plan. You have completed most of your plan; however I am concerned that the five observations have not yet been complete. I have a written summary from Dr. X, the Director of Special Education, and myself. I have no information regarding observations by your mentor teacher and the high school RSP teacher.

Please let me know your appraisal of the status on your plan and also if I can assist you in any way.

By February 1, 1993 I submitted the following letters:

From: my mentor teacher

Marianne Tong has been teaching a unit on improving reading skills to my entire afternoon Core class. During the unit, she has worked on reasons why people need to improve their reading, the differences between learning to read and reading to learn, and then how to increase their reading speed and comprehension. Our silent reading activities have become much more successful since these activities were instituted.

Marianne's use of Fred Jones strategies has been consistent and the students have responded well to her instruction. Her questioning techniques have been equally distributed between low and high achievers, boys and girls.

Marianne created a Jeopardy game format to review the key concepts that were included in the unit. This was a very high interest activity for the students. We were able to also incorporate some review questions on the current Core novel, Call of the Wild.

*The reading unit has been so successful in the afternoon Core
that I plan to borrow Marianne's materials to use in my morning
Core*

From: the high school RSP teacher:

*I had an opportunity to observe Marianne working in the
7th grade core class which meets in her mentor teacher's room
5th period on February 1, 1993. Marianne asked me to watch
2 Resource students and how she interacted with them during a
mainstream-collaborative lesson.*

*After 15 minutes of SSR (Sustained Silent Reading), Marianne
gave a short lesson about reading flexibility to the whole class.
The lesson was age and content appropriate, multi-sensory, and
engaging for the class. Techniques of skimming, medium paced
and slow-paced reading were reviewed. Students were allowed to
call out some answers because there could be more than one way to
answer. At other points in the lesson, hand-raising was required.
She used the technique of asking for a "key concept" to conclude
the lesson.*

*In my opinion, the "snapshot" which I observed showed
excellent pacing, use of materials, and personal interaction of
teacher and students. Marianne has developed a whole series
of lessons on reading and she and her mentor teacher apply the
reading techniques to the literature the class is reading. The long
range goal is to develop appropriate reading technique for each
situation. The collaborative relationship is strong and provides an
interesting and more varied experience for the students than they
would normally get.*

*In our post-conference, we discussed one of the Special
Education students who was never really on task the whole period.
We discussed strategies for how to get him on track, many of which
Marianne had tried with the young man. Positive reinforcement,
contract, and numerous parent contacts have all been tried. She
continues to work with him in two mainstream classes and two
Learning Lab periods, and she feels that he has made progress
in many areas. Lack of organizational skills and embarrassment*

at being in Special Education continue to interfere with his achievement.

Marianne explained to me that she's been working hard in the collaborative Core class to stop students from calling out "Mrs. Tong!" She has used Preferred Activity Time (PAT) to extinguish this behavior. There were no instances in this type of call-out while I was observing.

In conclusion, I have met with Marianne on at least three occasions in the past year to observe her teaching, discuss upcoming 9th graders, or sit in on an IEP meeting. I find that she has a very precise and careful understanding of each student's learning disability and how it affects his/her achievement in school. She covers her bases with parents, is learning special education laws and district policies, and is pleased to watch several student "miracles" happening in front of her eyes.

Marianne has earned a permanent place in our district, in my opinion.

On February 24, the SDC teacher observed me and wrote the following letter which I also submitted:

Thank you for the opportunity to observe your 2nd Period Math class on February 24. At your request, I noted a variety of student-teacher interactions and student off-task behaviors.

Upon entering the classroom shortly before the bell rang, I observed all five students on task, working busily on their multiplication time tests. All of the students remained on task during this period and were actively involved in the roundtable review of the answers.

The transition from the multiplication time test to the fraction/decimal/percent lesson had several good transition prompts including a reminder to students about their stars on the board which could be retained with a good transition period and tasks for each student to attend to during the transition.

The balance of the lesson on fraction/decimal/percent lasted approximately 18 minutes, with only 6 minor off-task behaviors noted consisting of 4 incidents of calling out when another was called on and 2 incidents of whistling.

The lesson contained excellent fraction visual clues. Analogies to money and test scores appeared to greatly enhance the student's understanding of decimals and percent. Good use of the overhead projector was made to maintain eye contact with students while an area was being pointed out or explained on the overhead.

The lesson ended in a timely manner, and in all was well planned and executed. It was a pleasure visiting your classroom, as it has been a pleasure working with you on grant requests and field trips over the past two years. Please do not hesitate to invite me into your classroom again in the future.

That same Wednesday, February 24, just before the Faculty meeting, the principal informed me that Dr. X wanted to see me after school—preferably alone. I wondered whether I was going to receive bad news. He shrugged. I told him that I would ask my mentor teacher to go with me. He immediately called Dr. X to let him know of this.

When we got to Dr. X' office, the principal was already there. I was informed that they had decided to make a recommendation to nonreelect (yes, that is the word they used) me for the coming year. I was then told that I would have until Monday morning to give him a final answer to the question," Do you want to resign or wait for the school board to make its final decision?" If he heard nothing further from me, they would go ahead with the recommendation to the school board. He then gave me a few moments to make any comments. I commented that my release would be the district's loss. I was not prepared to make a case for myself at that moment. My mentor teacher sat beside me and whispered that she was a shoulder to lean on; I appreciated that though I realized how powerless she had been to influence my future at Winters Middle School.

After this conference, we went to the Buckhorn Restaurant for a Ginger Ale. (I was afraid to have anything stronger because I was internally quite wrought up.) She called our Union Representative, to inform her of the turn of events and set up an appointment to meet her for the Grievance which I now planned to go through with.

After a meeting with the Union Rep and my mentor teacher the following Grievance was submitted:

Date of Occurrence giving rise to grievance: Dec. 16

Specific Provision Violated: 20.3.3

Grounds for Grievance: Grievant evaluation, specifically p. 2 # 6, was based on hearsay and undocumented information

Actions Taken to Resolve the Grievance: Grievant has met formally and informally with the immediate supervisor in an attempt to resolve this matter. The site rep (representative) and the mentor teacher in charge of the New Teacher program also have met with the grievant's immediate supervisor to attempt to resolve the matter. A resolution has been unsuccessful.

Remedy Requested: The grievant shall be granted her rights under section 20.3.3. Specifically, the grievant shall be evaluated according to the procedure outlined in the contract, and not on hearsay and undocumented information. A re-evaluation is requested.

March 2, 1993 – Level I

On March 12, I received the following letter from the principal:

Re: March 2, 1993 Grievance

Please be notified that your grievance submitted March 2, is hereby denied at this level due to the following:

1. *It is in violation of Section 23.3.1 of the Agreement by and between Winters Joint Unified School District and Winters Area Education Association 1992-1995. That section states in part:*

   "If an employee or the Association wishes to initiate a formal grievance, the employee of the Association must do so within twenty (20) workdays after the occurrence of the action or omission giving rise to the grievance by presenting such grievance in writing to the immediate administrator."

   The alleged grievance occurred on December 16, 1992 and the written grievance was submitted March 2, 1993, a lapse of 43 workdays.

2. *The contention that the evaluation was based on hearsay and undocumented information is not accurate in that the evaluation was based on information obtained directly by the evaluator.*

On March 19, 1993 I received the following letter from the WAEA:

Re: Grievance submitted March 2, 1993

Dear Mrs. Tong,

We regret that we will have to accept the District's decision to deny your grievance at Level I, and we will not be able to pursue the grievance to the next level. As you were aware the grievance was submitted in an untimely manner.

Our decision does not preclude you from pursuing the grievance on your own to the next level.

Yours truly, the WAEA Executive Board

A few days later the Union Rep brought me a letter to read. She and another teacher had composed this letter and would submit it to other teachers to sign and submit for publication in the Winters Express, the weekly newspaper:

March 22, 1993

An Open Letter to the Parents of Winters:

As a group of concerned teachers of Winters Joint Unified School District, we feel it is our duty to call the attention of Winters parents to the district administration's actions in having fired many competent teachers who are making outstanding contributions to our students' education. The list of qualified teachers who have been summarily dismissed in the past eight years numbers in the dozens.

Why were they fired? We wonder. Perhaps because of assertiveness, or personal appearance, or ethnic identity, or independent thought, or...who knows? What we do know is that we have lost many effective, caring teachers from whom our children could have continued to benefit.

For those who have left the district and are now teaching elsewhere, we regret that we were not able to discern this pattern earlier and publicly come to their defense. However, we have finally become aware of the high-handed, coercive manner used to dismiss so many of our colleagues. The reprehensible tactic repeatedly used by the administration in these cases boils down to the teacher being told: if you resign you'll get a good recommendation; if not, you won't be rehired.

Now, another of our colleagues is facing this all-too-familiar choice. Marianne Tong is a capable, intelligent teacher with much to offer your children. Several of her students, in fact, have made the honor roll. We believe it is time for parents to take note, ask questions, visit the classroom, and assert themselves for their children's sake.

It is time the administration be held accountable for its arrogant and unjust firings. We therefore ask the parents of our students to join us in protesting the dismissal of Mrs. Tong and in demanding that she be re-hired.

Sincerely, A Group of Concerned Teachers

(The teachers have requested that their names be withheld from publication for fear of retaliation by the administration.)

This letter was published in the newspaper, and a correspondence via the Letters to Editor continued.

Dr. X responded with a letter to the editor which included the following excerpts:

When I thought about the letter from the "concerned teachers," it wasn't really the unfounded allegations which caused me the most distress. It was the italicized editorial comment at the bottom of the letter which put such a letter into focus...

It is a privilege and an honor to be a teacher. The children we serve deserve the very best. Too often those who purport to know who is a "good" teacher were never in that teacher's classroom. They never observed his or her teaching. Who would you prefer to make the judgment on tenure for your children?...

When there are thousands of capable graduates of teaching programs every year, why shouldn't Winters continue looking for a match between a particular teacher's talents and our needs? Those released aren't necessarily bad teachers. Maybe there wasn't a fit in Winters. And in some instances maybe we don't see it the right way. Should the system be thrown out and instant tenure installed? We

> *think not. As much as we value our teachers, we value the children*
> *of Winters more. We will always make educational decisions based*
> *on the best interests of our students...*

During the two weeks of Spring Break, my face showed marked improvement. I returned to school relaxed and refreshed. I finished out the school year, holding my head proudly despite my badly shaken self-confidence.

Although I often experienced the "lame duck" feeling, I retained a positive attitude until the very last day. I made every effort to leave the RSP files and all the pertinent information about the students in order. I attended all meetings, including those that dealt primarily with the next year's schedules and students.

I received lots of moral support from well-wishing teachers and parents. Many were sad to see me go and wondered what they could do to change the administration's mind. Several wrote letters and some contacted the principal in person. Both my mentor teacher and the Union Rep expressed regret that they had encouraged me to wait with my grievance. The Union Rep urged me to contact a specific person at the CTA (California Teachers Association). She told me that I am entitled to one hour of legal consultation concerning my case. I learned from this person that my attempt to reverse the District's decision was futile. Besides, I had already decided to leave Winters School District. The entire experience had disfigured my face and embittered my heart.

On Promotion Day, Thursday June 10, 1993, my husband and I took the six 8th-grade graduates from the RSP program out to dinner at the Buckhorn restaurant. They had earned this promised treat by receiving no failing grades in any of their classes. I celebrated their success with a poem I read to them at dinner:

> *I just want to thank you, boys, for being you,*
> *So I'll favor this party with some words that are true.*
> *You have freely given me your energy and your art,*
> *Now it's time to recall a few things from the heart.*

> *Thank you, Jaime, for your friendly smile,*
> *And holding your temper every once in a while.*
> *We challenged some spelling; a story we typed,*
> *We struggled with fractions; math got us hyped.*
> *It was touch and go when "F's held you up,*
> *But thanks to your strength, you never gave up.*

Thank you, Sean, for your will to succeed,
When you went on vacation, you told us your need.
From teachers you gathered independent assignments
And arranged study sessions to protect you grade in science.
I thank you for talking to a seventh grader
About education now, so he can work better later.

Thank you, Chris, for your studious ways,
You worked on those root forms for numerous days.
I missed you when you left the Learning Lab
Because your enthusiasm never made me feel drab.
Most of all, thanks, for a great GPA.
A hard worker like you should really get pay!

Thank you Mike, for your resilience,
You bounced back from the lousy side of the fence.
I watched as you struggled through seventh grade
Then you gave me hope with the tiger you made.
While you were working to make eighth grade a success
You gave me much pleasure to wipe away any stress.

Thank you, Alfonso, for your spirit and heart
I knew you were special right from the start.
With the bag at your side, you gave me the sense
That your mischief was balanced with intelligence.
Thanks for the laughs, and thanks for the spiders
You have given me a reason to believe in outsiders.

Thank you, Ricardo, for your desire to learn,
If patience were gold, you'd have money to burn.
Last year we couldn't communicate,
This year you know how to help me translate.
I watched in amazement as you did book reports
And loved your current events event the ones about sports.

So, Boys, you can see that you've earned your dinner
Each one of you has a right to feel like a winner!

On the last day of school an awards assembly presented me with an opportunity to make a public statement upon my leaving. I had composed a short free verse poem which I read to the students and teachers at the assembly:

> *For a moment in time I taught you, and you taught me,*
> *Now that moment has passed, and I travel on. Thank you.*

Four Parents are Too Many

Why is this story so difficult for me to deal with? Even from my mature perspective, I have trouble sorting out the conflicted emotions that any thoughts about my parents evoke.

A child's love is simple, uncomplicated; then reality sets in. They were my heroes! Larger than life, the four people who were my parents gradually began to shrink until I discovered they were mortal human beings after all.

Attentively, I listened to their stories. Admiringly, I respected their courage. Guilelessly, I loved them. Each one of them was a good person in a corrupt world. Each of them was greatly affected by World War II. In turn, they influenced the twists and turns of **my** life. While each one of them did what they thought was best, they managed to send me to the brink of despair.

Perhaps I should retell the stories of their youth as I heard them from their own lips before recounting how their lives converged with mine.

Jakob

"Jakob, keep turning that handle! The wash needs to be thoroughly rinsed before I can hang it on the line!" Jakob's mother yelled from the kitchen.

In 1915 he was just a little boy of six, but he was expected to help with the laundry.

Jakob was thinking about the book he had started to read when his mother roughly dragged him into the washroom. "I'm working as hard as I can, Mother," he quietly said.

"You always have your nose stuck in a book! Do you expect me to do all the work around here just so you can fill your head with high-faluting ideas?" his mother had that wild look in her eyes that warned of a spanking.

"I'm sorry," whispered Jakob as he obediently cranked the handle on the washtub. Soon he would be going to school. "I'm not going to be a carpenter like my father," thought Jakob. "I want to read and think and go to school."

Despite the demands of World War I on German families, Jakob managed to continue going to school and pursuing his dream of becoming an educated man. At a time when most young boys had to start learning a trade at age fourteen, he attended high school until he was eighteen.

"No, I'm sorry, you can't go to college," his father announced when Jakob pleaded with him. "You need to start working and bringing in money. You know that my health is failing, and I can't support you and your mother anymore."

Though disappointed, Jakob accepted the circumstances. His high school teachers had recognized his academic and athletic talents and would have liked to see him go to a university, after graduation from high school, but there was no way to persuade the parents. One of the teachers helped him get a job in the largest insurance company in Germany, the Frankfurter Allianz. Jakob proudly contributed most of his meager earnings to the household budget for several years.

"Mother, I've met a young lady. She's beautiful, and I would like to marry her," Jakob carefully approached the subject at dinner one day.

"Well, our apartment is very small, but I suppose it would be good for me to have some help with the housework," his mother answered.

"What do you mean?" Jakob wondered.

"You can't afford to move out and support a wife. We need you. She'll have to live here."

Jakob became thoughtful, "I'm doing quite well at the Allianz. Soon I'll get another raise and…"

"No," his mother interrupted. "Your father and I depend on you. You are our only child, and it is your duty to take care of us in our old age. When you get married, your wife will live with us!"

Jakob knew that arguing was futile.

Tilly

Tilly was born at home prematurely on March 3, 1915 to a young German woman with an alcoholic husband and another baby of only one and a half years old. In fact, her father was too drunk to register the baby's birth until two days later. Thus Tilly's birthday was officially listed on her birth certificate as March 5. She weighed only two pounds, so the midwife said, "This baby won't live!" Tilly's mother bedded her down in a shoe box and fed her goat's milk with an eyedropper. Despite the violence of World War I raging through Europe and accelerating into a full-blown world war, Tilly's mother, Maria somehow managed to pull this tiny baby into adult life.

The little girl had many illnesses while she was growing up. There was her bout with rickets which left her with bowed legs. Rickets is a vitamin deficiency very common at that time and place. When the rambunctious little girl recovered enough from that disease to be allowed back to school, she had to endure quite a bit of physical abuse at the hands of teachers. Corporal punishment was commonly administered with a paddle across the backside or a ruler across the fingers for tardiness or talking in class.

"What happened to you? There is blood coming out of your ear!" shocked, Tilly's mother yelled, when the nine-year-old returned from school one day.

"I couldn't recite my catechism lesson for today, so the priest hit me," Tilly explained.

"That idiot!" Tilly's mother shouted so loud that her husband came into the kitchen to see what was going on. He was a huge man and easily roused to anger.

"I'm going to box his ears!" he yelled as he reached for his coat and walking stick.

"No, no! Please don't do anything! You might end up in jail," Tilly's mother pleaded with him. He had already gotten in enough trouble at his railroad job over his drinking and violence. "I'll take care of Tilly," she added as he huffed out of the kitchen back to his work on repairing a broken chair.

Tilly remained at home for a couple of weeks and fell even further behind in school. Her illnesses and weakened condition often interfered with her education.

Long periods of oral disease due to the unsanitary conditions and malnutrition during World War I also weakened her, but she kept surviving. Her ears continued to trouble her. Though her body was weak, her will to live and her talents were strong. One particular incident was a clothing design contest which she had entered in school. Her drawings were selected as winners, but due to her family's poverty, there was no follow-up training.

In later years she often told me about the art teacher's disappointment that she could not enter the school which would develop her skills. At age 14, she had to leave school and work as an apprentice to Mrs. Lahr, a seamstress. Tilly proved to be very talented and learned to design her own patterns and make new clothes out of older ones.

At sixteen, Tilly discovered that her ears still hadn't healed properly from the abuse. She had to have a mastoidectomy. (*Before the advent of antibiotics, mastoid surgery used to be one of the most frequent surgeries performed. Acute mastoiditis was common in those days and the treatment was a mastoidectomy to remove a cholesteatoma or a skin cyst in the ear.*) She had barely recovered from that surgery when her lungs had became infected with another common problem of the times, tuberculosis. Several weeks in a sanitarium restored her health and talents but left her with scar tissue on her lungs and a medical record which haunted her for the rest of her days. Despite her illnesses, she diligently continued to practice her seamstress trade.

John

When John emigrated with his parents, Gottfried and Johanna, from Germany in 1924, he was only two years old. A mechanic by trade, John's father knew that he could become rich in America where personally-owned motor vehicles were becoming commonplace. For several years, the small family lived in Texas, and John got a little brother, Werner.

Some relatives, who also immigrated before World War I, had established their new homes in agricultural Iowa. They urged, "Come on, Gottfried, we need good mechanics here. The weather is good. Lots of farming has become mechanized."

Once again, Gottfried and Johanna packed up their little family for the move to Osage, Iowa. Two more sons, James and Dean, were born there. John, the oldest, was expected to help with child care and other chores.

"You make sure your little brothers don't get hurt while I'm doing this laundry," John's mother chided.

"But I hate to change Deanie's crappy diaper," Johnny wailed.

"Look, I can't do it all," his mother yelled. "Dad is always busy in the garage, and I'm stuck with you four boys here in the house! Since you're the oldest, you need to help!"

Fourteen-year-old John was hoping to get on the high school football team. "Dad, I'm going to need time after school to practice with the team."

"And I need you to come help in the garage after school! Werner is old enough to help your mother in the house now, so you're going to come in after school to learn some real man's skills! No more discussion!" Gottfried was adamant.

Obediently, John demonstrated for a whole year that he could become a good mechanic just like his dad. "Dad, please let me stay an hour after school at ball practice. I'll work extra hard in the garage afterwards."

His dad grumbled something about foolish games but relented. "Okay, but you be here punctually at four thirty every day! And don't forget your homework! A good mechanic needs to be good at math and other stuff."

"Yes sir!"

By the time John graduated from high school, he had earned football and baseball letters for his jacket but his mom and dad had never watched him play a single game. He resented their stubbornness about "stupid children's games." Even though he had also become a good mechanic, he did not want to continue to "help" in the garage. World War II had started, and he wanted to enlist.

"Mom, Dad won't sign my enlistment papers. I'm not quite eighteen, so I need a parent's signature. Please, Mom," John wailed.

"Well, okay, but this is against my better judgment," she warned. "You're too young!"

"Look, the war is going on right now! Lots of guys are enlisting. We need to win against the Japs and the Nazis! I know I can help by working on engines. Dad has taught me well!" John argued his case.

Johanna signed the paperwork, and that same afternoon John joined the Army Air Corps. He served honorably and participated in several military campaigns, such as the 1947 Berlin Air Lift while he was stationed at Rhein-Main Air Base in Frankfurt, Germany and a mysterious U.N. deployment to Palestine in 1948.

While he was attending a party in the NCO Club he met Tilly, my mother, who had come to Frankfurt to sew for some friends.

Lottie

This beautiful little girl was born to a young German couple, Otto and Kathe in 1925. There were never any brothers and sisters, so her parents idolized her. During her childhood, Germany was experiencing a period of prosperity and peace. The little girl grew into a beautiful young woman.

Her father had honorably served in World War I, and World War II was far into the future.

Being a good student and obedient daughter were Lottie's only two obligations. After she finished school around 1939, she was employed by the Frankfurter Allianz, the same firm where Jakob Simon was working. The two met at their jobs in the office briefly, but there was probably no opportunity for a relationship. Jakob, a married man and father of a young daughter, was drafted into the German Army soon after the invasion of Poland in the same year. Besides, Lottie had a boyfriend.

Lottie and her mother somehow managed to survive the air raids in Koblenz while her father, who had already served in World War I, had to serve again during World War II.

The sacrifices of her immediate and extended families proved to be nearly overwhelming. She lost her first love to the war. When the war was over, Lottie was rehired by the newly reestablished Allianz, but the poverty of the post-war years caused Lottie to become extremely vulnerable.

Parenting

The events of World War II ensnared these four young people in an inescapable net. After the war, Tilly, a poverty-stricken sick young woman, faced the choice between Jakob, a broken prisoner of war and John, a victorious military hero. She agonized over the choice and even tried to pull me into her decision.

"Marianne, what shall I do?"

All I wanted was my mother to be happy. "Mutti, whatever you decide is fine with me." I hinted that I would rather have them create a happy family with me as their main focus, but that was not to be. In the terrible post-war years Tilly and Jakob could not recapture their youthful ardor. I was sent to live with my grandparents. Their divorce was bitter, and their fight over me ended in both of them getting custody though I was not living with either one.

Reluctantly, though apparently very much in love, Tilly consented to marry John and follow him to America. She had to leave me in Germany because Jakob, my father, refused to release me. I lived with my grandmother for another year while Tilly, Jakob and John corresponded regarding my future.

The three of them finally decided that I could follow my mother to America under the following conditions: John was to pay for my transportation; Tilly was to pay for some new furniture for Jakob; Jakob was to pay 50 Marks a month into a trust fund that I would receive on my twenty-first birthday; I was to travel by ship—no airplanes! I was to write at least one letter each month to my father; Tilly and John were to ensure my getting a good Catholic education in America.

At age twelve, I was only vaguely aware of these conditions set up by my parents. Even though nothing could have kept me from joining my mother, the separation from my German family was quite traumatic for me. I was only thirteen when I left my beloved grandparents. For years I blamed myself for my grandfather's broken heart. My mother didn't tell me that he had gotten so drunk one night that he fell against a rock wall and died as a result of the terrible head injury.

In fact, my mother appeared to become a different person from the one I remembered. She had been my hero through the war years, but I was not prepared to be her submissive little girl. Expecting me to take up in America where we had left off in Germany, she was not prepared to deal with a rebellious teenager in the midst of culture shock. Somehow we bonded over the ensuing five years. My stepfather, my mother and I had managed to become a happy little family by the time we moved to Bermuda where I graduated from high school. When I met my future husband, a U.S. Air Force sergeant of Chinese descent, she surprised me with a ferocious bigotry and hypocrisy that had never surfaced before. In an effort to dissuade me from marrying this wonderful man, she told me outright lies about him and his family on several occasions. Our relationship was severely damaged, and I shed many a tear over the loss of a mother I never had.

Eventually, I returned to Germany as a married woman with four children. My U.S. Air Force husband was transferred to Bitburg Air Base, only twenty-five kilometers away from Trier where my father had moved with his new wife, Lottie.

Yes, once my father recovered from his shocking experiences in combat and as a prisoner of war, he was re-employed by the Frankfurter Allianz. He and Lottie began to date and were married in 1952. He had opened a branch agency of the Allianz in Trier and become quite prosperous. I had heard about him from other family members; however, I had not been in touch with him personally for years. The intervening years between the divorce and my arrival in Germany were a chasm I was reluctant to bridge. How would my Chinese husband and I be received? How would our four children be received? Did I really want to reopen old wounds?

I found his address in the phone book and sent him a postcard. Within a few weeks we became truly father and daughter again. With his wife Lottie and my family, we spent many wonderful hours getting reacquainted while touring Trier and other Mosel towns as well as Luxembourg. We lived in a suburb of Trier, and I worked part time in his agency. He even bought me a used car to make getting to his home and office easier.

About a year after we moved to Germany, Tilly, my mother, came to visit. I was happier about my parents than I had been for a long time. Here they were both within my reach. Perhaps I could get them to meet and drop the vitriol that permeated every mention of "your father" or "your mother." I should have known better. Neither one was interested in meeting the other. Instead my mother presented me with the paperwork from their long ago divorce and custody agreements.

"Here, if you think your father is so great, you can get him to pay up!" she commented on the 50 Marks he was supposed to save up for me.

"He bought me a car, and they are very good to me. Can't we just let by-gone be by-gone?" I wondered.

"Whatever!" my mother dismissed the thought. "Do whatever you want."

"It's not up to me. Why didn't you do something when I was twenty-one? You were in Germany then and that would have been the appropriate time, not now." I argued.

"I didn't want to upset Daddy!" Daddy! That was how she referred to John whenever we referred to him. I remembered that she often, especially during my teen years, hurt **my** feelings in order to spare **his**.

"Then why do you want to upset me?" I wondered. "I've tried my best to get along with all four of you, and if I start bringing up old stuff like this, I'll be the one who has the most to lose," I explained.

My mother finally realized that this subject had run its course. Carefully avoiding touching on any mention of Jakob and Lottie, we had a nice visit for a couple more weeks. Then she had to return to her home in California.

A couple of years later, in a tearful good-bye, my father promised that he would visit us in California after his retirement. His plan was to retire in three years, and I looked forward to his visit. As the time drew closer, his letters began to hint that he would never make the trip. He wrote about their cats that couldn't be left alone and the vaccinations he didn't want to take. He didn't want to fly. Besides, his cough was getting worse.

In fact, his failing health was a legitimate reason for not traveling. He was hospitalized a number of times with lung problems. He wrote out a last will and testament, leaving me the heir after they were both deceased. Lottie attested to the stipulation that she would not alter the will if he died first. All I wanted was for him to enjoy his life as much as possible, but she did not trust me.

One time during a phone call, he was explaining this last will and testament. Suddenly, I heard her scream in the background, "Watch out! After you're dead, she'll come over here with a bunch of lawyers!" I couldn't believe my ears. Something like that was the last thing on my mind. My child-like heart loved my father not his money, but she didn't believe that.

On Christmas Eve 1985 our whole family, including four little grandchildren were opening presents in the living room. The phone rang, and one of my daughters ran to answer it.

"Mom, it's a call from Germany!" Lisa yelled.

My heart jumped. "It's my father wishing us a Happy Christmas!"

"No, it's Tante Lottie," said Lisa as she handed me the phone.

"Your father died this evening," said Lottie without any emotion. I began to hyperventilate but kept myself under control in front of the children around me.

"What happened?" I asked.

"The doctor already yelled at me, and I don't need you to yell at me, too," she continued in a mechanical voice.

I was stunned. "I didn't know he was back in the hospital."

She yelled, "You're just like a cow. I just lost my husband, and you have nothing to say to me." What did she want me to say?

All my bitterness about the broken promises surfaced, so I said, "Alright, now you can get yourself a younger husband and travel around Europe." For the past couple of years through letters and phone calls I had gotten the idea that she was tired of taking care of my sick old father.

She screamed something and hung up on me. A few days later I received the postcard she had mailed several days before he died. In a few words, she explained that he was at home but under heavy medication for his lung problems. He got up in the night to go to the bathroom in the dark apartment. He stumbled over a bathroom rug and fell against the tub, breaking three ribs. One of the ribs punctured one of his weak lungs. He lived for ten days in a semi-conscious state and then died.

Ten Days! I was outraged. I could have gone to visit him. I could have phoned him. I could have let him know that I loved him. The beast waited until he was dead before notifying me! I didn't know what to do with my anger. My husband and children did their best to keep me balanced, and eventually I was able to put the entire episode into perspective.

When I told my mother about this episode, she commented, "He really didn't deserve to be treated like that. We loved each other once, but the war changed both our lives!"

Yes, the war not only changed many people's lives, but it ended the lives of millions. I considered myself lucky. I was living life with all its ups and downs.

One of the worst experiences was yet to come.

My mother had been suffering for more than twenty years with rheumatoid arthritis. She and my stepfather were continuously attempting to find new doctors and new medical miracles to make her life more comfortable. They did not allow me to discuss the subject of health care. I was to stay out of their business. My mother often hinted that they would move closer to my home and our ever-growing family once "Daddy" retired, but that was just talk. Neither one of them had any intention of such a move. When my mother became too ill to make the eight-hour trip, we visited them several times a year.

During our last visit in July 1987 it was difficult to see my shriveled-up mother sitting in her wheelchair. Considering her condition, I thought it was a miracle that she was still alive. She was trying to finish the meal my dad had put on the attached tray, and we were just making small talk about the children and my college classes.

When she was finished eating, she pushed the tray forward a little and spilled a bit of the soup. I was trying to clean it up when my dad came in. He yelled "What the hell happened now?" and pushed the tray back into place.

Lifting her arm, my mother said, "I think you bumped my arm." Blood was dripping from her elbow.

My dad yelled, "Jesus Christ, you're more trouble than my sixteen kids!" I was rooted to my chair as I watched him tenderly clean her up and put her to bed. What in the world had just happened? I was stunned. His loud voice and his solicitous actions did not make sense. I had heard him make the "sixteen kids" comment before. My mother and I had always laughed at this joke.

When he left the bedroom, I went to my mother and asked her, "Does he treat you like that a lot? Do you want me to call your doctor?" I was prepared to pack her up and take her with me.

"No, Daddy is so good to me. He just gets a little rough sometimes.

Please don't say anything!" I was speechless. Then she dismissed me, "I'm going to take a little nap right now."

My husband was sitting in the living room while my dad was fussing around in the kitchen preparing dinner. My husband looked in surprise at my face, "What's wrong?"

"Love, don't ask. I can't talk right now." Then I laid my head in his lap and cried and cried.

In fact, a couple of days later I cried all the way from Los Angeles to Fresno where we stopped to visit my husband's mother. She noticed my sadness and made us tea.

Just six weeks later I answered the phone. It was my dad, "Marianne, your mother died. I found her not breathing, so I called 911. They worked on her for twenty minutes and brought her back a couple of times. When they took her away in the ambulance, I remembered that she had signed a Medical Directive with a DNR (Do Not Resuscitate). I followed the ambulance and gave them the paper at the hospital. They yelled at me about why I had them called them work on her then. I guess I just couldn't let her go." His voice kept breaking.

"Dad, I don't know what to say. We both loved her so much! It just wasn't enough. She's out of pain now." After I hung up, I sat down and cried hot tears until my husband came home from work.

He had been at my side throughout all the ordeals with my four parents. After a big hug, he picked up a basketball and took me outside, "Let's shoot some hoops," he said.

The Aftermath

January 23, 1988

Somehow, I feel the need to make another entry in my Emotional Outbursts Journal. Today, I feel very confused and don't know whether to love or hate the world. There is so much sadness in me about my parents that I find it very difficult to believe that my own life has some kind of continuity.

My mother's eyes keep haunting me. I'm very guilty about letting her down when my dad drew blood in a moment of domestic violence.

God, I'm so lost and alone. I feel that no one is ever going to understand me. The picture of my mother when my dad bloodied her elbow keeps hanging in front of my eyes whether they're open or closed.

My self-respect is completely gone. Right in front of my face, he had the nerve to treat her like that. He knew full well I wouldn't have the courage to do anything about it. How can I ever respect myself if I'm such a washrag that I let people do the most atrocious things right in front of me? I've tried to tell people, but either they don't believe me, or they just don't want to deal with such a complicated situation. Even the doctor I went to, said very glibly, "If that were MY mother, I'd have packed her up and taken her out of there." Oh God, I wish I had. I don't think I'll ever forgive myself or my dad for that day. I even blame my mother because she should have gotten out of there a long time before it got so bad.

My whole foundation of existence has been shattered. I've always been a great believer in the law and right and wrong. Justice! Ha! When the chips were down, I was too cowardly to call someone for help.

I ask myself, Marianne, what do you really want? I want to know that my mother was just as worthy of constitutional rights as any other citizen. She became a citizen of the United States in 1951 or 52, and she lived a respectable life. I feel right now that she was killed, and therefore, I can't get any rest until someone besides me gets punished. Right now, I'm bearing the whole burden on MY shoulders. I can't bear it much longer. I'm sinking in the flood! Please God, help me. I loved her so much, you know I did.

I think I've been a great disappointment to her from Day One, even though she always, always tried to make me believe that I was the most important thing in her life. I could never really believe it because she always made so many excuses for not living closer to me and our flesh and blood descendants.

Yet, the fact remains that I actually lived up to her expectations of establishing a nice big healthy family which she then did not participate in. That is what makes me so confused. What did you really want from me, Mutti? The tears are beginning to flow as I write this. I really am horribly mixed up about this. Here you are; I'm fifty years old, and you are dead. Will I ever be able to think coherently about the way things developed? I doubt it.

How could you live through the pain and horror of World War II and then when you finally had heaven on Earth, die? I guess, that's what's confusing me so much. Did you actually die because you no longer cared for us, or were you destroyed? If you were destroyed, should I, MUST I, avenge your death? Oh, Mutti, why didn't you leave me some clues, or better yet, why didn't you let me know how bad things were between you and Dad? Were you ashamed? Were you so drugged that you really couldn't see what was happening?

God, I'm going crazy! Not only my mother came to such a miserable ending that my own life is threatened, but my father also succumbed to forces which I don't really understand. Should I do something about his death? Why don't the two of you help me? You've opted out of life, didn't you? Isn't that what dying is? Opting out? Or is there really no choice? In that case, I'm dead, too. I do things; other people think I'm alive. But I'm dead. No one that I know of believes that I have the right to make a case for my parents. After all, they were old when they died. Old people die. No one in their right mind would take anyone to court about the death of an old person. In this country people have the constitutional rights to life, liberty and the pursuit of happiness. Maybe old people's pursuit of happiness includes death: Peace and quiet in a box six feet under; peace and quiet in the elemental atmosphere after cremation.

Too bad about me. I'm stuck with trying to untangle my emotions toward my mother's widower and my father's widow who in my opinion are the destroyers. They don't even know each other, but they acted as if they were part of a team that has the mission to make sure that my blood line disappears from the face of the Earth without a trace. Neither one of them ever wanted a child from my parents; however, I, as a reminder of my parents' potency, was in their way. I represented family life and dynamic growth, which neither my stepfather nor my stepmother had any ideas about. They wanted, and probably needed, status quo—an unchanging picture of the world. My parents were not allowed to think or talk of participating in their child's life. They HAD to feel guilty whenever they thought of me because thinking of me made them think of each other. What makes me think of these things? Hints. Telephone conversations. My own imagination? I don't know. My mother's favorite line: I wish I could, but I can't because of Daddy--"Daddy!" My father was more subtle in his rejection of me; in fact, I'm not sure that he rejected me at all. He just didn't know how to bridge the gap: an entire ocean--the Atlantic.

Gosh, I hated being reminded of my father's shortcomings by my mother, and I hated being reminded of my mother's shortcomings by my father. But they seldom missed an opportunity to let me know just what kind of people I came from. Once in a while they would realize that they were hurting me with talk like that and then they would quickly say something nice like, "your father was so smart and I loved him, but..." Or, "one wife would have been enough for me, but..."

What am I talking about? I'm not making sense. Being misunderstood, even by myself; having my love for my family turned into something ugly and pathetic--something that belongs in an insane asylum-- is my greatest fear. My step-dad would like that. Then he could walk around and righteously declare himself to be the victim of a bunch of insane women. All three hundred and eighty condescending chauvinistic pounds of him.

I remember my people as a very strong race. My ancestors survived the barbarian hordes and great plagues in Europe (they must have; otherwise I wouldn't be here) and they survived the wars as well. They lived in comfortable and clean homes, made clothes, cooked meals, tilled the land, participated in social efforts, and generally believed in life itself. My mother lived until 1987; my father, until 1985. They had been strong in crises, so why did they die when there was no national emergency? Why did they weaken? Why do I feel that their deaths are a personal affront to me? They brought me into the world, made a great fuss over me when I was a cute little baby, and then disowned me when I became an adult. Was I at fault? Was it me who killed them because I didn't share their enthusiasm in drugs and alcohol as an adult? Was it me who killed them because I shared my strength with others instead of concentrating on them? Was it me who killed them because I married out of my race? Was my presence on Earth their motivation to get out of life here? DID they disown me, or am I just feeling abandoned? I'm just guessing. Will I become the same way? I'm not that way yet, but I often have thoughts of the futility of trying to stay safe, sane and alive on this planet.

Hate. Hate and love. I feel them both. Since I am already dead, I can usually absorb my own emotions, so that is less of a problem for me than might be supposed. What really bothers me is my precarious position in American society. I have a family and there are laws here. Laws against murder. Courts which try and convict murderers. American prisons are full of people who have killed someone that society cares enough about to make a case for. My dilemma is my inability to decide whether my parents were murdered or whether they just died of old age. Should I come out of hiding, hire a lawyer and accuse someone of killing them, or should I believe that they simply died of their own accord? Why did they become invalid? I know what I THINK, but I don't know how to ACT on that knowledge. I have a husband and children to consider before I can spend money to chase demons that may not exist. What would my family gain by me avenging my parents' deaths? What would my family lose by me avenging my parents' deaths? Money. Time. Hate. Love. Faith. Would their lives become more or less valid if I try to straighten out their heritage and inheritance? Maybe the spirits of my mother and father will help me decide when the time comes. I haven't buried them yet, and I don't think I'll be able to bury them for some time. When I do, I'll go with them. December, 2010

Somehow, I've stepped back from the brink. I have finally become able to think, speak and write about my four parents, but I strongly believe that any child of a divorce would agree with me, "Four parents are too many."

My Aunt Elsa [10]

1913-2010

"But, Mutti, I'm not allowed to lie!" I complained.

"You don't need to lie. Just tell the conductor you are not four yet when he asks you," my mother tried to assure me. I wasn't convinced.

"But why?"

We were on the train to Berlin, and any minute, the conductor would come to check the tickets. "Look, Marianne, the tickets for children who are already four years old cost a lot more than tickets for children who are not yet four. I don't have much money, so I bought a cheap ticket for you."

"Mutti, now I understand. I'll be a good girl." Later in life my mother told me tales of how smart I was even when I was very young. Actually, I could already read the names of the cities as our train made its way toward Berlin.

"Will Tante Elsa be at the station waiting for us?"

"Yes, she's expecting us. We'll be staying with her for two weeks, and you are going to be on your best behavior!" my mother always admonished me before we went anywhere together. As far as she was concerned there was no greater crime in the world than her own child misbehaving in public.

For a moment I had to blink when the train pulled into the station. How could my mother be standing next to me on the train and also be waving at us from the platform? "Elsa!" my mother yelled.

"Tilli!" the lady on the platform yelled back. Ah, so that's my aunt Elsa. They were not twins, but they looked very much alike.

"I can't wait to show you off in our beauty shop," Elsa exclaimed, "What a big girl you are already!"

"I had to pretend that I'm not yet four," I was eager to explain. My mother and her sister looked at each other.

"You have to be careful what you say around this girl," they laughed.

My aunt had her own station in the Brandese Beauty Shop which was located on the Ulandstrasse, just off the Kurfürstendamm. The shop smelled good, but there was something in one corner that terrified me. I hid behind my mother as they tried to explain the old-fashioned electric contraption for permanent hair curling. Hanging from a six-foot high rack were perhaps fifty wires. A clamp was attached to each wire. My aunt showed me how she would put curlers in a lady's hair and then clamp the curlers to the wires. "You know that ladies like to look pretty with curly hair. This is how it's done."

"I'm never going to have my hair curled like that. My Mutti curls my hair with a curling iron she heats up on Oma's stove," I declared. Oma was Elsa and Tilli's mother who lived in Koblenz.

Several patrons in various stages of beautification had big smiles on their faces. Who was this precocious little girl? My mother gave my hand a tight squeeze, a signal that I had better stop talking now.

Elsa was amused, "Oh, let Marianne have some fun. She's just curious." I was introduced to Mr. and Mrs. Brandes, the owners of the beauty shop.

"Tomorrow you are coming to our house for dinner. Then you will meet our son. And on the weekend we'll all go to the Tiergarten. Have you ever been in a Tiergarten before?" Mrs. Brandes was very friendly.

"Tiergarten? Mutti, have I ever been to a Tiergarten? What is that?" I was full of questions.

"No, we don't have a zoo in Koblenz. A Tiergarten is a zoo where people can go see lots of animals."

"Will the animals bite?" I wanted to know.

My mother knew that she couldn't just placate me, so she was as truthful as possible, "Yes, the animals will bite, but that's why there are big fences between the animals and the people."

"Oh, good!" I was relieved.

My mother and I stayed with Elsa for a couple of weeks, and then we had to return to our home in Koblenz. Oma, my grandmother, was very happy to see me and allowed me to talk for hours about my adventures in Berlin. The winds of war had begun to blow, so my grandmother was careful not to mention anything that might alarm me.

"Next year Tante Elsa will come to visit us here in Koblenz," Oma explained. "Then we'll have a good time with her." Oma remained hopeful that good times would still be possible in 1942.

Our family life remained fairly normal. Elsa was able to come visit us in Koblenz a few more times before the bombings started, and I enjoyed her sense of humor. By 1943 the visits stopped. It became too dangerous and complicated to make the trip from Berlin to Koblenz, so we didn't see Elsa again until the war was over.

"Mutti!" I screamed as I saw her coming up the road from the bus stop. I was living with my grandmother after the war and seldom got to see my mother. All excited, I ran toward the woman walking towards. "Oh! Tante Elsa!" Everyone had always remarked how much my mother and her sister Elsa resembled each other, so I was momentarily confused. My disappointment must have been clear to Elsa.

"Sorry, Marianne. I'm not your mother," Elsa said as she gave me a quick hug. Then she started visiting with her mother and didn't pay much attention to me for quite a while.

My mother actually did arrive a couple of days later with her new fiancé. Her divorce from my father was final, and she had met an American serviceman. There was talk of moving to America, and Elsa was expressing her hope of eventually joining them. All this "grown-up" talk seemed very idealistic and sounded like a fairy tale to me. How could I possibly believe the things I heard about America after what I had already survived in war-torn Germany?

When Elsa arrived in Chicago in 1952, my mother, my step-father and I were at the O'Hare airport to welcome her. In the car on the way to Cedar Rapids, Iowa, my mother and Elsa were already squabbling in the back seat about money and who knows what. My step-father and I looked at each other, "It's their way of getting back together after a long separation," he whispered. "Don't worry! They'll be fine."

In Cedar Rapids we lived in a small mobile home in a trailer park. My parents had given me the only bedroom while they had to sleep on the couch. Now my aunt would be sleeping with me, and I had to give up two of the three drawers that held my stuff. At a time when a young teenager should have had a little privacy, I had to share my bed with a woman who was not particularly happy to be squeezed into a cramped trailer. We somehow managed to get along, especially when she showed me how to pluck my eyebrows, apply make-up and do my hair. Sometimes we talked late into the night about her childhood or the terrible times both of us had endured during the war years in Germany.

Elsa had been a very skilled and licensed beautician in Berlin, but now she was not employable in her trade. She didn't speak, read or write English; therefore, she couldn't obtain her license in Iowa. In those days, the laws made no accommodations for English language learners. Elsa enrolled in night school to learn the language, but it would take a long time before she would be able to pass the tests required for her beautician license.

John, my stepfather was still in the military and didn't earn much money as a sergeant, so my mother and Elsa decided to go to work at the Penick & Ford factory that produced such products as Brer Rabbit Molasses, My-T-Fine Puddings and Vermont Maid syrup. They told tales of how sticky the whole conveyor belt got when a bottle of syrup broke during the process. The only thing they , the beautician and the seamstress who couldn't work at their learned trades, liked about their jobs was the paycheck. Even though they earned meager wages, the money helped to support our household of four. They hated the work and the factory.

"How would you like to move to California?" asked John one day. Elsa and my mother got excited, but I was not so eager to change schools again. "We have to talk about whether we want to pull the trailer there or sell it here and take a chance on finding a place to live," John explained.

"That's a hard decision! Do you think our car could pull the trailer? We wouldn't have to stay in hotels and we'd have a home to live in as soon as we get there," my mother said.

"There! Where?" Elsa chimed in.

"I'm being transferred to George Air Force Base in Victorville, California. You can find it on this map," John answered as he pulled a map out of a desk drawer.

"Oh, my God! It's in the middle of a desert!" my mother yelled. "I'll have to sew us a whole new wardrobe!"

"And there'll be scorpions and rattlesnakes," John teased her.

In February 1953, the four of us sat in the Packard that was sure to pull the trailer without trouble all the way to California and waved "Good-bye" to Cedar Rapids. John declared that we were to keep any bickering to a minimum, and so we occupied ourselves with singing and reading road-signs, including the Burma Shave signs that were spaced at intervals along the highways with thoughtful slogans. We especially liked "The one who drives when he's been drinking, depends on you to do his thinking. Burma Shave." Another favorite was, "A Man who drives when he is drunk, should haul his coffin in his trunk. Burma Shave."

Victorville was no place for Elsa, a girl who left the city she was born in to work in the world city of Berlin at the age of seventeen. She was a city girl and found nothing to keep her in the desert town of Victorville. Unlike my mother, who had a husband, the privileges of being a military dependent and a family to take care of, Elsa suddenly realized that she needed to move on. She had continued with her night school classes and become quite fluent in English. Now she felt confident enough to apply for employment in San Bernardino and Los Angeles. Because she still couldn't obtain her license as a beautician, she accepted an offer to become a caretaker of a Los Angeles woman who had to live in an iron lung. And so, Elsa once again became an independent spirit in a large world city.

After only a year and a half at George Air Force Base, my stepfather was transferred to Kindley Air Force Base in Bermuda. We would have to move again. Elsa decided to remain in California. She had in the meantime met a man whom she hoped to marry. He was a widower with one grown daughter and two teenagers who still lived at home. They married in Las Vegas while we were in Bermuda.

"I wish I could have been at the wedding!" my mother cried. She always had a soft spot for her sister Elsa. "It's too bad she couldn't come to Bermuda with us."

After I graduated from high school, I started to work at Kindley Air Force Base. When I caused a family uproar by wanting to get married to an Airman of Chinese descent who was born in Los Angeles, Elsa wrote me a letter inviting me to come live with her in California.

The situation in Bermuda had become intolerable for me, so I accepted her invitation. In tears, I boarded the airplane in May 1956 and waved "Good-bye" to the two people I loved most: my mother and the man I wanted to marry. Elsa and her husband came to pick me up at the airport and tried to comfort me with talk about all the young men I would be able to meet now. They meant young men that would be white and well-to do. I wasn't interested.

For six months I lived with Elsa and her husband Jim. His two daughters were no longer living with them, but their sixteen-year-old son was still living at home and attending high school. We became good friends although we had completely different interests. I went to work and stayed busy writing daily letters to the man I loved even though I tried to forget him to please my family. Through an employment agency I had found a job as the cashier at a medical clinic. With my first paycheck I went to a sewing machine store and bought a simple machine at $30 a month. I spent my spare time sewing or going out with the young man Elsa had introduced me to.

Without much joy I went through the motions of living. Elsa and I got along okay. We both knew that our arrangements were only temporary, so I agreed to pay her $20 every two weeks. My stepfather's three-year tour of duty in Bermuda was about to end. He was assigned to a consecutive tour at Ramstein Air Base in Germany. My mother and he were coming to California for a short vacation before moving to Germany. It was my mother's great hope to convince me to move to Germany with them. "You might even meet a nice German boy there," completely dismayed me. Elsa, siding with my mother, encouraged me to update my passport and buy a winter coat. I acted as if I were serious about going to Germany. Neither one of them knew that I had accepted a phone call from the man I loved. He had called me at the Magan Clinic to ask whether I was serious about marrying him. "I can't go on like this!" he said after I finished crying. "If you want to go to Germany with your parents, then go. I can't promise that I will be waiting for you for all those years. We are both young, and we need to go on with our lives. If you want me to come to California so we can get married, all you need to do is answer this question: Will you marry me?"

"Yes!" was all I could get out. I knew that my family would be devastated, but they had set the example. Both my mother and her sister Elsa had left my grandmother behind in search of their happiness. I remembered my grandmother crying when my mother decided to marry an American and leave Germany. I also remembered my grandmother's stories of how Elsa had moved to Berlin at a very young age. Now it was my turn to do what I felt was the right thing to do. The man I loved was all that a girl could want in a husband except that he wasn't white. I could only respond to their objections with a, "So what?"

Elsa and her husband Jim actually defended my choice. When my fiancé came to pick me up, my stepfather yelled and started to beat me. Elsa and my mother screamed while Jim, a strong mechanic, pulled my stepfather off me. I quickly grabbed my purse, jumped into my fiancé's car and left the two crying women comforting each other in the driveway.

Before leaving for Bermuda, My fiancé and I got married in Los Angeles, and I made up with both my mother and my aunt Elsa. We went our separate ways with the promise to stay in touch.

The next time I visited Elsa was in 1958. My husband had reenlisted in the Air Force and was getting transferred to Florida. Our first child was born in Bermuda and I was pregnant again.

We both wanted to visit our families in California before settling down in Florida, so we made the trip across the United States in July in a very small car. Elsa was happy to welcome us and especially excited to meet our little girl. Elsa even offered to take care of her if we wanted to go to Disneyland. Our short California visit was very pleasant, and then we spent five years in Florida.

Meanwhile, my stepfather retired from the Air Force. My mother and he moved to Claremont where Elsa and Jim had also bought a home. Finally, my mother and her sister lived close to each other where they could go shopping, play cards and catch up with all the things they had missed for years. From the letters I received, I sensed that the two sisters were truly happy. I was a little jealous and would have loved to share my happy little family with both of them.

"Guess what, Love," My husband came home one day with the good news," I'm getting transferred to Travis Air Force Base. Do you know where that is?"

"In California!" I was thrilled. Our three little girls and I would be close to my family. We would be able to visit my husband's folks and mine several times a year instead of once every five years. I was looking forward to this move. "When are we leaving?"

"We'll be traveling in July again," My husband was almost apologetic. "This time we can afford to stop early at a motel every day and spend lots of time at the swimming pools when the hot afternoon sun gets to be too much," he assured me.

Our trip was a wonderful ten-day adventure. At ages six, five and two and a half, our girls were a joy. Even Lisa, the youngest, had already learned to swim in the mobile home park where we had spent the last five years. We sold our mobile home, and netted a small profit. Now we were on our way to California where my mother and my aunt were eagerly waiting to welcome us.

The children and I spent a month with my parents. My husband went ahead to Travis Air Force Base to sign in and prepare a home for us. Elsa came over to visit us every day and we played cards while the girls amused themselves in the roomy backyard.

For the next ten years, my husband remained in the Air Force, so we had to move around several times. Between moves, we visited my mother and my aunt in Claremont. Each time, I noticed my mother's attitude toward Elsa becoming more resentful. I tried to remain neutral and listened to my mother's complaints about Elsa's cigarette smoking, lying, and shop-lifting. When I didn't want to get involved, my mother explained, "I just need to pour my heart out to someone. I still love Elsa and promised our mother I'd always stand by her." Their love-hate relationship truly puzzled me.

In 1969, we were transferred to Germany. By chance our housing was close to the family members I had left behind almost twenty years earlier. I became reacquainted with my father, my grandmother and various other relatives. In 1971, my mother visited Germany for a month. She was already showing strong signs that her rheumatoid arthritis was crippling her.

"Will you be okay while you're visiting here?" I was worried. "Do you think you'll be able to do much traveling back and forth between all the relatives?"

"I took a cortisone shot before I left California. That usually helps me for six weeks or so, and then I have to suffer for it," she explained. "I really needed to come visit my mother, though. She's eighty-three now and probably won't come to America anymore. Her accident also took a lot out of her. Her leg keeps giving her problems. We're all getting old!" she added for good measure.

We spent a lot of time talking about Elsa. Actually, I spent a lot of time listening, and my mother spent a lot of time talking. I sensed that her life revolved around her sister more than it revolved around her husband, but I kept my mouth shut and simply remained compassionate. What could I possibly do? Our tour of duty would keep us in Germany until late 1973. The problems that my mother described were taking place in California. Besides, my mother didn't want my help; she just wanted to "pour her heart out."

A year later, my grandmother's health suddenly took a turn for the worse. She was hospitalized. She was no longer taking nourishment, and the leg that had been injured in the accident had swollen to three times the size of the other leg. Her spirit, that had been indomitable through two world wars and their aftermath, was obviously about to leave her broken body. My mother was too ill to travel, but my aunt Elsa arrived three hours after my grandmother's passing. We all gathered at my uncle's house for the memorial services.

My grandmother's estate was very tiny: a few personal belongings, a few pieces of furniture, and some jewelry. If there was any money, my uncle Jupp would get that because he had been her caretaker for many years. It was made clear to me that I was only a granddaughter and therefore not entitled to anything. The furniture went to one of my cousins who "needed" to furnish his apartment. All the clothing was donated to a charity, even though I would have loved to get one or two of my grandmother's smocks (a white dress-like garment she always wore while cooking to protect her clothes). Elsa laughed at me, "What do you want with those old smocks?" She didn't care about the sentimental value and memories attached to "those old things."

My uncle agreed that Elsa could take all the jewelry and share it with my mother. He probably didn't realize that my mother would never see one piece of it, but my intuition told me that something was going terribly wrong with my aunt. I just couldn't figure out what.

One of the first things my mother complained about when we returned to California was that she hadn't inherited anything from my grandmother.

"But Elsa told Uncle Jupp that she'd share the jewelry with you. Didn't she give you any of it?" I wondered.

My mother's eyes filled with tears. "No, Elsa said there wasn't anything left over, but then I saw her wearing a ring that I gave my mother."

"I'm sorry Mutti," I empathized. "I didn't get anything either. It's a good thing that my grandmother personally gave me the large picture I remembered from my childhood; otherwise, I'd have nothing to remember her by."

"Do you know that Elsa won't even speak to Jim's son anymore?" my mother asked.

"No. What happened?" I was puzzled.

"Last time Michael came to visit she chased him out. Jim was in tears. I felt so sorry for him."

On another visit my mother told me that Elsa had complained about me. "Marianne lived with me for six months, and she never paid me anything!" Elsa had said.

I explained to my mother that this was not exactly true. I had paid Elsa $20 every two weeks (my bi-monthly paycheck was only $120 or so at the time) and besides I left the sewing machine for her. I had made six months of payments on the machine, and there were only three more payments due. Elsa had agreed to keep the machine and pay it off. "Mutti, I guess that Elsa forgot those contributions."

"Mutti, you and Elsa need a break from each other," I offered one day a couple of years later. My husband had retired from the Air Force and we were now living in Fairfield.

"Dad and I realize that. He has accepted a job in San Diego. We've been looking for a house down there."

"You're kidding! I didn't think you and Elsa could ever be separated. You always told me that you couldn't move closer to us because you promised Elsa you would stay in Claremont." I was truly surprised.

"Well, Dad thinks that my health is getting worse because of the constant tension between Elsa and me, so he made this decision. We are having a house built in Escondido."

"I can't believe it!" I was speechless. "You're selling your beautiful house with the swimming pool here and moving to Escondido? This will mean a ten-hour drive from Fairfield for us. What is Dad thinking about?"

My mother looked wistful. "Well, he got a better job there and thinks that my health will improve away from Elsa."

This little experiment was doomed to fail from the beginning. My mother was completely miserable in Escondido. Only two years later, they moved back and bought a nice home in Azusa, a neighboring town to Claremont. Elsa and my mother were no longer within walking distance, but they were now able to spend lots of time going shopping together or playing cards. My dad and Jim both retired, and along with their mutual friends, they spent the next few years in relative peace.

Jim gradually became more and more ill and passed away in the early eighties. Even though this was a sad time for Elsa, she remained strong and spent a lot of time with my mother who was also getting more and more disabled. Whenever I went to visit, I could hardly endure the atmosphere in my mother's home. My dad's weight had gone over four hundred pounds, and his mobility suffered. He had become such a devout caretaker of my mother that it bordered on obsession, especially when it came to administering the enormous amounts of medication. I was not allowed to go to the doctor with my mother whose body was deteriorating right in front of my eyes. Appointments were cancelled when I arrived. My mother insisted that there was nothing I could do anyway. Every suggestion I made was countered with "What are you? A doctor?"

"No, I'm your daughter, and I care. I'm also a mother and have taken care of sick children," I tried to explain. "I would love to have you move to Fairfield, so I could take care of you. Remember, you used to say that you would move to Fairfield when Dad retired. He's been retired for three years now."

"You know I can't leave Elsa alone!" my mother's voice suddenly got strong. "You have your kids growing up around you, and you're going to college. You won't have time for me."

My dad chimed in, "Besides, we don't want to start over!" I was puzzled.

"Start over?" I asked my husband on the way home. "What do you think Dad meant by that? What's to start over? We're their family. There's nothing to start."

My husband, my sweet husband, just shook his head and made no comment. He must have had an inkling as to what was happening.

One of the mutual friends that Elsa had introduced to my parents many years earlier was Christine, an attractive widow. She and her husband Harry had been friends with Elsa when my parents moved to Claremont. There had been many parties and lots of good times in the years before death took Harry and Jim. Now that my mother was bedridden and close to dying, Christine was a frequent visitor. It never occurred to me to pass judgment on what adults to for their amusement even though I had always been somewhat suspicious of my dad's shiny face whenever Christine was around. Yet, his solicitous behavior toward my mother made me believe that he only had the best at heart. Elsa made no comments regarding Christine. They remained good friends.

In August 1987, my mother died. She had suffered great periods of pain with only occasional relief from cortisone or other medication for over twenty years. Even though Elsa donated a plot for my mother's urn next to Jim's gravesite, she did not attend my mother's funeral. Assuming that she was just too sad at the loss of her only blood relative in America, I didn't question her. I simply accepted this as one of Elsa's idiosyncrasies. She hadn't attended any of the weddings or graduation parties we celebrated in Fairfield, so it was not surprising that she avoided a funeral.

Within the next few months, my dad sold the house and bought a mobile home next to Christine's mobile home. He also started a diet and a fitness program. When he sent us an announcement that he and Christine were married and that they were going on a honeymoon in Germany, it became clear to me what he had meant by "Start over." It was also clear to

216

me why Elsa had avoided any meaningful conversations about my mother's physical condition with me: she must have known that Christine and my dad had just been waiting for my mother to die.

My feelings toward my aunt and my dad cooled significantly after my mother's death. I no longer felt the need to visit either one of them. I went on to earn my teaching credential and started teaching full-time. When Christine notified us that my dad had passed away, I felt a brief sting of sadness until I got to read his new revised Last Will. All emotion then left me. My dad had warned me nearly fifty years ago when I married my Chinese sweetheart that he would disown me. Now he had done just that. My name was expressly mentioned as being precluded from inheriting any part of his estate. Everything was to go to Christine, except for the contents of his mobile home which were to go to my aunt Elsa. I was neither surprised, sad nor angry, but I was disappointed. He had not even included the grandchildren that he had always considered as his own.

As my aunt Elsa became more elderly, my dad and Christine helped her sort out her financial affairs. After my dad died, Elsa depended more and more on Christine until she died. A mutual friend Ruth, who was also a neighbor of Elsa's, was recruited as the person who would help Elsa with her finances, shopping, and companionship as she became too old to drive and take care of herself. The rest of the family, including my uncle in Germany, was satisfied with this arrangement for at least eight years. Then things began to change.

The Timeline of my Involvement in Elsa's Financial Affairs

(On June 29, 2007, I wrote the following narrative report covering a few months of turmoil regarding my aunt Elsa. The quotations may not be verbatim, but they accurately reflect their substance.)

A few months ago I suddenly got a phone call from Elsa that truly puzzled me. She was angry with Ruth and wanted me to advise her. She kept asking, "Why should I have a will?" I didn't know what to tell her. I thought she already had a will, but she kept insisting that she didn't have any papers and didn't know what to do. I had been under the impression for years that her relationship with her neighbor Ruth was so close that she had named Ruth as the sole heir to her estate. I wondered what had happened to change this relationship. Throughout the phone call, Elsa must have asked the same question, "Why should I have a will?" four or five times.

Up until that time, I had completely stayed out of her financial affairs.

I had remained in touch with Elsa because, after all, she was my only surviving blood relative on this continent. My beloved mother had loved her, and that was reason enough for me to visit her now and then despite the distance between our homes. Whenever the conversation began to turn to finances, Elsa became intense, stating that the only reason people visit her is for her money. I always tried to change the subject deliberately, keeping our conversations to small talk. I certainly didn't visit her to get her money.

On one of our visits, Elsa complained that she had not inherited so much as a thimble from my mother's (her sister's) estate after my step-father and his new wife had died. She told me that a niece of Christine's first husband, Harry, had come from New York to claim the entire estate. This struck me as extremely odd. Rather than make a big deal out of this new information, I reminded Elsa that one of my mother's creations, a framed embroidery, was hanging in the dining room to refute her assertion. "At least you have that as a memento," I pointed out. She then told me that the dining room set also came from Christine's estate.

I wondered silently what else she might have gotten but decided against saying anything. Instead I agreed that the situation wasn't fair. "I can't do anything about it now unless I know more details. "Why don't you give me the name of the lawyer who handled the estate?"

I actually didn't know what I would or could do with that information except to get some clarity, but I was truly disappointed with Elsa's immediate reaction, "Oh, no! I don't want to make trouble! I don't know anything!"

I asked her, "Then why did you bring it up? Why tell me about Harry's niece?"

She just smiled and said, "I thought you wanted to know." I felt powerless and defeated.

My husband noticed my unhappy face and suggested that we leave soon. We made our good-byes and left. Naturally, I discussed my disappointment with my husband on the way home and told him that I really didn't want to visit Elsa anymore. I was particularly stunned that Elsa would not give me the name of the attorney. Why not? Did she just want to stir up my emotions? It seemed that my feelings got hurt every time we visited in the last few years. Every time we visited her, she made the comment that the only reason people visit her is because they want her money. It was never clear to me whether she meant me as one of those people. As a means of protecting my heart, we had no contact for a few years except for Christmas cards.

One day (I think it was after she received my 2005 Christmas card) Elsa called me to ask whether I wanted the picture my mother had embroidered. I said that I'd love to have it and that we would stop by the next time we were in the area. We visited her in the spring. At that time, she also gave me a box of all her photographs. I took them and put them in an album when I got home.

We phoned each other a couple of times, but only made small talk about her ailments. I had no expectations and no idea that trouble was brewing.

Now we come to January 2007. That is when I got the puzzling phone call from my aunt Elsa about making a will. I e-mailed my uncle in Germany (Elsa's brother) about this. He said he had been in touch with Elsa and Ruth and that there was a problem between them. She now wanted him (Elsa's brother, my uncle) to get the house. He wondered what had happened. I told him that I didn't know anything except that Ruth had been taking care of Elsa's needs and wants, and that she was Elsa's heir. I had never met Ruth. What did he want me to do? He told me to consider Elsa's age and that she was not well. "Give her a call once in a while." She would appreciate my contact. I told him that we had a Las Vegas trip planned for March and that we would make time to visit Elsa while we were in Southern California.

In a subsequent e-mail my uncle indicated that Ruth had written him. She felt that Elsa needed more help than she could provide. He wondered whether I would be willing to see to the matter. I told him again that I had never been privy to any information regarding Elsa's affairs. I had no authority to interfere in Elsa's affairs. I thought Ruth was handling everything. When I asked him about details, such as a will or the power of attorney that named Ruth, he said he had never seen a document about this. Even though he was sure that a will existed, he did not have Elsa's will in his possession. He sent me a copy of Ruth's letter.

Dear Jupp and Gabi

I believe that Elsa needs someone who can work with her, for the purpose of hiring house cleaning help or home assistants, and to help her with her finances (SHE HAS ABSOLUTELY NO CONCEPT ABOUT MONEY, BANKING OR ANYTHING FINANCIAL!!). I think her reasoning ability is slipping rapidly, and I am looking to you for guidance and help.

My problems with Elsa - again, are her dishonesty and out and out lies to me. Lying is often and continuous and it is hurting our working together.

ALL I ASK OF HER IS TO BE HONEST WITH ME! Which is something she will not do! You might think this is a power struggle. Not so. But she thinks that she must always be in full control.

Last week I talked to her about $1000 a month payments (as you mentioned in one of your e-mails) on the house and she rejected that idea immediately.

She still cannot find the "Original" trust legal paperwork and she asked me to send a letter to the attorney, asking for copies of her legal paperwork

(I sent you a copy of that letter). On January 16 the attorney signed the "postal return-receipt. Elsa said she has continually tried to call the attorney and "she doesn't call me back" - even today she told me she HAD NOT TALKED TO THE ATTORNEY SINCE WAY BEFORE CHRISTMAS! I called the attorney at 11:30am today and both the secretary AND Sherry (attorney) told me that Sherry HAD talked to Elsa yesterday! Elsa insists she DID NOT talk to them - once again, she is not being truthful. Does she REALLY not remember or what?? Over the years, her lack of truthful candor has been obvious. It is probably a lifelong trait in survival, but there is no matter of survival now, and it is unacceptable to have to deal with a chronic liar. Today she called, to talk with me about how I am reflected in the trust. In less than 5 minutes, she represented 3 different ways that I would be acknowledged by the trust. There is a saying in politics that states: " throw a lot of mud against the wall, and see what sticks". This is often used to demean the name of a political adversary. In this case, Elsa is using it to maintain the Matriarchal position with me. If one of the 3 representations is accurate and correct, then the other two are false.

I took Elsa to the doctor last week - the complaint about her throat bleeding?? The doctor gave her a referral to a throat specialist and she wouldn't let me make the appointment and says she will NOT go see him!

After many calls from Elsa to Amy, (Amy, the nurse, calls me, because she can't understand Elsa when on the telephone - you have probably have been on the phone with her when the phone drops down, and it is hard to hear her) the nurse in her primary doctor's office (over 20 calls from Elsa in the last two days, over 50 in the last 10 days), with demands for a multiple list of thing that she wants "free"; a social worker came out yesterday and gave Elsa a shower bench seat to put in the tub. Elsa immediately refused the seat. The social worker also brought a toilet seat riser with arm rails. Elsa called the girl and told her to come and take it away. Elsa said she does not want to wash it. I believe it would have made going to the bathroom much easier for Elsa. Elsa is having a problem with diarrhea, which frequently turns to an equally large problem with constipation. Every morning I have to check the floor from her bedroom to the bathroom and probably 2 times a week I have to clean up „accidents" on the carpet.

Some days Elsa is OK - other days she does not do well! Her memory is failing as every day she asks me how much money she has, or who is someone that I have talked about - she seems not to know. At times she asks who I am! I also feel that she needs someone to help her make decisions. SHE wants to hire someone and I told her she needs someone she trusts to help her hire a caretaker. She said she would and could hire someone (and I could just as easily fly the space shuttle)!! She cannot legibly write checks; the bank will not honor checks that she writes because they are not legible. She has me write the checks and she signs them. She questions every bill she gets, complains, and says she is going to stop paying all her bills including utilities, house insurance and property taxes, and all bills. She just says "take it out of the house!" She was going through the phone book to find someone to give her a loan on the house. I am concerned that she may sign something that she does not understand. Her doctor, Dr. Billings, has told her that borrowing money against the house was a bad idea! Just this week, she received the statement from the bank for the purpose of paying her taxes on the income. She hasn't paid taxes due, for years, and won't pay taxes for 2006 either. The interest added and penalties from the government might be very costly. I had mentioned this non-payment of taxes in a prior letter.

Elsa told me today that Mariana Tong is coming again (she was here at Christmas). Elsa told me that Mariana asked her if she had a Will and that is why she is coming down to see Elsa and see her will and papers.

In summary, Elsa needs a trustworthy conservator, who will work in her best interest. This is an immediate requirement, not something a week, month, or year away. She cannot function in even the most primary way (except for having a cigarette). She cannot cook, or prepare any meaningful meals, she cannot do her laundry, she cannot handle finances, she cannot pay her house aides without making mistakes (always in her favor) in the payments, she cannot acquire medical help when it is needed, and she cannot contract the services that she needs without assistance. Some of this is no doubt willful.

Life long traits:

1. Elsa trusts no one, and that distrust is now working against her best interest.

2. Elsa does not use what we call "common sense" (the ability to know the correct way, when it is not known what the correct way is).

3. Elsa is almost 100% reactionary; If I am for it, she is against it; If I am against it, she is for it; and so it goes with others.

4. Elsa believes that everything should be free, that the world (or at least this country) owes her everything she wants. Maybe that is the practice of your government, especially for the seniors, but the morality of our country is "pay your own way".

5. Stubborn; yes, rock hard stubborn, to the point of throwing childlike tantrums. Once Elsa has made up her mind, there is no changing it (especially, see 3 above). Later, in a week or so, it might become her idea, then it's alright to change her mind.

6. Elsa has to be right. Even when it's obvious that she is not.

It is a big waste of time and mental energy trying to deal with that thought process.

7. Insensitive to the feelings of others. You probably know what I'm talking about here. Elsa says (often loudly) whatever comes to her mind without the slightest sensitivity to the hurt caused to others. It is very embarrassing.

I'm not looking for sympathy here; I'm also not looking to have every interaction with Elsa being much more difficult that it needs to be.

We heard that the weather had finally turned cold in Germany. Hope your winter is not too severe.

Thanks, Ruth

I translated it into German, added comments of my own and sent it back. I also sent my comments to Ruth, offering to become the trustworthy conservator, that "someone who can work with her."

My uncle e-mailed me to tell me that he was upset with me. Apparently, I had over-stepped my bounds. I told my uncle that I was happy to stay out of the whole business and resolved to do so unless I was **asked** to step in. How was I to judge how far I should or could go? He apologized for over-reacting and we agreed to cross those bridges as we get to them (meaning that we would wait to see what Elsa wants to do.)

Somehow I was relieved that I wouldn't have to deal with Elsa's complicated story, but that didn't last long. My uncle thought I should visit Elsa and see if I could read the will and Power of Attorney authorizing Ruth.

The last time Elsa phoned me, I had told her that we would stop by to see her in March. I told Elsa that her brother had asked me to help her sort out her problems. I also said that it would be very helpful if she had all her paperwork there for me to read. She said she didn't have any paperwork, but that she wanted me to come by to visit her, though, and complained about how sick in bed she was.

When we visited Elsa, she was glad to see us and ate the food we brought. She got up and sat at the table with us. When I asked Elsa about the will or any other paperwork, Elsa suddenly became agitated, "I don't know! What are you talking about? I don't have any papers. What papers?" I was unable to determine whether she was truly confused or just playing. When I asked about the problems she had with Ruth, she said that everything was fine but didn't want to talk about it. I took some pictures to show my uncle that Elsa, smoking several cigarettes, was not as infirm as she had led him to believe.

My husband tried very kindly to get her to understand that we just wanted to read the will with our own eyes to assure ourselves that her affairs were in order. She insisted that there was no will and that her brother (my uncle in Germany) would inherit everything. I tried to tell her that the courts would follow the will she had written several years earlier and that Ruth would inherit the estate if that's what her will says. She continued to insist that there was no will and that her brother in Germany would get everything. I dropped the subject when I realized the futility of the conversation.

Then Elsa showed us a letter she had just received from Social Services. She was given a list of prospective in-home helpers from which to choose. She was apparently entitled to two hours daily (5 days a week) of help through MediCal. I explained the contents of the letter and told her that she could interview these ladies and then choose the one she liked best. She said she would take care of it. We left after making friendly and loving good-byes.

In the meantime my uncle and I settled our misunderstanding regarding Elsa. Instead, we continued to have fun via e-mail or Skype. com on our computers. The subject of Elsa only came up peripherally, as we were more engaged in telling jokes and discussing my daughter Lisa's impending Europe trip. She would be visiting in April and staying with him for a couple of weeks. Until then there had been no more discussion of Elsa's affairs. I thought Ruth had come back into Elsa's good graces and that nothing would be changed. Then I got another phone call from Elsa.

Elsa started by saying, "Why should I move out of my house? I want to live here until I die." Okay, now I got really confused! The subject of her moving out of her house and selling it had never been discussed in our conversations, even though I had offered her a place in my home if she ever needed more care. She kept asking, "Why should I sell my house? Why should I move?" I didn't know how to answer since I hadn't been the one who had told her to do that.

I asked again, "How can I help? What do you want me to do?"

She said, "I want to stay in my house until I die, but they want me to move out. How can I do that?"

"Who wants you to move out? What are you saying?" I wondered, but she just kept repeating the same question, "Why should I move out of my house?"

I told her that I have no information and no authority to do anything. I asked whether she wanted me to talk to her lawyer. I knew from Ruth's e-mail letter that Elsa had a lawyer named Sherry, but I had no idea of her last name or even where she practiced. Elsa happily accepted my offer to talk to Sherry, "Oh, would you do that for me?"

I said, "Yes, but I don't know her full name and telephone number."

Elsa gave me this information and told me that I probably won't get an appointment, "She never comes when I call." I said I would try to make an appointment and let her know. My husband and I would then meet Sherry and we could figure things out. At that time, I still didn't know just how I could be instrumental, so I discussed this with my uncle. He appeared relieved that I was willing to step in. He suggested that, I could be the Executor of the estate and have Power of Attorney. This was fine with me.

I e-mailed Sherry with my concerns, and she called me with a tentative appointment (unfortunately it had to be on a Tuesday when I was obligated to teach at the Senior Center, but oh well, this was important!). Provided that my cousin Gabi and/or my uncle (both in Germany) agreed to let me handle things, Sherry and I would meet in Elsa's house on June 26. I called my uncle and asked him to let Sherry know right away whether he still wanted me to get involved. My husband and I had pre-paid plans for a Reno vacation in June. We were preparing to leave on June 18 and planned to return on June 23. After that we could make the time to drive to Elsa's house. I notified the Senior Center of my absence, so we could leave on Monday, June 25.

Gabi then sent the following letter to Sherry:

Dear Sherry,

I hope the decision to name my cousin Marianne as Elsa's trustee with financial and medical power of attorney is the best we can do.

Regarding the trust we - my father, Marianne and myself - have decided that for financial, i.e. tax reasons, it is the most convenient solution making Marianne and myself half-and-half as the beneficiaries of her estate- provided Elsa agrees to this. My father has already sent his agreement to this via e-mail to you.

In case you need our personal data:

Gabi

Gabi also included other identifying information to assure Sherry of the legitimacy of this request.

I wrote a letter to Elsa on June 13:

June 13, 2007

Dear Elsa,

We'll be visiting you for a couple of days next week. We are leaving Fairfield on Monday, June 25 around 10 o'clock and arrive at your house around 7 o'clock in the evening. Don't worry about dinner. We'll take care of the food.

Then on Tuesday we can take you to the bank or anywhere else you want to go.

Sherry will be coming to your house on Tuesday, June 26 around 2 o'clock. We'll be there with you. Please don't cancel this appointment. My husband and I are coming to help you figure out exactly what you want to do. It's important that we get to meet her.

I've talked with Jupp and Gabi, and they agree that you should make the best decisions for yourself and that I can help you do that. We'll stay at your house for a couple of days until all the paperwork is straightened out with Sherry.

Till then, lots of love, Marianne

On June 19 while we were on vacation, I received a call from my daughter Lisa that Elsa had left several panicky-sounding messages on my answering machine. I called Elsa right away to see what was wrong.

"When are you coming?" was all Elsa wanted to know. I asked whether she had gotten my letter explaining our timetable. "Yes, but things can change." I told Elsa again that we were currently golfing in Reno and that I would be at her house on Monday, June 25 around 7 in the evening.

Sherry was coming on June 26 to document Elsa's wishes. "Okay, Honey," she said.

Our trip to Claremont was long but uneventful. We arrived around 7:15. We were hungry, so I sent my husband for a pizza and some beer. Elsa delightedly joined us and ate two slices of pizza with gusto. She even had a glass of beer with her cigarette.

We sat outside for a while and then prepared the pull-out couch for the night. I was surprised at Elsa's agility as she insisted on straightening the cushions and closing the drapes herself. We had brought our laptop, so I hooked it up where she showed me. I showed Elsa some pictures and then played a couple of computer games before going to bed. Elsa went to her bedroom and turned on her TV so loud that I couldn't concentrate on the book I had taken to bed. I closed the door, and soon Elsa appeared to open the door. I told her that the TV was too loud and I'd rather have the door closed. She agreed and then turned her TV down. I was soon asleep.

When I woke up the next morning, I noticed that my laptop had been disconnected and placed precariously on top of something else in a chair. I asked my husband whether he had moved the computer, but he hadn't. Elsa had apparently gotten up in the night and pulled the mouse out of the computer and moved everything. My husband told me that he came to bed after I had gone to sleep. He was reading in bed when suddenly a hand (Elsa's) appeared through the door and turned off the light. I laughed and asked why he didn't tell Elsa that he wanted to read some more. He just shrugged.

Anyway, moments later, people began to arrive. I was in the bathroom when I heard women's voices. Ruth and Betty, the 2-hour helper from the Social Services had arrived to help Elsa with her routine. They were trying to get her up to take her pills and get dressed. Elsa did not cooperate. She appeared to have leg cramps and was curled up in bed making pitiful sounds. Betty told me that her potassium pills were to relieve the leg cramps. Elsa steadfastly refused to take the pills. Ruth tried to get Elsa cleaned up and take her pills. Elsa continued to cry out and refuse to get up. This drama went on for about two hours. The two ladies left. I finally called my uncle in Germany to talk to Elsa. He talked to her for a while and then told me not to worry. He sensed that her apprehension about the appointment with Sherry was causing Elsa to act like that. After we hung up, I told Elsa to rest some more. "I'll be sitting on the porch with my husband, so let me know if I can help you with anything."

About 10 minutes later I went to check on Elsa. She was sitting on the side of the bed and already had put on some of her clothes. She didn't need any help and soon was fully dressed. When she wanted to come out, she was a little wobbly on her legs and used her walker, but otherwise appeared okay. She lit up a cigarette and then she asked me, "So, who is coming at three o'clock?" When I said, "Sherry," she asked, "Who is Sherry?" I realized that I was being played like a fine violin. I answered, "Your lawyer."

"My lawyer? Why do I need a lawyer? I don't have a lawyer." Elsa looked so innocent that I was actually wondering whether she was legitimately confused. Then she said, "Oh yeah! Sherry is my lawyer and she's coming today about the will."

I said, "That's right. You wanted me to make an appointment to make sure that you wouldn't have to move out of your house. Sherry is going to bring the paperwork for you to sign so you can make your own decisions. Then nobody can tell you what to do."

"Paperwork! What do I need paperwork for?" Elsa tried to convince me that she didn't need any paperwork to give her brother the house. She could do what she wanted without paperwork. I agreed that she could what she wanted but that it had to be written down; otherwise, a judge will follow the old will (which I had never seen but was told that it existed) and give everything to Ruth. "Okay, okay, I know!" she said.

Elsa then ate part of a croissant and drank some coffee. We made small talk until Sherry arrived promptly at two o'clock. Then the real drama began.

At first Elsa denied that she had initiated the current changes to her will. After Sherry reminded her of the letter she had written and the several phone calls for help, Elsa relented and agreed that she was the one who wanted to make the changes. Sherry was very thorough in explaining the changes and continually asked Elsa whether she understood and agreed. At one point Elsa tried to change her mind. She told Sherry that Ruth had been the only one who took care of her. At that point, Sherry made it clear to Elsa that it was her right to refuse a new will and that she was fully capable of making her own decisions. If Elsa wanted to keep the old will naming Ruth, then Sherry's work here was done and she would leave, indicating that Elsa could choose any other lawyer in the future. Sherry was simply stating a fact without being confrontational. Sherry continually assured Elsa of her right to make decisions, but that she, Sherry, could not, in all good conscience, continue to be her attorney. Honestly, I was somewhat surprised at Sherry's vehemence. What had transpired to bring on such an adamant stance? I began to wonder just how much information was being withheld from me. Some clarity gradually came in as the discussion went on, and a little more light was shed on the situation in today's phone call from Ruth.

Before I go into Ruth's phone call, I want to describe a little more of Sherry's visit.

After much questioning and explaining, Sherry offered the documents for Elsa to read. She wanted to make absolutely sure that Elsa really understood the importance of the changes that were about to be made. This would be a completely new Amendment to the will, and the old one would no longer be effective. The new will (actually, not a new will but an amendment to the Living Trust) would not mention Ruth's name at all. I, Marianne Tong, would be named successor Trustee in place of Ruth, with my uncle and his daughter being the fifty-fifty heirs. A medical directive was also presented. I was to have Power of Attorney in medical decisions regarding Elsa's health care. Elsa listened carefully and occasionally asked a question which was promptly answered. Elsa appeared to be fully engaged. Sherry asked Elsa whether she trusted her niece Marianne. Elsa said yes. For some reason, Sherry needed to know Elsa's Bank account number. When I produced two recent statements, Sherry questioned a $27,000.00 difference from one month to the next. Where had the money gone? Elsa said she had sent it to my cousin Gabi. I was surprised; this was news to me. Neither my uncle nor Gabi had mentioned such a transaction. No problem: this was between my uncle and Elsa and didn't concern me. Sherry also seemed satisfied with the explanation.

The discussion went on, and after a while, Sherry sent me into the neighborhood to invite someone to be a witness to the actual signing. The neighbor on the left turned me down but referred me to a lady in the house next door. There was no answer, so I marched over to the house on Elsa's right. The young man, a sheriff's deputy, was willing to come over.

When Elsa asked, "Who are you?" he quietly commented that dementia seems to be starting. He and Elsa had known each other for years, so why didn't she recognize him. The she said, "Oh yeah! You live next door. Why are you here?" In order to dispel any notion of dementia, Sherry questioned Elsa who gave coherent and logical answers. Mark, the neighbor, was satisfied that nothing strange was going on. He witnessed the signing and left shortly afterwards. I told Sherry that I had a few questions and produced some notes I had printed out. Elsa noticed her name on the paper and snatched it from my hands. She focused on a couple of sentences dealing with some alternatives my uncle had suggested. Elsa wanted to know what these notes meant. Sherry and I finally convinced Elsa that these notes were **not** part of the official will. They were simply questions about options I had written out before our meeting. I asked Elsa to give the notes back to me, but Elsa absolutely insisted on keeping them. I suspected she wanted to show them to Ruth who was mentioned a couple of times.

Anyway, I yielded and told her she could keep the notes. Sherry was then able to redirect Elsa's attention to the official papers and more relevant matters.

Now we were ready for the "piece de resistance." I was unprepared for the theatrics that ensued when Sherry presented her bill. The invoice carefully itemized the phone conversations and e-mails that led up to the will-signing. Elsa declared, "I'm not going to pay that. I have no money." Sherry tried to convince her that she was simply charging for the time she spent working on this case and deserved to get paid. Elsa countered with, "I don't have any money." Sherry reminded her that she had seen the bank statements and that she had plenty of money. Elsa refused again. In fact, at one point she became quite abusive and declared, "That's all you lawyers want, my money."

The argument between a calm Sherry and an agitated Elsa became quite embarrassing, so I gently handed Elsa her checkbook and told her to write a check now. She yelled that it was none of my business. I quietly reminded her that she had made it my business when she asked me to help her. When she again pushed the invoice away, I said, "Elsa, you can either write a check to Sherry now or write one to a judge in court." Sherry had not told me (and I didn't know) that my uncle had told her to send the bill to him; otherwise, I would have kept quiet. I pointed to the checkbook. She finally wrote the check and received her invoice marked "paid in full." Elsa then declared that she would send it to Gabi since many of the charges had to do with the time spent phoning with Gabi. Sherry agreed that this would be fair. In my own mind, I was still wondering why a check for $27,000.00 had been sent to Gabi at all, but I decided not to ask. By now it had become clear that I wasn't going to get all the answers, anyway.

When Elsa kept asking, "What do I do now? I want to live and die in my own house," and complaining about not having any money, Sherry asked me whether I had ever heard of reverse mortgages. I said that my husband and I had attended two seminars but decided not to take advantage of this program. Sherry then explained to Elsa that she could use money out of the house by getting a reverse mortgage. She could use this money to pay for any kind of help she needed. All she needed to do was contact a certain Steve S… who deals in reverse mortgages. He would be able to help Elsa receive enough cash every month from the house to pay for any services she needed. Elsa wrote his name and phone number down, but she was not happy to hear that she might have to pay for services. Again, Elsa commented unkindly about lawyers taking all her money. I had heard enough and declared, "Elsa, you could have gone to law school and become a lawyer yourself!" I immediately realized that this was somewhat harsh, but Elsa's comments and complaints had honed me to a sharp edge. Elsa did not respond to my unkind comment.

After a stressful hour and a half, Sherry promised to mail me a copy of the documents and then left. Elsa would also receive the originals via registered mail. My husband was sitting on the porch throughout the ordeal, so I got me a glass of tea and joined him. Smoking another cigarette, Elsa also came to sit with us. She wanted to know, "So what are you now?" I wondered what she was getting at and finally understood that she wanted to know my new title in the will. She thought I had now accepted certain responsibilities as a care giver. I told her that I was Executor of the estate after she died, but as long as she is alive, she is her own boss. This was what she had wanted. "Well then, who's going to give care of me?" she asked. I told her that she could pay someone if Ruth was unwilling to continue her services out of friendship. That was why she should get a reverse mortgage. Then Elsa focused again on the notes I had written. She wanted to know what certain sentences meant. I was becoming more and more annoyed, telling her that these notes had nothing to do with the actual will. They simply represented the questions about whether I could make Elsa my dependent and include her on our insurance. I had intended to ask these questions of Sherry. I asked her to return the paper to me since it obviously caused her so much concern. She adamantly refused to let it go. Since her name was mentioned, she wanted to keep it. I said, "Okay, okay, keep it then."

My husband noticed that I was getting increasingly frustrated with Elsa, so he quietly said, "Looks like we're driving home this afternoon." I nodded. I went inside to straighten up the bedroom we had occupied and packed our things. Within the hour I was ready to depart. It was clear that there was no chance that Elsa and I would come to any kind of agreement.

"Elsa, the whole idea of this appointment was to give you a way to stay in your own home. That is what you wanted. If you get a reverse mortgage, you can stay in your home as long as you want. You'll have the money to pay someone to take care of you," I tried to explain, but my words fell on deaf ears.

I told Elsa that her two-hour helper from Social Services would be here in the morning.

"Yes, Betty is nice. She can help me," Elsa agreed.

I told Elsa, "If you need additional help you'll have to pay somebody. I can see that you don't want any help from me." There was nothing else I could do until I had the paperwork in hand. We made our good-byes and left.

We stayed overnight in Bakersfield and drove home the next morning. Elsa had already called and left a very short comment on our answering machine. In mid-afternoon, she called again. "Who's going to take me to the bank? **You** can't come every time I need something." Again I reminded her that a lady from Social Services comes in every day for two hours. This lady could help her go places and get whatever she needed. If two hours in the morning wasn't enough, she could pay someone to stay longer. She grumbled something about not having money for that, and then she gave the phone to Ruth who revealed a few more surprises to me.

Ruth asked me whether this whole new situation had developed as a result of her being accused of stealing money. (Another surprise!) I told her that I had never heard anything about stolen money but that Elsa had mentioned a fight over a set of dishes earlier in the year. Ruth then explained that she had written a check to herself in September in the sum of $18,750.00. $18,000 of this was to repay her for the nine months that she had given $2000.00 a month to Elsa and $750 was to repay the cost of making the original will and Living Trust. I was stunned. "Why were you giving Elsa $2000 a month?" I asked.

Ruth told me that Elsa was always complaining about not having money, so she provided money to her. The $750 was to repay the money she had spent on getting the original trust that had named her trustee and heir. She stated that Christine had advised her to get Elsa's promise in writing. Another stunning revelation! I suspected all along that my step-father and Christine had something to do with Ruth's interest in Elsa's affairs, but I had dismissed this as an absurd assumption on my part. Ruth expressed her disappointment in Elsa and admitted that much of what she had done for Elsa was in the hope of inheriting her estate. She also told me that much of what she had done was out of friendship and that she loved Elsa despite everything. I certainly understood that feeling because despite a very bumpy history with Elsa, I still loved her.

"I still don't understand how this $18,000 has anything to do with Elsa's wanting to change the will," I asked Ruth.

"Insisting that the $2000 a month was coming out of her house, she thought I was stealing her money when I wrote the check to pay myself back," Ruth explained.

"Why did you suddenly stop giving her $2000 a month and want your money back?" I wondered.

"Elsa keeps changing her mind. One minute she says that I would inherit everything; the next she tells me that she talks about selling the house and moving to Germany," Ruth explained. "My husband and I just couldn't afford to keep giving her the money without some assurance that we would get it back one day."

"Boy, I can certainly understand that," I said.

"Right after I got the check cashed, Elsa arrived at the bank and changed her account to take my name off," Ruth added.

I had heard enough. The situation in Claremont with my aunt manipulating Ruth and everyone who came in contact with her was like a bad soap opera. I had fallen into a trap when I accepted my uncle's advice to get involved in my Aunt Elsa's affairs. Now my name was in the Living Trust. I was committed.

Gabi Comes to Visit our Aunt Elsa

In July I was informed that Gabi, my cousin, with her husband and her son were flying to San Francisco in August. They planned to stay with us in Fairfield for a few days, travel around California, Nevada and Arizona for a couple of weeks, and then visit our aunt in Claremont before returning to San Francisco for the flight back to Germany. Gabi said she would feel more comfortable visiting with Elsa if I could also be there to speak with her doctor, so my husband and I made the third trip in one year to visit Elsa.

Our two-day visit proved to be fascinating. We arrived to find Elsa in bed fighting with Betty about a $125 telephone bill that was due. Elsa didn't want to pay; Betty said she had to. I tried to get Elsa to sign a check, but she said the man at the telephone company told her she could just pay $5. My argument was futile, so I left the room. Elsa barely paid attention to her niece Gabi, but made remarks about her handsome husband. She remained in bed and said we should come back later. She also appeared to be more irritated that Ruth had gone to Oregon for two weeks rather than be happy to have us visit her. Elsa continued bickering with Betty regarding the phone bill.

Gabi and I decided we should all leave for a few hours and come back later with food and drink. Away from the house, we left a message at Dr. Billings' office to get some information and direction regarding our position in Elsa's physical and mental condition. We also expressed our concern that according to her caretaker, she was smoking in bed. The doctor called back later, but we got very little information. As far as he was concerned, Elsa was perfectly competent to make her own decisions. He knew that she was a smoker, but he had no specific suggestions.

The five of us stopped to have lunch and drive around the area for a couple of hours. Then we stopped at a supermarket to buy some food for a nice dinner at Elsa's house. We were apprehensive but looking to make the best of the warm Southern California evening.

Back at the house, Elsa was very happy to see us. She realized that she had not been friendly in the morning and was ready to be a sweet hostess. She mentioned that Ruth always calls her at nine o'clock in the evening to check on her. With a happy smile and joking around with us, Elsa seemed to be a different person from the one we had found in the morning. Elsa sat on the floor near the front door and smoked several cigarettes while we chatted and took some pictures. Finally, Gabi and my husband got busy in the kitchen, while Gabi's husband and I were preparing the picnic area in the backyard. We used a folded-up bed sheet as a tablecloth for the weathered picnic table and found enough seating places. Soon all six of us were having a wonderful time sharing a bottle of wine and some good food in the balmy evening air. Elsa was having a great time, and so were we.

Suddenly, Elsa decided that she was tired. "I'm going to bed now. I'll see you in the morning. Good night." She got up and went into the house without assistance.

"What just happened?" Gabi wondered.

"It's nine o'clock." I answered.

"So what does that mean?" Gabi's son was puzzled.

"Remember that Elsa told us that Ruth was going to phone at nine o'clock? She wants to be in bed near her phone when Ruth calls," I explained.

"No! Do you really think that Elsa knows it's almost nine?" Gabi's husband wanted to know.

"That's how smart she is! She loves to act as if she were on her last leg and confused to keep everybody under control and concerned. She used to do that to my mother. Elsa's illnesses and problems were always more severe than my mother's. My mother died twenty years ago, but Elsa is still going strong" I commented.

Sure enough, the phone rang exactly at nine. As Elsa and Ruth declared their love for each other, we cleaned up the kitchen. Then we wrapped up the evening and went to our motel with the promise to come back in the morning.

The next morning my husband and I arrived at Elsa's house a few minutes before Gabi and her family. Elsa was glad to see me and told me in confidence that she really didn't like the lady that Gabi had brought to her house the day before.

"Elsa, that was me!" I tried to explain.

"No. Gabi brought this stranger along. I didn't like that woman. You're Marianne, my sister's daughter." Elsa insisted.

When I told Gabi about this, we all had a good laugh. No specific decisions regarding our aunt's care were made during this visit. It seemed to all of us that Elsa's arrangements with Ruth and her caretaker Betty were satisfactory all the way around. No changes were made. Soon we were back on the road. A few days later, Gabi and her family flew back to Germany.

I stayed in touch with my aunt by telephone and also through her caretaker Betty who kept me informed regarding her health. MediCal had in the meantime discovered that Elsa was no longer eligible for any further financial assistance. The information that had been used to allow the two hours of in-home support services was out-dated (from a time when Elsa's husband Jim was still alive) and no longer valid. Betty was distraught at the thought that Ruth, who according to Elsa only visited a few minutes a day, would be Elsa's sole caretaker. I got in touch with my uncle, and he sent some money to pay for Betty until some other arrangements could be made. For a few months, I paid Betty privately to remain with Elsa. This arrangement worked until September when the money my uncle had sent for Elsa's care ran out. We told Elsa that she would have to pay for any in-home care out of her own finances. It was difficult to make her understand that no more contributions would be made by the family. I reminded her to get in touch with Steve, the agent recommended by Sherry about a reverse mortgage. There was sufficient equity in her home to pay for her care. Neither my uncle nor his daughter were particularly interested in inheriting the house, so a Reverse Mortgage would be the ideal way to make sure that she could continue to live in her own house for the rest of her life and have enough money to pay for her in-home care.

"What do I need a Reverse Mortgage for?" Elsa demanded.

"Remember, you wanted me to make sure that you could stay in your house for the rest of your life? This is what started the ball rolling with the appointment with Sherry and the new will in the first place. You say you don't have enough money to pay for someone to take care of you. This is the way to make sure you have enough money from month to month," I tried as gently as I could to bring her up-to-date.

"I don't need anybody to take care of me!" Elsa yelled into the phone. "I have friends!" Of course, I knew that she meant Ruth, her neighbor, who had helped her for years. Unfortunately, Ruth had become bitter about no longer being the heir. She refused to accept our offer to pay her monthly for Elsa's care. I certainly understood.

"I don't want to take the responsibility of being a hired caretaker. Up to last year I was taking care of your aunt as a friend and eventual heir, but she keeps changing her mind. My husband told me not to get involved anymore," Ruth explained on the phone.

Actually, I couldn't fault with Ruth for that. Elsa's promises to put this or that person in her will were highly unpredictable. From one day to the next, she said "My brother is getting the house after I die." Then she declared, "Ruth has been giving care of me. She should get the house." Depending on whatever momentary whim, she named different heirs in each conversation. The only thing I could be sure of is that I would definitely not get anything. Of course, I had indicated often enough that I didn't want anything from her anyway. All I was interested in was my aunt's contentment. I knew from our history that she had always been independent and worked hard to achieve her own place in the world and her own home. I simply wanted to help her stay out of the nursing homes she so steadfastly feared. Whatever arrangements Ruth and Elsa could work out was up to them.

By November 2007 we had reached an impasse. The following journal illustrates the trying time as my family and I tried to be helpful in my aunt's life.

Elsa's Visit

Saturday, November 16, 2007 at 8:29 AM, I received a call while still in bed. It was Elsa, crying, "Please come get me. People are taking everything. I want to come to you. You can have everything. I'll sign you the house. Please come get me."

I asked, "Do you mean right now? I can't just come over. What happened? I thought you didn't want to come."

She said, "No I changed my mind. Please come get me."

I said, "I'll talk it over with my husband and call you back in an hour." Then I got up and went to the bathroom. The phone rang again. My husband took the phone and said, "Oh, hello Betty." Then he handed the phone to me.

Betty told me that $500 in cash had gone missing. Elsa was very upset and they were looking for it all over the house. There were other "little" things too. I asked about the doctor's visit. Betty said, yes that she had gone to the doctor and that he was sending someone over on Monday to evaluate her in her own home to see what should be done next. I asked Betty about the forms that she was going to send me. She said she had told me that she would send them after the doctor's visit. I told her that I remember her promising to send the forms the day after Columbus Day. I asked, "Did Ruth have anything to do with me not getting the forms?" She said no and that Ruth was coming in right now. Could I hold on to talk to her? I said yes.

Pretty soon Ruth was on the phone. We talked for a long time. She told me about the doctor's visit and some of the other things that had occurred lately. When I asked her directly, "What has occasioned this crisis this morning, she said, "Maybe it has something to do with me pretending to call the police yesterday." Then she explained how she and Betty had searched the house for the $500, and when they couldn't find it anywhere, Ruth went to the phone and pretended to call the police. Elsa had apparently gone ballistic. She kept worrying about the police, and when they didn't show up, Ruth told her that they might be busy with an emergency, and that they might come by later.

Suddenly it became quite clear to me why Elsa suddenly wanted to come to me. First of all, she didn't want to be home when the doctor's representative was coming on Monday, and second, she is deathly afraid of the police.

Ruth suggested I put off coming to get Elsa till after the doctor's representative had seen her. I said I would talk it over with my family and call Elsa back.

I skyped my uncle in Germany, talked it over with my husband and called my daughter Lisa who offered to go to Claremont with us. My uncle called Elsa and asked her repeatedly whether she was sure about me coming to get her. Together we decided that we would go down that afternoon and bring her back. I called Elsa and asked her again, "Are you sure? If I have to make another trip to your house, you are coming with us. Don't change your mind once we are down there."

"No, no, I'm not going to change my mind. I want to come live with you."

"Okay then, we will be there this evening. Then we will bring you to Fairfield tomorrow."

By one o'clock we were on the road.

We got there around eight o'clock and stopped to buy pizza. Ruth opened the door for us, and Elsa was already in bed. After Ruth left, Elsa got up and ate two large slices of pizza and drank a glass of wine with us. We noticed that she had already packed a plastic bag with some clothes and underwear. Her phone book and checkbook were also in the bag. She was obviously still planning to come with us. I called a locksmith for a Sunday morning appointment to change the locks. There were so many keys floating around, that I was worried we wouldn't be able to establish who had entered the house if anything were missing when (or if) we got back.

Sunday, November 18 around 8:30 AM, when we arrived, Betty and Ruth (plus Woody, the dog) were already there. There was great excitement. Elsa was sitting up in bed declaring repeatedly, "I'm going nowhere! That's it!" She didn't want to eat or take her pills, and was yelling like crazy. Ruth and Betty were trying to calm her down, and that made it only worse. The telephone rang, and it was the locksmith. He wanted to know where the house was. He arrived a few minutes later. We let him change the locks (It took about an hour). In the meanwhile, the drama in the bedroom continued.

While I was in the living room, Ruth had called Gabi, and now they wanted me to talk to her. She asked me, "Marianne, what do they want me to do from here in Germany?" I told her it wasn't my idea to call her. I gave the phone back Ruth, "Here, Gabi wants to know why you called her." More yelling. Elsa got the phone, yelled at Gabi, "I'm going nowhere," and hung up.

A little later, Jupp called to try to remind Elsa that she was the one who wanted me to come get her and that she had promised not to change her mind this time. Elsa hung up on him, too.

I finally had had it and asked everyone to leave the room. I could just imagine how Elsa must have reacted to all of us at once trying to make her realize that the decision had been made, and she would have to live with it. Betty finally got her to accept a little food and her meds and then they left the bedroom. Betty went out to talk to my husband and Lisa while I stayed with Elsa who was still not calm. She absolutely insisted that she was not going with us. I told her that I was not leaving without her. "We'll take you with us for a visit. If you aren't happy with us, we'll bring you back in two weeks." Elsa finally relented.

Ruth came back in for a tearful goodbye (Ruth was the one crying; Elsa was unaffected)

Eventually the three people, the locksmith, Betty and Ruth, left.

Elsa got up and led us through the house to see what had to be taken with us. She said, "Take the Hummels and anything you want." We packed up a few more clothes and shoes. I found some more pictures and some paperwork. We looked for her billfold, but that was nowhere to be found. Her red handbag was hanging over the headboard, but it was empty, so we didn't take it. Suddenly Elsa must have realized that we were serious, so she went back to bed and wrapped herself tightly in the covers.

Lisa and I went in. I gently removed the coverlet and then the top sheet. I folded it up. Elsa asked, "What are you doing?" I said that we were taking her bedding with us so she would have a familiar feeling in my house. Again, she said that she wasn't going. Then I removed the contour sheet out from under her. Lisa was talking to Elsa the whole time. After I had the sheets folded we also took her pillow and got the car ready. At that point Elsa realized that she could no longer resist us. Willingly, but with some physical difficulty, she got into the car, wearing her nightgown, a robe and my Minnie Mouse bozo. Since she didn't want to put her clothes on, we were willing to take her just like that. We put her walker into the trunk. Soon we were on our way.

The trip went surprisingly well until it got dark. We even stopped at an In and Out Burger in Bakersfield. Elsa ate a whole hamburger and fries meal, plus half of Lisa's fries. As soon as it got dark though, Elsa began to worry that we didn't know where we were going. She insisted that this was the wrong way to get to her house. From five to seven o'clock it was a very stressful trip. Elsa's yammering almost became too much for my usually calm husband. When we arrived, she was, of course, exhausted. She ate a slice of pizza and shortly went to bed.

Lisa and I organized the medications and soon called it a night. She would be back tomorrow after work.

Monday, November 19, This day started with great hue and cry and ended with everybody happy.

The first thing she said when she woke up was, "I want to go home." When I answered, "You are home, Elsa," she got mad. She told me that some people had taken her out of her house and now she didn't know where she was. She wanted me to tell her who she could call to take her home. She even talked about calling the police. She looked around our house and told me that I must have stolen all the things I had in my house. Surely, I couldn't have paid for all the things I have. I told her that my husband and I had worked hard and earned everything we have. She just shook her head. Mostly she repeated, "I want to go home," over and over again. She was up and around and still kept repeating that. I decided not to react and went to make her a breakfast. When she wanted to go out to smoke a cigarette, I told her to wait with the smoking until she had taken her pills and had her breakfast, I placed the coffee and food and her pills on the patio table and left. Soon all the food was gone. She accused me of stealing her cigarettes. When I showed her the package in the pocket of her walker and offered her one, she said, "You're mean."

I went inside and set a yeast dough for a Streusselkuchen (a crumb cake with a yeast base and apple topping). I knew that this was a favorite. Then I e-mailed my uncle to turn Skype on. I couldn't wait to see what she would tell him. Well, it turned out that they had a yelling match. Lisa arrived just as Elsa was yelling "Shut up!" at the computer screen. Finally, she walked away. When my uncle and I were telling a few jokes and laughing, she came back and got mad. She told him, "Shut up!" a few more times before we finished skyping. Lisa couldn't stay and my husband had to leave for his SIR's meeting, so for about two hours I was alone with Elsa. We got a few things out of our system. It helped, though, when I let her smoke another cigarette outside. The weather was quite warm and it was very pleasant on the patio. I brought a nice liverwurst sandwich and another cup of coffee. She still wanted to go home, but we talked about that it couldn't happen today. I made a calendar and showed her that she would stay at least two weeks. I called Betty to see whether we could depend on her to come back to care for Elsa. I told her that I was trying to make a deal with Elsa for a two-week trial period, but that could only work if I could depend on someone being there. She said she would.

I showed Elsa the two-week calendar I printed out. She argued about the "Bank Business" entry. "What bank business? I don't have bank business." I reminded her that all she had was one dollar and that she had wanted to go to the bank about her account. She couldn't grasp that and kept mumbling, so I dropped that subject. I called the Senior Center to let them know that I had a family emergency and wouldn't be able to come in on Tuesday.

I baked the streusselkuchen. It was done just in time when Lisa came back. Elsa was happy to see Lisa and even more happy to see the piece of streusselkuchen and a fresh cup of coffee. She also took her afternoon pills without too much commotion. Lisa kept Elsa entertained. My husband came back and I started to cook dinner. I made a delicious chicken ala king and some schnitzels. James, one of our grandsons came over for dinner, so the five of us had a good time. Elsa told Lisa about our two-week deal. Apparently, she had reconciled herself to the situation. Kathy came by in the evening and had a nice long conversation with Elsa.

Tuesday, November 20 this day was much better.

My husband went golfing. While she was still in bed, Elsa and I looked at my mother's photograph album. She ate her breakfast (scrambled egg, toast, and fried potatoes) and took her pills. When I skyped my uncle, she wasn't interested though. I think she felt embarrassed about yesterday's yelling match. She finally did peek in and say a quick hello to him. Lunch went okay, and later we all finished off the streusselkuchen. Lisa came over, and we were talking when my husband came back around two o'clock. She went shopping and bought some hair-dye for Elsa. She also brought a shower stool so Elsa could safely take a shower. I invited her for a good goulash meal which I was planning to cook for that evening. Lisa came back for dinner. All in all, it was a pretty good day. We even worked together on a pair of foot warmers I was crocheting. After a long day, I sat down at the computer to play some solitaire. It was around 9PM. Suddenly, Elsa wanted her phone book. I told her I was tired and not getting up now. She got somewhat abusive, but when she noticed that I was really not jumping up right away, she went to bed.

Wednesday, November 21 I had a hair appointment at 9 AM, so my husband promised to stay home.

When he noticed that the envelope with two checks he had put by his phone was gone, he realized that the noise he heard in the night was

241

Elsa moving around the house. He looked in her room, but couldn't find the envelope with the checks. I went in her room and noticed that a large manila envelope was lying on her night table. I took it, and sure enough, it was the one I had prepared for a friend with a picture and two CD's. The check envelope was also in the manila envelope as well as the contents of one of my purses. I gave the stuff to my husband and left for my hair appointment. I got home around eleven o'clock, but Elsa still hadn't eaten any breakfast. I fixed her a plate and put it in front of her, so she ate and took her pills with a cup of coffee. Then Lisa came over with her little granddaughter Kimmy, and we all (including uncle and his wife over Skype) had a good time watching the baby. Later in the afternoon, Lisa took the baby home and we just hung out until dinner. I had some yeast dough left over, so I made another streusselkuchen. My husband went to get some Kentucky Fried Chicken. We ate and then looked at some pictures on the computer. We reminisced about Germany. Elsa went to bed around 8:30. My husband and I went to bed around 11PM. At 12:15 I heard Elsa walking around. She was in the kitchen leaning over the snack bowl. She was surprised to see me. I put her back in bed and put a second quilt over her. I noticed that she had a baggie with three Bayer aspirins on her night table. That was the baggie from my purse which is still missing. Since I use my fanny pack for my ID's and money, there wasn't anything much in that purse except some theater tickets. I offered her a sleeping pill, but she didn't take it. Fine, but I told her not to get up anymore or smoke in the room during the night. I told her, "You can smoke tomorrow," and went to bed.

Thursday, November 22, 2007 When I got up at 7:30 AM, she was still in bed.

I looked for my purse, but it's not out in the open where I could find it. I made Elsa a cup of coffee, and then I made her a scrambled egg and heated up a cinnamon roll. She only nibbled on it and didn't take her pills either. She got up and went to the bathroom. Then she went back to bed. Around 9:00 I heard her yelling her usual "O wei, o wei." What I suspected had happened. She was sitting on the toilet, but had dropped a couple of turds on the carpet. Fortunately, it was not diarrhea. I picked it up and cleaned up the spot. She went back to bed, but had to get up and do more business in the bathroom a few minutes later. Then she went back to bed.

When she was finally through with her bathroom duties, I talked her into a nice shower. Lisa had bought a shower stool, and we had a flexible hose for the shower head, so the clean-up went very well. She washed her hair, and later took another nap.

For Thanksgiving I made a nice dinner. Lisa, Kathy, plus our granddaughters, Kaala and Janine came to eat with us. Elsa was okay with the girls there. She visited and then went to bed early.

Friday, November 23, 2007 Thanksgiving Dinner at Lisa's house! The morning and afternoon went on uneventfully.

We skyped with my uncle, and she talked with him a little. When we got ready to go to Lisa's house, Elsa didn't want to go. We got her dressed, and she got into the car, but she complained all the way over there.

There were lots of family members, and Elsa was a little overwhelmed, but she sat in the living room and admired the big TV. Kevin and Ted took her outside to smoke several times, but she didn't eat much (only a little bread and some spinach dip). After taking some pictures we went home around 8:00. Her evening routine has been to go to bed, rest for a little while and then come shuffling out for a cigarette. Then she sits with us for a while, smokes another cigarette and goes back to bed. We had been taking the knobs off the stove and taking them upstairs with us because in her own house she turns the burner on the gas stove on to light her cigarette. But in our house, the knobs turn on the gas without lighting it unless you turn it past a certain point. Elsa hasn't figured out how to do this yet. She simply lets the gas escape. I'm worried that she would let the gas out and then perhaps try to light the cigarette with her lighter. The escaped gas is likely to flare up! I was beginning to worry more and more about her cigarette smoking because of the fire hazard. We installed an additional smoke alarm directly over her bed.

Saturday, November 24, 2007 Elsa slept late but took her pills and had breakfast without a problem.

When I was making Elsa's bed, I noticed a little bump under her pillow. I checked, and there was my purse! When I asked Elsa how my purse got under her pillow, she insisted that it was her purse. Actually, it was a purse that my mother had given me. Perhaps it was familiar to her. Anyway, I didn't make a fuss about it and simply removed it. Elsa did not comment.

Our daughter Vivienne and granddaughter Leah spent a few hours with us today. We skyped my uncle, and I even took a movie of Elsa and my uncle talking with each other over Skype. Leah and Elsa got along fine. Leah seems to have a lot of empathy for people who need help. After

Viv and Leah left, we had a good dinner, and the rest of the evening went okay.

Sunday November 25, 2007 Elsa slept very late again.

I think she gets up at night and roams the house. She had breakfast and took her pills. Lisa came over around dinner. My husband went to get Chinese food, but Lisa didn't want any. Elsa ate a huge plateful. Then she went to lie down for a little while.

Suddenly she came out and declared, "You have to go buy me some cigarettes." I told her we don't "have to" do anything. Lisa looked harshly at me. I explained that a person can get a lot more out of me with a nice "Please."

Anyway, Lisa and I discussed shopping with Elsa for a while. Finally, Elsa wondered how she could pay us. I said, "You can write me a check, and then whenever you need something, we can take it out of the money." That was fine. I wrote a $100 check out of her checkbook, and she signed it. Lisa and I then went to look for the kind of cigarettes she wanted. Long's Drugs didn't have them. The smoke shop near Raley's was closed, and Raley's didn't have them. We tried Rite-Aid, but they didn't have the right brand, either. Lisa called Dad to see if Elsa would take some other brand. She said, anything is fine, so we bought a pack of Pall Mall's.

Elsa was so happy when we came back. Right away, she lit one up and went outside. I also got the crocheted bed socks finished for her. She was happy to wear them to bed, but I don't know whether she kept them on. Doesn't matter, she doesn't really get cold feet.

She went to sleep around 8PM, but got up again around 10:30 to declare me crazy for still sitting at my computer. She thought we should all be in bed already. She went outside to smoke another cigarette. Then we all went to bed around 11:30.

Monday, November 26, 2007 Elsa got up around 9:30.

I brought coffee, a roll, a scrambled egg and a bowl of applesauce with her pills to her bed. She ate her breakfast and then got up to go outside to smoke a cigarette. I noticed that five cigarettes were already missing out of the pack.

I baked another Streusselkuchen, and my husband started a pea soup. Elsa was sitting on the lawn pulling weeds. I took a picture and was about to e-mail it my uncle when he skyped me. We talked for a few minutes because he was about to get his weekly massage.

My husband left (with some Streusselkuchen) to pick up Lisa and drop her off at the bus stop. Lisa is spending the next two weeks in San Francisco for training as a tour guide.

Tuesday, November 27, 2007 My husband went golfing.

Elsa stayed in bed, and I went to the Senior Center where I give computer classes. I left hot coffee, her medicine and breakfast for her. I came back between classes to see whether she was okay in the house. Then I returned at 1:15. She then got up and spent some time in the yard. Elsa told me that she was ready to sign the forms to put me on her bank account, so I made an appointment for 2PM the next day. She had lunch. Later my husband came home from his golf game, and we had Schnitzel for dinner. The day was uneventful.

Wednesday, November 28, 2007 I stayed home all day.

Elsa refused to get up until 2PM. I called the bank to cancel the appointment. Elsa was then quite fine until Ruth called. After their conversation, Elsa wanted her house keys. I had overheard her telling Ruth that she would send her a key. I refused, and quite an argument started. She wanted to know why I didn't want Ruth in her house, "There must be a reason!" Remembering the e-mail from Ruth, I agreed, "Yes, there is a reason." Elsa wanted to know it, so I said, "I have a reason, but I'm not going to tell you because I don't want to hurt your feelings." I'm sure Elsa would be devastated if she read what her "friend" had said about her. This is the e-mail that started all the changes and hullabaloo with the New Will and all.

My husband went bowling, but I didn't go. I just couldn't leave Elsa. Later Lisa called. Her training is going well, and she's having a good time in San Francisco.

Thursday, November 29, 2007 Elsa got up around 10AM.

I had already given her pills, coffee, and a nice breakfast. Betty called to tell her that the check from Germany had arrived. She then called back after she had taken it to the PO. I told her that Elsa will probably not be coming back to Claremont. It seemed that she was settling in.

My uncle skyped us, but Elsa couldn't concentrate on anything beside her money. She kept saying she never got the money from Germany. Then she said the bank should send her the information about how much she has in the bank. When my uncle tried to tell her to put my name on her account so that I could be more helpful, she kept saying "No" or "Why should I?" or later, "I don't know, I don't know what you are talking about." He was quite upset, and sent her an e-mail. I printed it with his explanation of the word "Vollmacht=Power of Attorney" and why I need her to sign me on the account. I hope she gets it. She later went outside to smoke wearing only her flimsy nightgown. I brought a warm pair of pants (mine) and put them on her. A short time later, she was wearing her own pants, and mine were folded up on the couch. Her agility and strong will is amazing! She spends a lot of time sitting on the lawn picking weeds. I am somehow uneasy about this, but she tells me that she is not cold and she likes to do this.

Friday, November 30, 2007 Today was a peaceful day.

My friend Gertrude came over with her dog, Roxie. We will be keeping Roxie for a week over Christmas and wanted to get her acquainted with the house. Elsa took to the dog right away. Gertrude invited us to her boat for the Christmas tree lighting and boat parade in the Suisun Marina. She also offered to come over and keep Elsa company when we needed her to.

Saturday, December 1, 2007 What difference!

After breakfast, my uncle skyped us again. Elsa and he had a hair-raising fight! I had gone to the bank and discovered that the Power of Attorney written in June was useless. It only becomes valid if Elsa becomes incapacitated as confirmed by at least two doctors. (I still haven't told Sherry about it.) I told him the bad news about the useless Power of Attorney. My uncle wanted Elsa to pay me, but Elsa didn't think she needed to pay me. He suggested $2000 a month, and I thought she would go ballistic. He kept trying to tell her to pay me, and she kept telling him to shut up. Rather than get loud with her, I spent most of the day upstairs. Her mail, including the check from Germany arrived, but I didn't even look at it. I just handed it to her and went back upstairs. Just before 5 o'clock, I fixed her a nice hot meal of egg noodles and goulash. Then we told her that her dinner was on the table and we were going out for a couple of hours. We really enjoyed being on the boat with Gertrude. Her husband was home nursing a terrible pain in his leg, and the other two couples that had been invited had other plans so there were just three of us. When we got home around 7 o'clock, Elsa was truly angry and hungry. She hadn't eaten and kept wanting to know why I wasn't talking to her. I told her I just didn't want to get loud and have a fight, so I was avoiding her. Around 10 o'clock, she came out and asked my husband for a piece of bread. I knew she was hungry, but I was determined that she would have to ask me nicely if she needed something.

Sunday, December 02, 2007 Today was again completely different. After thinking how mean I had been, I made her breakfast and coffee and brought it to her bed. She got out of bed around noon, and from then on it was quite pleasant. She signed her check from Germany over to me. "Here, now if I need something, you can buy it for me," she explained. If she decides to stay with us I plan to establish a separate checking account with the money she gives me that can be used for her personal needs and a helper for a couple of hours a day. This way I won't feel taken advantage of. We talked about going to the bank tomorrow to find out her balance. She also wanted to buy some personal items.

Monday, December 03, 2007 What a day! At 4:45 AM (!) Elsa was making noise downstairs.

I went down to see what she wanted. I thought maybe she was hungry and looking for something to eat. When she saw me, she yelled, "Where are my cigarettes? I want my cigarettes!" I told her she had a package that still had at least 10 cigarettes. Besides, I didn't want her to smoke in the house in the middle of the night. We yelled at each other for a few moments until I realized what I was doing, and then I said firmly but quietly, "Go to bed!" She grumbled, but she went to bed. I told her if she insisted on getting all her cigarettes, I would no longer bring her breakfast to bed, and she would not be able to sleep during the day anymore. I wanted her to sleep through the night.

My husband got up around seven o'clock, and Elsa got up around 8:30. He gave her a cup of coffee. I got up at 8:50 and fixed more coffee. Then I went to buy some croissants. We had a pretty decent breakfast, and I thought we would go to the bank to take care of her business. She didn't want to go. I was going to buy her a hamburger and let her do some shopping, but she didn't want to go. She searched through her address book and found the page where I had written that I received money from her. She demanded her money back and wanted to know why she had given me money. When I explained that she had given me the money as part of the payment for her care here and to provide things she needed, she got very abusive and demanded to be taken back home. Yelling several times throughout the day, "I want to go home now!" she did not let up. My husband has finally had it and told her that we would take her back on Friday. I wasn't sure that would be a good idea.

We had enchiladas for dinner and an apple cake for dessert. After complaining about a stomachache, Elsa drank a cup of tea my husband offered her. Then she went to bed.

Tuesday, December 04, 2007 I woke up at 4:30 AM and couldn't go back to sleep until I had a big cry.

Not only the difference of opinion with my husband regarding my aunt, but also the grief over my friend Xochitl's sudden death, kept me very sad and awake. Finally, I dozed off, but I had to get up because I had classes at the Senior Center. I was grateful to see it rain, so my husband couldn't go golfing. I put out the pills and told him what she liked for breakfast, then I left. Classes went very well.

When I got home, Elsa was cheerful. We had a nice lunch together. My husband had made some delicious egg salad, and she scarved it up like crazy—me too! I called the 800 number for Social Security for an appointment. We need to get Elsa's Medicare card replaced and her address changed. I also called the Area Agency on Aging and left a message about my Power of Attorney. I don't know whether Elsa will agree to making a new PoA, but I have to try.

She was talking about getting some new hair dye, so I offered to take her shopping. She actually got dressed and let me take her. I went to the Dickson Hill Raley's Store because I was hoping she would see the WaMu bank and want to go in. I had brought along her Pass ID and her checkbook and asked whether she would like to go to the bank, but she said no. We bought the hair dye and a new eyebrow pencil. She actually wanted to look around the store and touch all kinds of things, but I got her out of there as quickly as possible after I caught her opening a jar of cream and dipping her finger in it. When we got home, she grumbled to my husband that going shopping with me wasn't any fun, "She just gets what she needs and then leaves the store." She's right! I've never really liked trolling for bargains, etc.

My husband made a great dinner of fish filets, delicious fried potatoes, salad and peas. We also had a glass of wine. Later we had dessert, and then she went to bed around 9 PM.

Wednesday, December 5, 2007 What a day! Damn!

I don't even know where to start. Ruth called before Elsa even woke up. I told her that Elsa really wants to come back to Claremont. I asked her straight up whether she would be willing to take on the responsibility if I brought her back. She said absolutely not, yet she was not willing to tell Elsa this. After she had some coffee and a little Danish, she colored her hair. My uncle and I skyped for a little while, but Elsa refused to talk with him. She kept saying that he has no idea. Because my uncle got another call and Elsa wanted something, stopped skyping. She shampooed her hair, and then I helped her put some curlers in her hair. Then we had good hot dogs for lunch. Things seemed to be going alright when she suddenly asked why we didn't take her home. She reminded us that we "promised" on Monday that we would take her home on Friday. I tried to tell her that we didn't "promise" anything. What we had told her is that I would see whether someone in Claremont would be there to receive her, and besides, it is only Wednesday today. We still have another day to try to figure it out. She got extremely abusive and perseverated on "but you promised." I took a couple of videos of her tantrum. She threatened that she would sleep outside and not eat anything anymore. Then she would get a cold and die. Her tantrum lasted nearly an hour. At two o'clock I went to Rosanna's for a Kaffeeklatsch with the German ladies, including Gertrude who promised to come over with Roxie to sit with Elsa while we went bowling.. When I got back home, I took a nap. Elsa's tantrums were really wearing me out.

I bowled lousy and we lost all four games. I felt like I was dragging a box of rocks around with me. When we got home at 8:45, the doors were locked because Gertrude had left already. Elsa called me from her bed. She wanted another cigarette. She told me that the lady with the dog was visiting for quite a long time. She was trying to be all sweet. When I told her that she had really treated me like shit this afternoon, and that I was still angry, she wondered what she had done. She asked "What did I do? I'm nice to everybody. I don't get mad at anybody." I didn't explain. Those tantrums are producing too much tension in our home. At this point, I'm ready to do whatever I can to return her to Claremont. I'll try Social Services tomorrow. Perhaps they can make some arrangements with their counterpart in Claremont. I just don't care about trying to save her money and her house anymore. I wasn't getting anything out of her estate, anyway. Back in Claremont, she will just have to pay for her own care.

Thursday, December 06, 2007 Calling for Help! Early in the day before Elsa got up:

1. IHSS 784 xxxx confusing machine
2. Public Authority 438-xxxx Michael, very nice and helpful
    a. LA Public Authority, 1-877-565-xxxx to report that I'm taking her back
    b. State Info line 211 ask for Public Guardian or State Conservator Office
    c. suggested I call IHSS 784-xxxx to see what they can do
3. called 211, young man gave me 1-xxx-300-xxxx to make local call to Claremont

4. Called 1-xxx-300-xxxx in the Claremont Area, a girl told me that I need to make a call to Elder Abuse Hotline (1-877-477-xxxx) and report "Self Neglect" before I can drop her off. Actually, I feel that this is a little over the top.
5. I did call 1-877-477-xxxx but I got a message that this number can't be reached from this area
6. Called our local Adult Protective Services 1-800-850-xxxx and left a message
7. Called 784-xxxx talked to a very nice young lady. She told me to call LA Area Agency on Aging, 1-213-738-xxxx for LA County. They might provide MSSP (Case Management)
8. Called 1-213-738-xxxx, left a message to assign a case manager to my aunt.

Elsa woke up at 9:30 and called me that she is ice-cold. She had slept on top of the covers all night and only covered herself with one blanket. Her bed actually has nice warm flannel sheets, lots of pillows, and two thick coverlets. I told her if she had slept between the two flannel sheets, she wouldn't have been cold. She wanted me to hold her hand, but I reminded her of how she treated me yesterday and walked away.

I made coffee, toast and a scrambled egg for her, and put her meds on the plate, too. My husband brought it to her bed. At 10:10, she walked out to smoke a cigarette. She now has four packs left in her carton.

This turned into a very interesting day. While my uncle and I were skyping, Elsa came out and actually had a fairly decent conversation with him. Then I had to get ready for the Christmas luncheon at the Senior Center. I told Elsa that we'd be back at one o'clock, and that we would have Kathy and Ted over for dinner. By the time we came back, Elsa had cleaned up the kitchen and gotten herself dressed. I made scalloped potatoes and a pineapple upside down cake. My husband went shopping and then made a couple of meatloaves.

We invited Roman for dinner, and he brought a couple of bottles of wine. While I finished up the dinner, my husband, Roman and Elsa started on the wine. Around 6:30, Kathy, Ted and Janine arrived. Kaala was also expected, but she had to go to work. We had a lovely dinner with wine. We had coffee and the cake for dessert. While I was cleaning up, Elsa helped. In her well-intentioned effort to put the remainder of the cake in the refrigerator (even though I had asked her to leave it on the stove), she lost her balance and tried to find something to hold on to. It was a good thing that I was standing right behind her because she reached out and hit the cake pan which went down with a bang. The Pyrex exploded into tiny little shards and our delicious cake became instant garbage. Elsa stood paralyzed among the shards and asked, "What happened?" Kathy came to help me move her to the other room. My husband came to clean up the mess while I finished washing the rest of the dishes.

Elsa went to bed around 9 o'clock, and our company left around 10 o'clock. Around 11 o'clock, Elsa came out and showed me her empty pack of cigarettes. She asked (very politely) for another pack, so my husband handed me one. I pretended to get it from behind her ear and said, "Let's see if there's another one behind the other ear." Elsa got a good kick out of that, and we both laughed. After she had a smoke she went back to bed.

Friday, December 8, 2007 All Hell broke loose today.

Still assuming that Elsa would live with us and not return to Claremont any time soon, my husband brought a Change of Address form from the Post Office. After breakfast and Elsa had settled into her routine, I showed her the filled out form. All she had to do was sign it.

"I'm not signing anything unless I read it, and I can't find my glasses," she added.

"Here are your glasses," my husband handed them to her.

"After I've had my cigarette!" She grabbed her stuff (including the P.O. forms) and went on the porch with her walker.

Some time later she came back inside. "I'm not going to sign this. I want my mail at home."

"But, Elsa. It would be so much more convenient to receive your mail here. At your house it's probably stacking up, and then someone has to mail it up here."

"I want to go home!" She started yelling.

I was a little surprised at her immediate reaction. Yesterday has gone so smoothly that I thought she had begun to feel more at home. "I haven't been able to reach anybody to take care of you in Claremont," I tried to convince her.

"I don't need anybody to give care of me. I have friends," she shouted at me.

"Elsa, be reasonable. Stay with us till after Christmas. Your house will be alright for a couple of weeks, and I'll have time to make better arrangements for your care," I was beginning to whine.

"You don't have to do anything! I want to go home! You told me you would take me home on Friday! I'm ready to go!" she yelled.

I went to her room, and sure enough, her stuff had been packed into two shopping bags. She had even stripped her own flannel bed sheets off the bed and rolled them up in a bag. She stubbornly kept yelling, "I want to go home." By three o'clock she still hadn't calmed down.

"Okay, let's go! We're leaving at four o'clock," my husband suddenly appeared in the room and firmly repeated, "at four o'clock we're getting in the car and taking her back."

"Love, I haven't been able to make any firm plans for her," I reminded him. "It's Friday, nothing will be open tomorrow."

"Ruth is at home. She talked to her only yesterday. Betty is ready to start coming back for a couple of hours a day. You've done all you could. I can't stand watching you being treated like a slave. We're leaving in an hour!" my husband was serious.

For an hour I busily got ready to make another eight-hour trip to Claremont while my mind was racing with mixed emotions. I felt a certain sense of relief combined with resentment, guilt, love, concern and anger.

Leaving at four in the afternoon caused us to drive most of the trip in the dark. As we passed Bakersfield and approached the grapevine, Elsa noticed the first road sign pointing to Los Angeles.

"Los Angeles! I don't want to go to Los Angeles! I don't live in Los Angeles. You don't know where you're going! Turn around! I'm not going to Los Angeles!" She yelled and yelled.

My husband kept still. I said, "Elsa, we will be going to Claremont, but this is the highway to get there."

"No, you're just taking the long way on purpose. You just want to torture me!" she was not to be calmed. "You're taking the long way just to make me mad!"

For over a half hour she kept up this harangue until we turned on I-210 toward Pasadena. "See, Elsa, now we are on the road toward Claremont."

"You took the long way on purpose. You're mean!" she had to get that point in even though she finally realized we were heading in the right direction.

"Here is the cell phone, I've dialed Ruth. Talk to her and tell her you're coming home," I handed the phone to her.

"She's probably asleep now," she didn't want to accept the phone, but I held it to her ear. "Hi, Honey! I'm coming home." A few moments of silence and then, "We're on the way right now. I'll see you in the morning. Bye."

I was relieved, "See, Ruth is home, and your life will be back to normal. I was just trying to help when you wanted me to come get you that day."

Elsa just grumbled something about the long trip. She seemed surprised that we actually returned her to her familiar home. I asked her to pay me for services rendered and handed her the checkbook. She laughed at me and said, "I'm not paying you. For what?" I really hadn't expected her to pay me for the trips and the extra expenses incurred in her behalf, but by this time, I was playing her game and just wanted to confirm my suspicions. She simply expected me to do things for her without compensation—now or in the future.

At midnight, my husband and I fell into bed at a motel. Elsa was in her own house again.

The next morning we drove by to see whether she was alright. We notified her doctor and talked to Betty. Then we drove home.

A few months later, Betty called me several times with concerns about the new will Elsa had made with a new lawyer. Betty had been fired by Ruth, and things were not going well. She gave me the name and e-mail of the new lawyer, so I e-mailed her to ask about the current status. She wrote me that I was no longer welcome in Elsa's affairs. From the lawyer's letter, I learned that Elsa had told her that I had initiated the changes. She had told this new lawyer that I had arrived one day with paperwork and forced her to sign it, and that I had come to take her out of her house. I was therefore not to interfere in her life anymore. In a rebuttal letter, I reiterated the story of how I got involved and how Elsa had initiated the changes.

One day Betty called me from the Claremont police station. She had tried to visit Elsa, so Ruth called the police. I spoke to one of the officers and tried as briefly as possible to explain the situation. He advised me to try calling my aunt on the phone. If I couldn't get through, I was to call him back. I tried three times within an hour to call her house. Even though the phone was picked up two times, no one answered. The third time, the phone just kept ringing until I finally hung up. Then I called the officer back. He promised to go over to check if everything was on the up-and-up. Betty had told him of her suspicions that he needed to follow up on, especially since I couldn't get anyone to answer the phone.

A couple of hours later, the officer called me back to assure me that even though my aunt appeared to be very frail and in bed, she was clean and coherent. The house was in order, and a nurse was preparing something in the kitchen. He promised to stop by every now and then to check on her.

A few months later I was notified that my aunt Elsa had passed away peacefully in her own home in the presence of the hospice folks on March 9, 2010.

I did not receive a copy of the Revocation of the June 2007 Amendment to Elsa's Living Trust until several months later. Ruth had replaced my uncle and my cousin as the heir. Not surprisingly, I was specifically named as the one who caused Elsa to agree to the 2007 Amendment "under duress." I was also accused of "removing" seven Hummel figurines. It was clear that the new attorney hired by Ruth believed the stories my Aunt Elsa told about me. No one ever asked me whether the stories were true.

"Oh, what a wicked web we weave when first we practice to deceive!" I guess someone should have told her when she was a little girl that she wasn't allowed to lie.

A Story of Hardship and Survival [11]

Part one -- Peter and Maria Hammes

"You know Luz, I haven't been feeling well since my baby died last year," a very pale Elisabeth explained to her friend Lucille in 1835.

"I noticed that you haven't done much baking lately," Lucille answered. The two friends had come to the Backes (a public bake house with two brick ovens) along with three other villagers to decide their starting times for the next day's baking. As customary, each woman had carved a distinctive design into a tiny piece of wood and placed it in a bag. "Come here, Tilly," called Lucille to a small girl playing nearby. "You get to draw the lots." The order of the draw determined the order of the starting times of the following day's baking.

After chatting for a few more minutes, the women went home to prepare the dough for the next day's baking. In a wooden trough, specially reserved for bread-making, a large amount of flour was heaped high and shaped into a crater. The sourdough leavening saved from the previous week's baking would be mixed with liquid and poured into the hollowed-out spot. Some of the flour was mixed with it and then left to rise. Later, the kneading would begin. The dough had to be kneaded several times and left to rise. That evening, the house always smelled promising. By the next day, the dough would be ready to be shaped into loaves.

The dough, along with enough wood to bake it, was taken in bulk to the Backes. The ovens had to be fired up first. While the fire roared behind the metal doors, there was time to shape several loaves out of the amorphous mass of dough on a rough wooden table. Once the fires in the ovens burned out, scrapers on long sticks were used to remove the cinders, and then the loaves were pushed far back into the hot brick chamber on great paddles. Sometimes there would be a little lump of dough left over; not enough for another loaf of bread but just enough for a small loaf of apple-bread!

A couple of apples were peeled and diced and kneaded into the dough. A bit of sugar (sometimes a kid would be sent home for it) was sprinkled on top of the scored round form before it was placed just inside the oven. There were always plenty of children around to wait for this special treat.

Elisabeth had drawn the first shift. She was up at dawn to drag her sore body to the Backes. By the time Lucille brought her dough and wood to the Backes, appetizing aromas of fresh-baked bread wafted in the air. Elisabeth was handing her seven-year old daughter Liz, a bite of the pungent apple-bread.

"Elisabeth, are you okay? You look terribly pale," Lucille was the midwife in the village and therefore particularly observant about the other women's health. She had already noticed Elisabeth's sad face the day before but didn't want to say anything.

"I think I'm going to have another baby! It's too soon! If I counted right, I'll have the baby in February! I'm not even completely healed from the last one. I just don't know whether I'm ready to manage another one right away. What am I going to do?" Words were tumbling out as Elisabeth was using her flour-stained apron to wipe some tears from her cheeks. She grabbed the paddles and started pulling the baked loaves out of the fire chamber.

"I'll help as much as I can," said Lucille, "but February is always a very cold month around here. Will you be able to keep the house warm enough?" Lucille had spread out her dough on the butcher block counter. Her capable hands kneaded the dough while her thoughts were busy with Elisabeth's problems.

"My husband Peter has been doing quite well in his blacksmith shop. We have brought in plenty of wood for our fireplaces, and the root cellar has plenty of potatoes, turnips and preserves. Also, I've put up a huge crock of sauerkraut and another one of pickled green beans. Our crop was good this year, so we also have plenty of dried peas, beans and lentils. Our chickens are producing eggs, and our cows are giving milk. It's not that we don't have enough food; I'm just feeling weak all the time and have to force myself to go on. I'm just not ready to have another baby!" Elisabeth quickly dried her tears when her little two year old son, Anton, whimpered in his carriage.

Lucille began loading the ovens with blocks of wood. There was no more time to discuss Elisabeth's problems. The fire would have to be started soon and her loaves baked. At least three other women had planned to do their baking that day. "'Bye, Elisabeth, let's talk later."

The familiar metallic sounds from the blacksmith shop told Elisabeth that her husband was working hard. She hoped he had repaired the outhouse today. She had to use the chamber pot until he could put a new seat board in the place of the broken one. What a bother! At least in the outhouse, unpleasant odors blended with the manure pile next to it. Her nose was accustomed to those farm smells, but a chamber pot in the house was something she truly hated to deal with.

"Mommy, Mommy, Anton is grabbing my hair!" Liz screamed. No time for self-pity, she thought as she rushed toward her children.

Elisabeth untangled little Anton from Liz and gave both of them an affectionate pat on the butt and a chunk of apple-bread. Then she put the six freshly baked loaves in the bread box. It was time to prepare the main meal which consisted of a bowl of whey, a gelatin-like by-product from the cottage cheese she had made the day before. There would also be fried potatoes with bits of bacon and a dish of applesauce.

"Peter, I'm really afraid to have this next baby, and I don't know why. We had such high hopes when we got married, and life is so good here, but I feel so weak all the time," Elisabeth told Peter just before Christmas.

"Don't worry, I'm strong enough for both of us," Peter tried to assure her, but inwardly he was wondering what he would do with his two children if Elisabeth died in childbirth. A no-nonsense blacksmith, he had very little empathy for his young wife who seemed to be constantly complaining about her health. "See if Lucille has something to help you."

While January was unseasonably mild, February brought a harsh snow storm. Lucille fought her way through large drifts to be at Elisabeth's side. The baby was due any time now, and Lucille knew that her help was sorely needed. Elisabeth had already spent the past three weeks in bed. Neighbors had been taking care of the two children and brought food, but there was little hope for Elisabeth.

"I baptize you Maria Margaretha," the village priest sadly intoned. Silently he said a prayer for the infant's young mother who had been buried the day before. There was no mother's milk for baby Maria. She was so tiny. Not even the nurturing care of the neighbor women could help the baby now. One week later the tiny body was buried among the many little graves marked with white marble statues of angels. The cemetery was filling up.

A great puzzle settled over the village. What was the secret of death in a time of plenty? No answers came.

The grief of losing his wife and baby in one stormy winter week hit Peter hard. Little Liz and Anton needed a mother! He needed a wife! He could not depend on neighbors forever. His spirits mirrored the dreary weather. As spring arrived with colorful flowers and warm sunshine, his heart began to hope again.

A number of young ladies, dressed up for Easter, had gathered on the village square. Attracted by a particularly vivacious girl from a neighboring village, Peter walked toward the group with his little Anton.

"Oh, how cute! What's his name? How old is he?" Maria Korzelius asked boldly. The other girls tittered.

"Careful, Maria, he's a widower! Probably looking for a new wife," whispered a curly-haired blonde named Magda.

"Well, I'm looking for a husband, so that's a perfect match," whispered Maria to her friend. Turning to Peter she said, "I'm sorry, I didn't mean to be so bold."

Peter smiled, "His name is Anton, and he'll be a great blacksmith like me one day." He tipped his hat and straightened up ever so slightly.

Magda poked Maria with her elbow and whispered, "See, what did I tell you? He's definitely ready to find himself a new wife." All the girls tittered again and in a great flutter of pastel-colored skirts ran into the church for the Easter services.

Little Liz caught up with her father and brother. "Daddy, who was that lady? She's nice! Is she going to be my new Mommy?"

"Hold on, Liz, what makes you think I'm looking for a new mommy?"

"I want one, and she looks nice. You shouldn't be sad anymore, Daddy," Liz expressed what he'd been thinking.

Peter took advantage of the beautiful spring that year and courted Maria. Almost every evening he took time out after a busy day in his shop to walk to Maria's village and meet her family. She welcomed his advances and their wedding took place after the harvest was in. She moved into the house which had been badly neglected for over a year. Before the harsh winter arrived, Peter even repaired the outhouse. The water well in the backyard was given a new pulley, rope and wooden bucket. A new stove was purchased for the kitchen.

Maria brightened up the entire home with her hustle and bustle. At twenty-eight, she was already an accomplished home maker, and doing her chores came easily. In the spring of 1837, she became aware of life stirring within her. Her little Balthasar was born in June. He was a robust little boy and another blacksmith candidate judging by the looks of his strong little arms. The home sparkled with signs of life and joy.

Liz gladly took on the care of the baby while her "new mommy" worked on preserving and storing food for the coming winter. Lucille had helped bring Balthasar into the world and introduced Maria to the women who frequented the Backes. Soon Maria was able to produce the same delicious aromas of freshly baked bread as the rest of the women.

Despite a rather difficult winter, little Philip was born in February 1839 without a hitch. Peter breathed a sigh of relief when Lucille assured him that his third son was a healthy little boy. His family was growing, and life was good. Liz became quite a little caretaker of her three little brothers. Anton grew into a strong young man who would start school in the following year, and the two babies, Balthasar and Philip thrived.

Two years later, baby Johann joined the family in January. Peter prayed that the dark cloud that had hovered over his first family had disappeared forever. His daughter Liz and his four sons gave him plenty of reasons to work diligently in his blacksmith shop.

Bright, strong and energetic, Maria did not anticipate trouble. The village did not receive much news from the outside world. If they had learned of the cholera pandemic moving across Europe, they might have been able to protect and defend themselves. Within the isolated village, now and then a baby got sick and died. It had happened in Peter's own family, but no one suspected that these incidents might be related to the outside world. When little Philip got diarrhea in July of 1842 Maria simply cleaned up the mess. She had no reason to worry.

"Lucille, Philip has been messing his pants for three days now, and he won't eat. What do you think might be wrong?"

"Maria, it's just a "bug" that some kids get," Lucille assured her. "Philip is a strong little boy, and he'll be alright. Just give him some of this tea until his appetite comes back."

"Mommy, I don't feel so good!"

"What? You too, Balthasar?" Maria was exhausted from the constant clean-up. Now both boys were having diarrhea and wouldn't eat. Several other children in the village had become ill.

"Help, help! My little Philip has stopped breathing!" It was a very hot day in July, and Maria's panicky voice rang throughout the sleepy Sunday afternoon village.

"Are we going to die, too?" asked Liz, as she was holding one-year-old Johann. No one knew.

Peter tried hard to remain calm. What was it that was bedeviling his family? Even baby Johann was beginning to show signs of the illness.

"No-o-o-!" The same blood-curdling scream had been heard from other farm houses throughout the village several times in the past week. "All three babies gone!" Several wailing mothers of dead babies had gathered in the street. "What's happening to our children?" Their sobs were accompanied by the frenzied hammering in the blacksmith shop. Sparks of anger and frustration flew off the anvil with each blow of the hammer. Peter was disconsolate; Maria was unaware that she was already carrying another child.

A new spring brought new hope. Life goes on. The baby was coming. Liz and Anton had been spared, but a great sadness had settled upon the village. Maria dragged her swelling body through her chores. The animals, the fields and the vegetable garden had to be tended. Fires had to be kindled. Bread had to be baked and food cooked. The house no longer sparkled.

Little Lorenz was born in the middle of April. Like his brothers, he was robust and likely to become a blacksmith like his father. Maria and Peter dared not hope that this little man would have a future. They clung close to their older children and the new baby.

"Liz, how would you like a little sister?" Maria asked one day.

"What do you mean? Are you going to have another baby?" Liz brightened up.

"Yes, in March we'll have another child, but I don't know whether it will be a boy or a girl," Maria knew it was time to explain the miracle of life to Liz, and this was a good opportunity. They had been busy shelling dried peas in preparation for the winter. There was always so much work to do after the harvest. Liz' capable young hands deftly opened the pods and with one motion of a finger, she rolled the peas into a bowl.

"Do babies grow like these peas?" Liz wanted to know.

"Well, not exactly," Maria was pleased that the moment of truth had arrived. "Let me explain how a woman's body can grow a baby once a man has planted the seed, okay? You've already watched how the bull on Lambert's field has given our cow a calf, so you can understand how a man can give a woman a baby, right?"

Liz nodded. "But you are not a cow, Mom!" A little outrage strained her voice.

"You're right, but there is a certain similarity. A man and a woman start by loving and respecting each other because we have souls; however, we are after all, an animal species. When we are ready to have a family and we want children, then we have the ability to, to..... oh, you know!" Anton had walked in and Maria was suddenly a little embarrassed. Liz nodded with a knowing smile.

"Come on, Anton, grab some peas and help us. We still have a lot of work to do!" Liz quickly changed the subject.

Baby Margaretha arrived in March. It was an early spring and the winter rains had already stopped. With Lorenz thriving, and two older children helping around the house, Maria recovered quickly. Margaretha eagerly nursed at her breast while Peter looked on with a satisfied smile. His heart had begun to heal. Surely, the loss of his first wife and five babies had hardened him, but he and Maria firmly held their family together.

"Maria, this is going to be a lean year. The weather conditions are worrisome. It is planting time, but we need more rain soon." Peter explained one day. "There isn't enough rain to grow the crops."

"Peter, let's pray that our family will stay safe through a difficult year. We'll just eat a little less." Maria tried to put on a brave face despite her heartfelt misgivings.

The summer of 1846 did not provide an abundant harvest. Last year a good crop of wheat had promised plenty of bread for the winter, but this year's crops had remained sparse. Lack of clover and hay threatened the farm animals, and even the usually plentiful potatoes had not supplied the village with enough provisions for the winter. Help from neighboring villages could not be expected because their weather conditions were similar. The whole country was looking toward a difficult winter, but if they were very careful and rationed their reserves, they could sustain their lives.

"Please get me some water from the well, Anton. I need to clean up little Margaretha. She threw up, and her bed is all messy." Maria's heart was beating in fear. This was exactly how baby Johann had begun his illness. She tried hard not to show her frightened eyes to Anton and Liz. "It's probably just the soup I just fed her, Liz."

"Mom, then what is wrong with Lorenz? He didn't eat that soup, and he just pooped all over the floor. It's kind of liquidy."

Maria looked up. "Liquidy? Do you mean he had diarrhea?" Now she stopped disguising her fear. "Come on. We have to wash everything!"

"But, Mom, the well is almost dry. We don't have enough water for cooking. How can we wash everything?" Liz began to cry. Peter walked in.

"What's going on? Anton just came to complain that he had to get water, but he couldn't lower the bucket low enough to get any." Peter's face was stern, and the muscles in his cheeks worked furiously.

"Peter, Lorenz had diarrhea and Margaretha threw up. I'm so afraid. It's just not fair. Why are these babies being punished? Why don't we have fresh water to clean them up?" Maria was overcome with tears. "I can't, I can't!" she stormed at Peter.

Just then Margaretha vomited again. Peter shuddered. The evil had returned to their home.

Two more babies dead! It was impossible. How is a family to survive such tragedy?

In Peter's mind the answer was obvious. Only eleven months later, baby Catharina was born. Her strong cry heralded a fertile spring. Signs of a very good year could be seen everywhere. The animals were thriving and the fields were ready to be tilled and planted. The entire village anticipated an abundant harvest.

"Wow, Mom! This is going to be a lot of work." Liz commented as she watched Anton unload a mountain of cabbages from a wagon.

"Yes, but you should be glad. Remember how we starved last year? This year we'll have lots of sauerkraut and enough food for the winter and even some left over to take to the farmer's market. Now let's get started on our preserves. Maria had already gathered a couple of bushels of blackberries for the delicious jam she planned to put up in jars.

"Mom, what are we going to with all these apples? There must be a ton of them hanging on that tree!"

"We'll peel and slice about half of them. Then we'll thread the slices on this string. When we hang them in the spare room, the apples will dry. When they are good and dry, we can put them in this wooden box your dad made just for this purpose. All winter long, we'll have apples to use for snacking, making apple sauce or even baking an apple cake or two. What do you think of that?" Maria sounded more cheerful than she had for several years. A good harvest meant a comfortable winter and, most of all, enough food for her children. "We'll put the rest of the apples in the root cellar and eat them fresh. Have you seen all the bags of grain we reaped this year, Liz?" Maria asked. "There's plenty of wheat for cakes and rye for bread."

"Do we have to turn the grain into flour ourselves? How can we do that?" Liz was becoming more and more curious about how food was produced.

"Liz, remember when your father took you to the mill in Dommershausen a couple of years ago? The mill has those two huge round stones, remember? This is where the miller grinds the grain into flour. The farmers bring in the rye or wheat in big sacks. After all the grain is ground up into flour, the miller keeps some of it and gives the rest back to the farmer. The miller can then sell flour to the baker who can sell bread to folks who can't do their own baking. This way everybody is happy. I can use the flour to make the dough and bake our own bread in the Backes. If you promise not to get too close to the fire chamber, I'll let you help me with the baking this year. Would you like that?"

Liz was happy. She had a little baby sister, Catharina, who was not throwing up. Anton was spending a lot of time with his father in the blacksmith shop, so he wasn't bothering her. Best of all, she spent lots of time with Maria. Together they prepared the turnips for the molasses and the cabbages for the sauerkraut. Liz especially enjoyed cranking the little machine for cutting the string beans into "French cuts" for the pickled bean salad. Throughout the summer and into the crisp autumn days, the two worked from morning to night preserving the food for the winter. "Are we going to have any more babies?" she asked one day.

"I don't know. I'm not growing one right now. Maybe I won't have any more. It's not completely up to me, you know. Sometimes, a man and a woman just don't have any babies. That's the whole mystery. Maybe one day in the future, doctors and scientists can figure it out, but right now, I have no control over whether I'm going to have a baby or not," Maria explained.

Liz was quiet for a moment. "Maybe my father is afraid of what will happen to his babies, so he doesn't want to give you any more."

"Liz, you might be right, but your father is a good man. He works hard in his shop and in the fields. I don't think he is afraid of anything. It's not his fault that the babies died or that I'm not growing one right now. It's just nature. You will learn that for yourself after you are married. By the way, you're almost nineteen. Have you thought about marriage yet?"

Liz blushed. "Well, there is Gerhard. He tried to kiss me last Sunday after church."

"He's a nice boy, but don't be in too much of a hurry." Maria tried to remain matter-of-fact. She would have to speak with Peter about this budding romance.

"Guess what!" Maria had invited Lucille over for coffee and cake. "I think I'm going to have another baby!"

"You must be the bravest woman I know," Lucille admired Maria. She thought of several mothers who had lost babies in 1842 and 1846 that continued to wallow in their grief. Maria was different. She actually seemed content. "I can't imagine how you can be happy about having another baby."

"I just believe that I'm destined to be a mother of a great family. Who knows what my children and children's children can accomplish some day. Somehow, I believe that the world will be alright. I've heard that some scientists and doctors are beginning to find cures for these terrible illnesses. I'm still strong and young enough to have more babies. With your help, I'll have this next one. I just can't believe that these babies will also be taken away from me."

"Maria, you know you can depend on me. I'll be with you when you are ready to have that baby. Have you picked out a name yet?"

"No. Peter doesn't want any of the boys to be named after him. He joked that there are already enough Peters in his family." Maria smiled at her own joke.

"There's still plenty of time to think of a name. When do you think the baby will be born?" Lucille quickly changed the subject.

"It's due in April. By then the weather should be warming up. It might still be raining a lot, but that's okay. Peter has been very good about keeping the house repaired. He just put a new roof on, and all the windows are nice and tight. He even built a new outhouse after I told him about my hearing that dirty outhouses might have something to do with the babies dying of that terrible disease. He's not completely convinced that they died of a disease that can be caught from one person to another. He still thinks he might be cursed and punished for something. But at least he's willing to listen to me when I tell him about something I've heard from city folks traveling through our village."

"Maria, be careful about what you believe. Those city folks don't know everything, either," Lucille cautioned.

"I know, but they do stop in my little parlor to buy food," Maria reasoned. "You've heard of my little money-making venture, haven't you?"

Lucille nodded. "Yes. I think it's a great idea to offer your parlor as a place to gather on Saturday and Sunday afternoons. City folks traveling through can have a place to rest and have a bite to eat, and village folks have a place to go after church. Do you ever have too many people in your place?"

"No, it's a large parlor which we never use anyway. Liz helps me with the cooking, and Anton takes care of serving the food and cleaning up while little Catharina runs around entertaining the visitors. There are never very many travelers, so it's just perfect," Maria seemed proud of her place. "I'm trying to think of a name to call my place. Do you have any suggestions?"

"Well, this house has almost been like a hospital, and now you are offering your hospitality. Why not call it "Hospese?" Lucille had always had good ideas.

"That's a wonderful name, Lucille! Maybe Peter will make me a nice sign to hang outside. I'm beginning to feel very confident about the future. I even hope this one will be a boy." Wistfully she thought, "Peter deserves another son."

Part two -- Moritz

"Mother, where shall I put these new glasses?" Moritz, now a strapping young man of sixteen, was carrying a wooden crate of beer mugs. It was early November, and the restaurant would be a busy meeting place for the local farmers throughout the winter.

"Those shelves over there behind the bar for the glasses, but don't put them there until they've been washed," Maria answered. "I wish your father were still alive to see how well his family is doing now." Maria wasn't talking to anyone in particular. Moritz had been only seven and his little sister Maria Anna barely four when Peter died. A horse had kicked Peter while he was shoeing it. Anton had called for help right away, but Lucille and the new village medic couldn't save Peter. He had received a fatal blow to the head.

The Hospese restaurant had become the social center of the little village of Macken. Maria's cooking attracted the pickiest eaters. Catherina, who had become a beautiful nineteen-year old blonde, served the guests. Sometimes she had time to play a couple of memorized songs on the harmonium, a small foot-pedaled pipe organ, to delight the diners. Even thirteen-year-old Maria Anna, nicknamed Marieche, was learning the business. She was in charge of keeping the floor swept and the dishes clean when she wasn't busy decorating the tables with fresh flowers or winter foliage.

Liz and her husband Gerhard had moved into the upstairs rooms and helped to maintain the fields and animals. Anton, now thirty-five years old had taken over the blacksmith shop. With Peter's training, Anton had become the official blacksmith for Macken and several neighboring villages. He often bragged about the "Hospese" and drew in guests from far and wide. He and his wife lived with her parents in a farmhouse three houses up the street, but he was a "regular" at Hospese. His group of friends played cards by candle light at the same corner table every Saturday evening until midnight and made plenty of noise while demanding their beer and sausages.

Moritz admired his older brother Anton, but he was not inclined to become a blacksmith. Maria didn't mind that he preferred entertaining guests with good food, singing and telling jokes to working with horseshoes and wagon wheels. During the planting and harvesting season, he worked side by side with his sister Liz and brother-in-law Gerhard in the fields but was always preoccupied with his restaurant.

"Mother, I'm really worried about Catharina," Liz had just finished churning the butter. She's been slouching around and hasn't smiled in several weeks. "What could be wrong?"

"Liz, I wasn't going to tell anyone. Catharina made me promise to keep it a secret, but now I have to tell. A couple of months ago, she was attacked by Schmitze Alois. He got a hold of Catharina and raped her. She was so ashamed that I had to promise her not to make a fuss."

"But, Mother!"

"Look, if I had said anything, your brothers Anton and Moritz, and perhaps even your husband Gerhard might have gone and beaten up Alois. Catharina and I didn't want them to start that kind of trouble, so we thought we could just forget it."

"So what does that have to do with Catharina's problems now? She looks really sick, Mother."

"Do I have to spell it out for you? She's pregnant!"

"Oh no! What are we going to do? She's not married! By Christmas the whole village will be gossiping about her."

"Liz, if our friends in this village can't be more understanding with our family after all I've been through, I'll, I'll...." Maria was at a loss for words. She knew how vicious the local gossips could get. More than once she had heard whispers about this or that. More than one young man or woman had been ignored or worse for months at a time.

For three weeks, Liz and Maria were keeping a worried eye on Catharina. They tried to get her to eat, but Catharina grew steadily weaker.

One morning in December, Catharina's voice weakly called, "Mother! Liz! Please help me!"

The two rushed upstairs to Catharina's bedroom. "Quick, call Lucille, Liz!" Maria yelled. "There's blood all over the bed!"

Maria rocked Catharina in her arms. Liz came back with some tea. "Lucille is on her way." They tried to get Catharina to drink, but it was useless. Catherina was too weak. When Lucille arrived, a flicker of hope shot through Maria.

Lucille shook her head after her thorough examination, "I'm sorry, she was too far gone. I couldn't do anything for her."

Maria stood rooted to the floor. "Another child dead! How much more am I supposed to endure?" she asked no one in particular. "Our family is filling up the cemetery."

Lucille walked over to Maria and put her arm around her shoulders, "Come let's have a cup of coffee. We've been friends for a long, long time. We'll plan a lovely funeral for Catharina, and then we'll talk about the wonderful future your children, Liz, Anton, Moritz and Marieche are going to have. Okay?"

Like a statue Maria allowed Lucille to move her out of the room, leaving the emaciated body of her precious Catharina on the bed. They entered the kitchen where Moritz was preparing food for the restaurant. Liz, pale and quiet, soon joined them.

"You three ladies look terrible! What is wrong?" Moritz looked up with his cheerful sparkling eyes.

"Moritz, Catharina is dead."

For a moment all movement stopped in the room. Moritz's hand was holding a ladle in mid-air. Finally, Lucille said, "Come, let's sit down," as she pulled the chairs away from the table. "Moritz, come here and sit with us. We are going to predict the future for you."

Moritz sensed the goose bumps on his skin. Here he was, an eighteen-year-old boy surrounded by three women who wanted to predict his future--and a dead sister upstairs! This was too bizarre, but he could not tear himself away.

"Let me make some coffee first," he tried to avert the inevitable. "Mother, you know it's not possible to predict the future!"

"I know nothing!" Maria's face had become soft and shiny. "Liz and Lucille know nothing! Yet we are here to tell you about life! Don't you think you ought to listen?"

Moritz felt a prickling sensation in the back of his neck as he brought the coffeepot to the table. For a few minutes he heard only the sounds of cups, saucers and spoons clanking against each other. "Somebody, say something!" he thought frantically.

"Moritz, life is good," his mother started. "You're going to get married some day."

"And you're going to have six, no maybe seven, children," Liz added.

"And the Hospese restaurant will make you rich!" Lucille threw in for good measure.

Moritz was fascinated. "Will my wife be beautiful?"

Liz commented, "That's up to you. You can choose your wife from any number of beautiful girls, so we can't tell you what she'll look like or what her name will be."

"Okay, tell me more about the children. Are they going to die like my little brothers and sisters?" Moritz had heard stories about the horrible time his mother and father had endured during the cholera epidemics. There hadn't been any difficulties like that in his lifetime, but the little graves in the cemetery had kept the terror alive. Now and then news of terrible world events was brought to the village by travelers. There had even been a big war in America, a place where nothing bad was supposed to happen!

Lucille cleared her throat, "Moritz, anything is possible. There might be another epidemic. There might be another war. There might be more bloodshed. On the other hand, there might be good health and peaceful times and prosperity. Some of your descendants might even travel all over the world. Why not think the best?"

Maria brightened up a little. "Yes, I've lost five babies and now my daughter is lying dead upstairs, but I have you and Marieche. And your father gave me Liz and Anton. I can't ignore the wonderful family I have. You are my son, and you will have the strength to care for your own family."

"Gerhard and I will be here to help you, too," Liz promised. Liz had remained childless. Lucille and Maria had quietly discussed the possibility that Liz had seen too many babies die in her youth and become barren as a result.

"Hey, what's going on?" Marieche, an energetic teenager, bounded into the kitchen. She had been tending the chickens and was carrying a basket of eggs. "Brr! It's cold outside! There's work to be done! What are you all sitting around for?" she demanded.

"Please sit down Marieche," her mother looked stern. "Your sister has died."

"What? I don't believe you!" the young girl screamed and started for the stairs.

"I said, 'Sit down!'" Maria's voice hissed through clenched teeth.

Marieche picked up a towel and sat down. Tears were welling up. "Does Anton know?"

"If you promise not to upset him and his pregnant wife with hysterics, I'll let you go tell him," her mother's voice had softened.

"Can I go see Catharina first?" the upset teenager wanted to see for herself. It was all just too unreal. "How can a healthy twenty-one-year old woman suddenly get sick and die for no reason?" she wondered to herself.

"Okay, go upstairs for a little while. Then wash your face before you go talk to Anton," Liz had taken command. "Now we women really have to talk about the funeral. Moritz, do you have an idea now of what's in store for you?" she teased as she dismissed the young man.

"Yeah, yeah! Now let me go do my chores," he mumbled as he left the three women at the table talking about Catharina's funeral.

The Hospese Restaurant needed his attention.

In 2005, the "Hospese" house in the story won an architectural prize.

Author's Notes

1. Thoughts while sharing my Kentucky Fried Chicken with the ducks at the Fairfield Civic Center Pond.

2. *Wong Hoo Chun* was my husband's maternal grandfather. We had been curious about him for years, but the family lore was scanty: he was an herbalist in San Francisco. When we went to the National Archives & Records Administration (NARA) in San Bruno, California, we found a treasure trove of materials, including pictures of my husband's mother as a four-year-old. I compiled the knowledge we gained into a coherent narrative.

3. In the study and teaching of World War II history I have often thought it was unfair that the name of evil personified is known by every schoolchild while the names of good people like my grandmother disappear into the mists of oblivion. One day I was so annoyed after coming home from school that I wrote *Parallel Lives*.

4. For years there was a show after dark in Disneyland that people lined up for hours ahead of time. Spectators sat shoulder to shoulder on the pavement on New Orleans Square in order to get a glimpse of Fantasmics. A lucky few who had the money could sit on a balcony above the Disney Art Gallery and view Fantasmics in comfort while enjoying refreshments. Each time we visited Disneyland, I promised myself that one day I would sit on the balcony with my

husband. It finally happened.

5. New Blood for the Nation was written as my assigned college response to Richard Crashaw's, "Upon the Infant Martyrs:"

To see both blended in one flood

The mothers' milk, the children's blood,

Makes me doubt if Heaven will gather,

ROSES hence, or LILIES rather.

Roses symbolize occasions that celebrate life; Lilies, on the other hand, symbolize funerals.

6. Having to fill out forms and answering questions about my political and other affiliation, I finally got disgusted and wrote this "What Am I?" poem to get over my emotions.

7. If a young man enlists in the armed forces of his own free will, he serves his country. If, on the other hand, a young man is drafted, he becomes government property. The mothers of draftees ought to be compensated. After Jimmy Carter reinstituted the draft registration, I became irate and thought about all the effort I had put into raising my son. This letter was sent to the President and all the U.S. Senators.

8. In the media and in conversations, I am sometimes pressured to express a political opinion. From my perspective as an immigrant who had to jump through all kinds of hoops to come to this country, I am usually hard-pressed to have an opinion about people who arrive without legal standing. I do have opinions about those who come to commit felonies. This letter was a response to the news that nearly 30% of inmates of our prison system are incarcerated illegals.

9. When I was not rehired as a teacher in one school district, I wrote this story. I didn't know what I expected to accomplish, but just compiling the information was helpful. Subsequently,

I taught successfully for years in two school districts before I retired.

10. All the names have been changed, but the story is based on facts. Writing and documenting this unpleasant episode of my life was very therapeutic.

11. From family lore and very sketchy documentation of my ancestry, I constructed this fictionalized story. Moritz, of the story was my great-grandfather. He and his wife Barbara (not mentioned in the story) became the parents of seven healthy children who survived into adulthood. The youngest, Maria, became the grandmother who raised me in the same house in Macken after World War II. Many of the old homestead's features, such as the outdoor toilet and lack of running water had remained the same over a century.

About the Author

Marianne was a robust and healthy little German girl until the ravages of World War II took their toll. She barely survived a mysterious illness, terrorizing air raids, and her parents' divorce.

When her mother married an American and emigrated to America, Marianne was expected to follow. Her ocean voyage from Italy to New York changed her life into that of a normal American teenager.

In a twist of fate, Marianne met a Los Angeles-born Chinese American serviceman in Bermuda, causing a great uproar in her family.

Eventually they got married and raised four children while remaining active in a variety of community events, including earning University degrees._Her Memoir, <u>The Little Girl That Could</u>, was published in 2009.

Marianne's desire to learn about her ancestry has led her to discover precious information in documents from Germany. Her curiosity about her husband's ancestry led her to do research at the National Archives & Records Administration in San Bruno. Among the aged files from Angel Island, she has found a wealth of materials to weave her tales.

Marianne and her husband Lee make their home in northern California within easy driving distance of their children, grandchildren, great-grandchildren and their extended family.